Behind Our Backs

Post 45 Loren Glass and Kate Marshall, Editors
Post•45 Group, Editorial Committee

Behind Our Backs
Feminized Poetry and
Capitalist Abstraction

Amy De'Ath

Stanford University Press
Stanford, California

Stanford University Press
Stanford, California

© 2026 by Amy De'Ath. All rights reserved.

No part of this book may be reproduced or transmitted in any form or by any means, electronic or mechanical, including photocopying and recording, or in any information storage or retrieval system, without the prior written permission of Stanford University Press.

Library of Congress Cataloging-in-Publication Data
Names: De'Ath, Amy, 1985– author
Title: Behind our backs : feminized poetry and capitalist abstraction / Amy De'Ath.
Description: Stanford : Stanford University Press, 2026. | Includes bibliographical references and index.
Identifiers: LCCN 2025028518 (print) | LCCN 2025028519 (ebook) | ISBN 9781503643840 cloth | ISBN 9781503644847 paperback | ISBN 9781503644854 ebook
Subjects: LCSH: Poetry—Women authors—History and criticism | Feminist literary criticism | Marxist criticism
Classification: LCC PN1091 .D43 2026 (print) | LCC PN1091 (ebook)
LC record available at https://lccn.loc.gov/2025028518
LC ebook record available at https://lccn.loc.gov/2025028519

Cover design: Michele Wetherbee
Cover art: Julia Dzwonkoski; courtesy of the artist

The authorized representative in the EU for product safety and compliance is: Mare Nostrum Group B.V. | Mauritskade 21D | 1091 GC Amsterdam | The Netherlands | Email address: gpsr@mare-nostrum.co.uk | KVK chamber of commerce number: 96249943

For my parents, Sue and Paul

Contents

	Acknowledgments	ix
	Introduction	
	Hidden Abodes and Inner Bonds	1
1	Consciousness-Raising and the Problem of Value	42
	Bernadette Mayer and Kay Gabriel	
2	Two Senses of Abstraction	79
	Bhanu Kapil and Alli Warren	
3	Abolition of What?	113
	Annharte, Anishinaabekwe, Granarchist	
4	Recasting Dialectics	147
	Hannah Black's Deep Cuts	
	Notes	181
	Index	225

Acknowledgments

The idea for this project initially took form in Vancouver, on the unceded and occupied territories of the xʷməθkʷəy̓əm (Musqueam), Sḵwx̱wú7mesh (Squamish), and səlilwətaɬ (Tsleil-Waututh) nations. I'm grateful for the time I spent living on Coast Salish territories, and for what I continue to learn about capitalism and all our relations from the First Peoples of that land, and from Indigenous organizers and scholars elsewhere on Turtle Island. Such learning—and more than just learning—seems especially pressing as I move to Boston and the unceded, stolen territories of the Massachusee (Massachusett) and the Mashpee Wôpanâak (Wampanoag) First Peoples—an area initially colonized in part, along with neighboring Nipmuc lands, by people from my hometown of Sudbury in Suffolk, England.

I must also begin by acknowledging this book's huge debt to Chris Nealon, though he gave everything freely. He generously shared his sharp and expansive knowledge, as well as solidarities and jokes; he supported me in numerous other professional ways; but above all, as if it were no big deal, he allowed me to think of this work as part of a larger project we share.

At Stanford University Press, Erica Wetter supported this project from the start and in ways that went beyond the call of duty. I am also thankful to Caroline McKusick, Chris Peterson, and Natalie Rovero for their kind and expert assistance, and to Jennifer Gordon for her precision and sensitivity in copyediting. And I want to say a huge thank you to the *Post45* series editors, Kate Marshall and Loren Glass, and especially to Kate for her invaluable feedback at various stages.

A previous version of Chapter 4 appeared as "Recasting Dialectics: Hannah Black's Deep Cuts," in "Lyric and Containment" (special issue), *differences* 36, no. 2–3 (2025), edited by Sarah Dowling and Claire Grandy, and previous versions of sections of the Introduction and Chapter 1 appeared in "Hidden Abodes and Inner Bonds: Literary Study and Marxist-Feminism," in *After Marx: Literature, Theory and Value in the Twenty-First Century*, edited by Colleen Lye and Christopher Nealon (Cambridge: Cambridge University Press, 2022); and in "Manly Things," a *Post45* "Contemporaries" cluster on Bernadette Mayer, edited by Kristin Grogan and David Hobbs. Previous readings of Bhanu Kapil's *Ban en Banlieue* appeared in "L(a)ying Down in the Banlieue," *Mute*, 21 September 2016. Previous readings of Marie Annharte Baker's poems appeared in "Decolonize or Destroy: New Feminist Poetry in the United States and Canada," in *Women: A Cultural Review* 26, no. 3 (2015).

I've been lucky to have had several chances over the years to present thinking that informed this study, and I am deeply appreciative of conversations with audiences at the Amsterdam School for Cultural Analysis at the University of Amsterdam; the Centre for Research in Philosophy, Literature and the Arts at the University of Warwick; The Program in Critical Theory at the University of California, Berkeley; the Contemporary Art Research Forum at Northumbria University; the Marxism in Culture series at the Institute of Historical Research, School of Advanced Study, University of London; the School of Politics and International Relations at Queen Mary, University of London, and the Sexual and Political Economy Network of Historical Materialism; the Postgraduate Research Forum in the School of English and Drama, at Queen Mary, University of London; the Department of English at the State University of New York, Albany; the Department of Women's, Gender, and Sexuality Studies at Emory University; the Institute for the Humanities at Simon Fraser University; the Centre for Modern Poetry at the University of Kent; the Interdisciplinary Critical Thought Workshop at the University at Buffalo; the Image Text Ithaca MFA program at Ithaca College; the Marx & Philosophy

Society Annual Conference, and last but not least, I'm grateful for energizing conversations at Performing Arts Forum in France and with comrades in the Marxist Literary Group.

It would have taken even longer to write this book had it not been for a period of research leave at King's College London in 2022. But most of all, I am deeply grateful for the company of my colleagues there, both on and off the picket line. Seb Franklin read multiple iterations of what eventually became *Behind Our Backs*, and his insights and encouragement, like his friendship in general, have been gold. For their brilliance and solidarity, I also want to especially thank Luke Roberts, Clare Birchall, Adelene Buckland, Jane Elliott, Christine Okoth, and Sita Balani. Alan Marshall has been a most thoughtful, sincere, and supportive Head of Department. I am also grateful to the many brilliant students I've been able to work with at King's, especially on the MA Contemporary Literature, Culture and Theory, and especially Fintan Calpin. Lastly, I'd like to thank my new colleagues in the Department of English at Tufts University for the generosity they've already extended to me.

I'm indebted to friends and colleagues who read parts of this book along the way. First of all, I am deeply grateful to Colleen Lye and to the other anonymous reviewer who provided sharp and generous feedback on the manuscript, truly helping me to improve it. For their advice, conversation, and precious time, I'm so grateful to Beverley Best, Andrea Brady, Sarah Brouillette, Seb Franklin, Sean O'Brien, Marina Vishmidt, Naomi Weber, and Brian Whitener. I want to thank Bev for the tools she has given us all for critiquing capital: an immense gift, as is her luminous company. I'm grateful to Andrea Brady for her enduring support, and for the deep care and precision of her inspiring thinking. Thank you to Sarah Brouillette, for being our comrade and being unceremoniously brilliant. Thank you, as well, to Sarah Dowling, for getting me into all this in the first place and for still being my teacher without saying so. I will always be grateful to Marina Vishmidt, who is (still) unbelievably no longer with us, but who pressed me to hurry up and publish this book and treated me as an intellectual peer long before I deserved it.

It was with some naïveté that I began a PhD, but I was nurtured, encouraged, and financially supported by the English Department at Simon Fraser University. Lucky for me, Jeff Derksen took me seriously and gave me a language for talking about poetry as a mode of critique, among many other gifts.

Stephen Collis supported me intellectually and pastorally, from start to finish, with uncommon generosity and openness. I also want to thank Carolyn Lesjak for her fine-grained read of my dissertation and for joyfully teaching me how to read Marx better. This book owes a lot to her teaching and her writing.

This project has followed me a long way, from Vancouver to London to Buffalo to Boston. Thank you to the following people for the meaningful conversations and friendships that make trying to write a book worth pursuing: Catrina Baker-Bassett, Kate Baker-Bassett, Bret Benjamin, Shane Boyle, Marie Buck, Marija Cetinić, Chris Chen, Sarika Chandra, Kevin Davies, Martin Dines, Diego Espíritu Chavez, Fer/Cari Fuentes, Kay Gabriel, Lenora Hanson, Edmund Hardy, Danny Hayward, Emma Heaney, Leigh Claire La Berge, Amy Ching-Yan Lam, Trisha Low, Dan Nemser, Chris O'Kane, Dawn Paley, Angus Reid, Margaret Ronda, Jordy Rosenberg, David Schulman, Robin Simpson, Juliana Spahr, Sam Solomon, Syd Staiti, Arabella Stanger, Laurel Uziell, and Stephanie Young. Special thanks to Angie Knowles for her exceptional kindness. And in memory of Sean Bonney, who grasped it all so clearly.

For our delightful time in Vancouver, thank you to Andrea Actis, Clint Burnham, Nate Crompton, Ryan Fitzpatrick, Anahita Jamali Rad, Natalie Knight, Danielle LaFrance, Cecily Nicholson, Catriona Strang, and Fred Wah. Heidi Antolick, thank you for giving me family there. Thank you also to friends in Buffalo who embraced me: Carlos Amador, Aaron Bartley, Anna Falicov, Judith Goldman, Matt Kenyon, Laura Marris, Elisabeth Paquette, and Andrea Pitts. Thank you, Julia Dzwonkoski, for making the cover art for this book and for the joy of your friendship.

Thank you to the Whiteners—Mary, Doc, Sarah, Marcus, Frank, Katharine, Tony, and Harper: clear eyes, full hearts, can't lose! Thank you to Sarah Manning, especially, for your encouragement during the last stages of this book. Thank you to my other parents, Lesli Tunbridge and Tim Tunbridge, and to Emma Tunbridge-Hibbert and the formidable Holly Tunbridge.

Naomi Weber, you've always been what "heroic" means to me. I love you, Mr. Toastie.

Teresa O'Brien lovingly encouraged this project, and understood its questions and anger, and I will always carry her memory. I am deeply thankful to Bob and Clíona for sharing so much with me too. And I am abidingly grateful to Sean O'Brien. These pages contain so much that we learned together and in daily conversation—the most meaningful act.

Thank you to Deb De'Ath, Auntie of This Parish, whose love is always felt, and to my superb siblings, Dave Gibbons and Gill Clayton; to Jericho Clayton-Gibbons and Eli Clayton-Gibbons; to Kate Fox, Louie De'Ath, and Alexander De'Ath; and especially to my smart, loving brother Jack De'Ath.

I somehow hit the jackpot with my parents, Sue De'Ath and Paul De'Ath—two funny, brilliant people who know what it's like to spend nights stacking shelves or Saturdays in a distribution warehouse, and who also know how to party. Thank you, Mum and Dad, for the freedom, understanding, and constant support you've given me, and for the open-hearted and courageous way you both move through the world. This book is dedicated to you.

In no small measure, Brian Whitener helped me to the end with this project, and in his typical way, made life gorgeous. *Have it!*

Introduction
Hidden Abodes and Inner Bonds

IN THE *GRUNDRISSE*, KARL MARX famously argues that human beings are ruled by abstractions.[1] By this, he means that the apparent freedom of individuals—the freedom to work, to own property, to have a family, to speak freely—appears as freedom only as a result of a complex, constantly reconstituting array of social relations propelled by the movement of value. Capitalist abstractions may not be something we can clutch at, but they are real: they arise from the paradoxically collective but uncoordinated actions of individuals, in the process of production and in the sphere of circulation. As such they arise "behind our backs," independent of conscious thought and outside of language.[2]

It may seem neat enough then, that in conversations about contemporary poetics, the abstract has often been associated with the idea of formal experimentation and the non-referential, as opposed to the communicative or content-driven operations of language.[3] At the same time, as is especially the case in financial literature and journalism, it can also be a byword used to assert the obfuscating complexity and immateriality of financial transactions.[4] In G. W. F. Hegel's thinking, however, the abstract idea is conceived dialectically and in relation to the concrete: not only are abstract thoughts relational and derived from each other, but they are an objective part of a process of "pure activity" that Hegel calls "spirit," a holistic abstraction that realizes itself in being and essence.[5] It is here in this method of processual activity and relationality that we can begin to see the basis of Marx's own dialectical critique of capital's abstracting movement.

Indeed, Marx has something uniquely important to say about the strange objectivity of economic relations in a capitalist society, as he highlights their simultaneous dependence on the collective actions of individual agents and power *over* those same agents—their status as objective forces "that determine individual existence, even in its most hidden recesses,"[6] and their "socially binding action."[7] In the years since the 2008 global financial crisis, there has emerged a renewed critical effort to understand how capitalist society is "form-determined" by value, to use another helpful Marxian term.[8] This book argues that contemporary feminized poetry constitutes an important part of that critical project, and that it does so by pursuing a dimension of theory that draws its power from the dialectics of aesthetic experience. Second, it argues that a recent reinterpretation of Marx's concepts to examine capital's internal logics and their relation to its historical forms of expression provides the basis for a new, more capacious type of Marxist literary criticism—one that is sensitized to the reproduction of social difference and able to systematically account for a world of infinite diversity. Here, I read contemporary writing by feminized authors to demonstrate a Marxist method of interpretation that is open to being reworked by the literary object itself and the forms of critique it engenders. In this vein, both the works under study and the reading method laid out in these chapters grapple with the fragmentary nature of lived experience, in which moments of a systematic whole take on forms that appear to be disconnected from that whole. As Diane Elson, a major contributor to the field of value-form theory, noted in 1979:

> [T]hose who experience capitalist exploitation do not need a theory to tell that something is wrong. The problem is that the experience of capitalist exploitation is fragmentary and disconnected, so that it is difficult to tell exactly what is wrong, and what can be done to change it.[9]

Attuned to this problem, the works considered in this book strive to tell us that "something is wrong" on several different registers, from the level of sense perception to world system, and in doing so they offer fresh and previously maligned insights regarding how capitalism works. They suggest how gender and race are bound together at a conceptual level by the logic of capital, for example, and they point to the way capitalist social forms are always constitutively tied to other temporal and spatial moments. Take Bhanu Kapil's metaphor, "the strength of the British Pound," with its amalgamating overtones of empire and masculine sexual aggression; or the way Kay Gabriel gestures to the antagonistically embodied and abstract character of sexual difference in the moving image of a false nail, ripped at the involuntary climax of a queer sex scene: "He wants to turn around / I know your name! But his orgasm / rips out of him, an acrylic nail caught / off a finger and torn."[10] Despite their deep and obvious differences, the set of poetic cases I read here suggest a shared desire to transcend the gendering histories of separation that define subjective experiences of being socially bound by the logic of capital.

What does it mean to be "bound" by capital, or "form-determined" by value, though—descriptions that can seem both economistic and conspiratorial? Poetry has some answers, and Marx has a congruent one based on an analysis of the relationship between capital's hidden internal movement and its historical forms of expression. Value, Marx's concept for the socially average labor time it takes to produce commodities, exerts a determining force on society because it is the only socially valid measure of productivity in a capitalist mode of production—and competitive productivity rates are the *sine qua non* for capitalist enterprises. Value never appears directly, however. Surplus value produced by workers and appropriated by capitalists appears in the actual world as profit. This inversion, whereby the movement of a social relation undergirded by the actions of humans takes an objectivized and apparently natural form in what we call economy, entails what Marx calls a "practical truth"—a situation in which the labor of actual people has "ceased to be organically linked with particular individuals in any specific form" and acquires an abstract dimension that, for the first time in history, governs the way society is organized.[11] In a dynamic Marx initially analyzes in *Capital* as the commodity's fetish-character, the value that arises from this process appears to move to its own tune—and in a sense, *it does*, because when social relations between producers are reflected as natural relations between commodities, value acquires a semblance of independence that (never mind having "real-world effects") becomes the dominant driving force of all society.[12] This dynamic is what Beverley Best calls capital's automatic fetish and its "function of abstraction."[13] As she explains, capital takes on social forms of appearance that mystify its singular inner logic and movement, the point of which is simply to expand—to make more capital. She characterizes the process of value-in-motion as a "perceptual physics," a term that potently captures the unity of a system in which the production and circulation of value presuppose each other, and where value dissimulates itself from the social forms it produces and determines. Value disappears, in fact, because it is only ever expressed in an equation between one thing and another.[14]

As the poetry in this study seems to intuit, capital is also nothing but the social forms in which it takes shape. It works on and through the subjects who reproduce it, whether they do so consciously or not. Capital is not a force of human nature but the expression of a dynamic social configuration, a logic realized every day, "a collective doing and making that inadvertently invents a world—a mode of sociality that excretes an assemblage of objectivities taken to be natural and intractable."[15] Importantly, this process is unplanned and contingent, but it is never random. Rather, it is syncopated to the rhythm of value-in-motion, what Best calls the "gravitational force" of expanding value, "the means by which value becomes capital." Capital therefore poses a unique representational problem, as she clarifies:

> A gravitational pull on capital's bearers towards a certain way of seeing, categorizing, and understanding the world is an objective dimension of the movement of capital. Capital generates a pantheon of self-representations that inform by both betraying and confirming (on different registers) our experiences in the world. At the same time, people are constantly challenging, analyzing, and disassembling these surface stories.[16]

Value's dissimulating movement occasions a "perceptual delinking,"[17] not only making it impossible to know how a historical moment—experienced or imagined—is constituted within a social totality, but also generating a representative regime where, as most people well know, some ideas run an easier course than others. At the same time, as Fredric Jameson emphasizes, these representations do not belie an obscured systemic poison to which we might awaken; rather, they constitute our reality:

> [T]he realm of separation, of fragmentation, of the explosion of codes and the multiplicity of disciplines is merely the reality of the appearance: it exists, as Hegel would put it, not so much *in itself* as *for us*, as the basic logic and fundamental law of our daily life and existential experience in late capitalism.[18]

What is both unique and devastating about capital, then, is that it acquires an objective propulsion of its own. Marx demonstrates this in *Capital I*, when he compares earlier forms of commodity societies (such as existed in ancient Greece) to the economic laws specific to capitalism, where money is transformed into commodities and then into money again ("M-C-M"):

> In simple circulation, the value of commodities attained at the most a form independent of their use-values, i.e. the form of money. But now, in the circulation of M-C-M, value suddenly presents itself as a self-moving substance which passes through a process of its own, and for which commodities and money are both mere forms.

How does value manage to appear "self-moving"? Marx explains:

> But there is more to come: instead of simply representing the relations of commodities, [value] now enters into a private relationship with itself, as it were. It differentiates itself as original value from itself as surplus-value.... Value therefore now becomes value in process, money in process, and as such, capital.[19]

Industrial capital "is money which has been changed into commodities, and reconverted into more money by the sale of these commodities," which Marx shortens as M-C-M' to denote value's movement from money to commodities to *more* money (the latter Marx calls "money prime"—money as the "prime mover"). This is the general formula for capital,[20] and it helps to explain how the products of human social labor assert themselves as apparently natural economic laws over and against the very subjects whose activities produced them in the first place, in a world where "man" is "governed by the products of his own hand."[21]

Believe it or not, the significance of value's automatic and non-representational character to the study of literature and culture is only just beginning to be recognized.[22] While a counter-tradition of critical social theory began to develop in the 1960s—initially from the Frankfurt School as the New Reading of Marx (which was prompted in part by Hans-Georg Backhaus's transcript of Adorno's 1962 seminar, "Marx and the Basic Concepts of Sociological Theory"), but also as an analysis of "social form" and Open Marxism in the UK and US—these methods, with their emphasis on the objective illusions of economic categories and the fetishistic inversions of capital's social forms, have tended not to travel far in the study of "soft" areas of social theory such as gender and race, let alone have much impact in literary studies.[23] Even where they centrally inform the work of an influential literary critic like Sianne Ngai, their political ramifications can be eclipsed by attention to the zanier aspects of her own analysis—see one reviewer's enchantment with the stainless steel banana slicer.[24] It is as if (imagine!) Ngai's own early observation, in *Ugly Feelings*, that "forms of negative affect are more likely to be stripped of their critical implications when the impassioned subject is female" held also for the elision of critiques of political economy when they are voiced in the work of feminized critics.[25]

Reading Feminization

A number of recent studies in contemporary poetry have bucked this general trend, nonetheless, where Marxist critics have argued that the movements of capital and its periodic crises have long been overlooked themes in twentieth-century poetry, especially through the era of "long downturn": a period of economic stagnation often traced back to the oil shock of 1973. See, for example, *Remainders: American Poetry at Nature's End* by Margaret Ronda; *The Work of Art in the Age of Deindustrialization* by Jasper Bernes; *The Matter of Capital: Poetry and Crisis in the American Century* and *Infinity for Marxists* by Christopher Nealon; and a number of influential articles by Sianne Ngai and Joshua Clover.[26] Five more important books—Luke Roberts's *Living in History*; Christopher Chen's *Literature and Race in the Democracy of Goods*; Walt Hunter's *Forms of a World*; Samuel Solomon's *Lyric Pedagogy and Marxist-Feminism*; and Andrea Brady's *Poetry and Bondage*—have helped to turn our attention to the specifically capitalist mediations of gender, race, and Indigeneity in postwar histories of capital accumulation.[27] Deeply informed by this turn to a critique of capitalism in contemporary poetry studies, *Behind Our Backs* argues that, in fact, contemporary feminized poetry from North America provides an even more radical story of capitalism as a total system when it directly links the hidden abodes of social reproduction to the inner bonds of capital's logic. The poetry studied here is not only sensitive to capital's processual remakings of gendered and racial difference, but to the way it purports to ameliorate the differences and divisions it has itself violently produced. We thus find, in feminized writing of the late twentieth and early twenty-first centuries, an alertness to the recompositions of gender as social form and an attempt to grasp how the lives of feminized people are shaped by the zombie-like abstractions of capitalist value production—an adaptable system that supersedes historical periods precisely because it is the force that drives them.

As a feminist challenge to gendered and generic approaches to literary forms, a renewed interpretation of Marx's concepts and their ramifications for reading literary texts, and a demonstration of how feminized poetry offers sensory and dialectical insights into capitalism's workings, *Behind Our Backs* asserts that feminized poetics can actually contribute to Marxian critique. Yet among other things, a long baked-in allergy to Marxism in literary studies, coupled with the institutionalized consolidation of liberal and capitalist-friendly ways of thinking about social difference, have precluded such readings of feminized writing. Consider, for example, the question of how to read the following lines from Dawn Lundy Martin's 2015 collection, *Life in a Box Is a Pretty Life*:

> Representation falls away. Chokehold "blackness." Swallowed "brown." Your "black" father whose "blackness" precedes him. Stumble in laborious "black" gait toward "absence." Cross your "black" hands, empty your "black" pockets, hold your "poor" "black" baby against "brick" "wall" as instructed . . .   In absence of wholeness catch glimpses of the sides of selves.[28]

A socially progressive reading of these lines might proceed in terms of identity: "blackness" is a constrictive marker, generationally and paradoxically reproduced as the negation of "representation." Blackness prohibits a "whole" view of a self. Importing intersectional methods, such a reading could note the trinity of race, gender, and class invoked by the phrase, "your 'poor' 'black' baby," showing how each of these structural axes oppressively shape the "life in a box" that Martin's collection promises to explore.

It is notable, though, that this approach need not refer to poetry at all, since poetry is just one of many possible objects for a theory of structure reliant on positive social identities (even if poetry's supposed authenticity might be invoked as evidence for that theory). A more agile and consequential reading of these same lines, however, would attend to the way they highlight feminization, racialization, and the class relation as matters of dynamic repetition and perennial renewal, as well as how they connect their immediate surroundings to elsewheres of various kinds. In attending to questions of capitalist social form, this way of reading reveals a series of techniques and strategies that feminized poets have been using to write about what fails to be recognized as "social" in the first place. And while I do not want to belabor the point, it is worth repeating that it is a reading method based on Marx's demonstration, in *Capital*, that as value moves through the world acquiring and shedding various forms—labor, commodities, money, for example—the value-form is not any particular thing but an expression of a relation between things: an objectively existing but abstract process that shapes our social world in ways that are impossible to out-think. Indeed, what makes this analysis so useful to both literary and feminist criticism is that it allows us to grasp value as a form that, by abstracting labor into socially necessary labor-time, operates behind our backs as a set of impersonal compulsions. It explains how it is action rather than thought that produces capitalist abstraction.

Re-reading Martin's lines above, then, we might compare the solidity of the image of the brick wall to the other abstract yet objective categories invoked by the poem as limits: "poverty," "blackness," "brownness." Though representation "falls away" and a "whole" view is absent, the speaker's frustration—marked here by the use of jarringly short sentences and scare quotes to relay images of anti-Black brutality—points not to a demand for recognition, but to a fragmented experience where cause and effect are not merely obscured but obliterated. Far from a critique of totality-thinking, we can read in Martin's own appeal to abstraction a desire for a view of the whole otherwise foreclosed by capital's self-representations. Rather than confirming a set of gendered properties often attributed to lyric poetry in the feminist tradition—embodiment, plenitude, unknowingness, authenticity, or something like, in Marina Vishmidt's words, the "pseudo-concreteness that often accompanies theoretical projects intolerant of the (real) abstraction that organises contemporary social life"[29]—such a reading suggests how the poem's form, language, and movement hold dialectical contradictions in sight so that we might grasp them for a moment. In this instance, "absence" can itself be understood, to stay with Marx's terms, as a form of appearance thrown up by the real-but-obscured movement of capital. Along with "Blackness," the term "absence" is one of only two abstract nouns to be conspicuously placed in quotation marks in this section of Martin's poem, and the precise nature of both are drawn into question. The poem thereby evinces what Nealon has recently called "intuition," a type of perception that is less epistemological, more sensory and theoretical in its mapping of a social totality, and one he identifies both in the Hegelian dimensions of Marx's work and in contemporary "Marxist" poetry.[30]

Behind Our Backs thus marks the difference between a simple notion of the structural and an understanding of social forms in motion. The initial works I study, by New York City–based poets Bernadette Mayer and Kay Gabriel, link processes of feminization to the destabilizing effects of deindustrialization since the 1970s, quite literally tracing the concretization of gender and the production of whiteness in relation to systemic shifts in labor markets. Subsequent readings show how, in distinct ways, the British Indian poet Bhanu Kapil and Anishinaabe poet Marie Annharte Baker highlight the conceptually immanent relations between processes of feminization, racialization, and the class relation, in part via poetic descriptions of the ways racial representations of feminized subjects are reproduced and circulated during this period. Their work presents challenges to now-institutionalized versions of intersectionality theory when it is revealingly read through lesser-known methods drawn from value-critical Marxist feminisms, as well as Indigenous Marxisms, to suggest a dialectical concept of the reproduction of racial categories.

When literary texts engage the dialectics of aesthetic experience to think about the relation between sense perception and a total system in this way, they are themselves doing a type of theorizing. And yet, literary works cannot really do it for themselves: they need dialectical readers. To this end, I aim to offer a novel interpretive practice for feminist literary criticism, one that shows how feminized poetry not only unfemininely dares to theorize a social totality but requires our participation as readers in the co-production of that theoretical knowledge. Yet this approach is neither symptomatic nor reparative. It looks a little like the collaborative reading practices proposed by Language poetry in the 1980s, but it is different: rather than reader-as-agent, managing the deferrals and signifying chains of what Lyn Hejinian referred to as the "open text,"[31] the chapters ahead demonstrate how much contemporary feminized poetry enables reader and poet to meet as dialecticians. Deliberately or not, these poems encourage us to make the speculative leap of faith inherent to all theory, and to engage in a practice of "seeing what we know" rather than, like good surface readers, "knowing what we see," as Carolyn Lesjak puts it.[32] The point of this book, then, is not primarily to argue for the (nonetheless revelatory) capacities of feminized poetry, but to underline the breathtaking capaciousness of poetry and critiques of capitalist value when they are put together, particularly as they help us grasp the processual reproductions of gender, race, and class in their dynamism as social relations.

It is this dynamism that I intend to foreground when I refer to such writing as "feminized," a category that should not be understood as ethically good or bad. Unlike "women's" or even "feminist" poetry, the grammatical orientation of the term "feminized" points to an unfolding, active process. Indeed, along with racialization, the concept of feminization is increasingly used in contemporary theory to link analysis of the capitalist management of populations to questions of feminized labor.[33] Even more pertinent for this study, though, is how the term "feminized" has provided a tool for queer Marxism to think specifically about the relationship between distinct orders of economic and cultural "devaluation," notably in Rosemary Hennessy's argument that the cultural vehicle of (validated) masculine and (degraded) feminine significations mediates a disposable labor force in which "all subjects who transgress this prescribed distribution of gendered bodies are feminized, whether they are men or women."[34] Writing about maquiladora laborers in Nuevo Laredo, a Mexican city close to the US border, Hennessy argues that:

> The disposable, feminized worker is the one capital pursues across the globe and continually reinvents because she above all others gives away more of herself for free. As [Melissa] Wright delineates in *Disposable Women and Other Myths of Global Capitalism*, to be feminized means that the value of your labor power lies in the value of your devaluation. This seeming paradox is actually a long-standing capitalist strategy that discloses the intimate relation between cultural value and surplus value. To be feminized is to bear on your embodied second skin the mark of (de)valuation, which is indeed quite valuable to capital. It legitimates your potential disposability, the low limit on the wages you can command, and the excessive value-added charge your labor will produce.[35]

The counterintuitive insight that the low price of feminized labor is in fact a sign of its high value is a view shared by Best, who explains how women command a lower price for their labor because they disproportionately bear the burden of unpaid reproductive work, meaning that feminized labor is "costlier to reproduce" for capital as a whole.[36]

But also significant here is the methodological device Hennessy offers for pinpointing capital's mediation of the gender-sex binary. Insisting on the embodied (and not purely discursive) aspects of identity formation, Hennessy describes the brutal treatment to which maquiladora workers are subjected—from pills to force them to work for days without sleep to homophobic bullying—and draws on Jay Prosser's concept of a "second skin" to describe these practices as feminizing operations. For Prosser, the concept of a second skin offers a way to narrate trans experiences of a "second" material body that is subject to dominant social ascriptions, experiences of nonidentity that sit in antimony with a more personally felt sense of gendered embodiment.[37] And so, in transposing the concept of a second skin to her analysis of the exploitation (physical and temporal) of maquiladora workers, Hennessy finds a way to connect both the embodied and discursive dimensions of feminized subjectification to Marx's category of surplus value. In doing so she theorizes value's relationship both to an embodied subject who can be disproportionately exploited, a subject who physically and mentally "forfeit[s] more of themselves in the labor relations that produce capital," *and* to the cultural impress of the sign of feminization, in her words, "a feminized second skin folded into the conditions of exploitation," which is legitimized by "the cultural values circulating outside the factory."[38] In Hennessy's hands, "second skin" thus becomes a dialectical device that helps to flesh out the meaning of terms like "socially-binding" and "form-determining," enabling us to see how the capitalist strategy of lowering the price of feminized labor reproduces a materially *and* discursively feminized subject—a form of appearance that, not insignificantly, conjoins two generalized social abstractions called "gender" and "sex," and does so in part through another one called "race."

Hennessy's way of thinking about feminization is informed by Donna Haraway's claim that "to be feminized means to be made extremely vulnerable; able to be disassembled, reassembled, exploited as a reserve labor force," and made "reducible to sex."[39] Yet because feminization is understood here from the standpoint of capital's logic, her analysis not only allows for the possibility that feminization could, in a different world, mean something other than "the mark of (de)valuation," but also suggests how vulnerability, hyper-exploitation, and bare sexual difference make up just one (dominant) dimension of what constitutes a feminized subject in the maquiladora, since no one on earth is identical to the form of appearance their person takes in capitalism. Recent work in transfeminism insists on this point. In his critique of how the figure of the abolitionist Sojourner Truth has been recruited by feminists to argue for the inclusion of trans women in an expanded category of liberal womanhood, Cameron Awkward-Rich points out that "people have long struggled precisely for the right to *exit* the terms of 'the colonial/modern gender system,' have long lived, been made to live—with all that living entails—askance to its terms." Arguing that we should instead retain the more radical possibilities of Truth's famous and ambiguous question—"Ain't I a Woman?"—Awkward-Rich compares her to the Russian immigrant Mamie Rubles, who was brought before a court in San Francisco in 1890 for wearing masculine attire (thereby violating the city's 1863 cross-dressing ordinance), but who refused to concede, inviting the judge to feel their muscular arms and arguing that they were "neither a man nor a woman," indeed had "no sex at all."[40]

Given that social relations are by nature abstract, the rubric of feminization helps us to ask how it is, exactly, that those relations produce and transform the phenomena of the world. How do abstractions such as gender and race mediate the formation of subjectivity? How do they organize our material relations, our living arrangements, our capacity to sell our labor, our vulnerability to state violence? And how do those modes of social reproduction, all too real, take their place in the production of an objective reality of capitalist social forms: subjects, institutions, industry, media, finance, infrastructures, all kinds of paraphernalia and detritus—forms that often find their expression in the realm of signs but, rather than sharing a mutually constitutive relationship with the economic, as Stuart Hall once argued, are in fact dominated and driven by capital's automatic, rapacious, senseless movement, even as they are not reducible to it?[41]

Behind Our Backs contends that feminized poetry holds some answers to these questions, and not only at the level of identity-production. Indeed, the poetry I study here helps us to see how abstraction becomes "real" not by suddenly becoming a "thing"—a commodity, a woman, a subject, per se—but by coercing participation in a whole process that constantly discards and returns to those "things." Thus, for example, in her "granny boot camp" poems, Annharte (as she prefers to be called) critiques the stereotype of a mawkishly maternal Indigenous woman by taking this persona to parodic extremes in order to reclaim her as a desirous and queer figure, and one with an ambivalent critical-political stance. In one poem she writes, "I will proudly wear a button MEDICINE WOMAN NOT"; in another, "Tipi room creep on all fours then / switch genders," and "Cyber Gran ejaculates."[42] Her poems denaturalize the care work performed by a hyperbolically racialized matriarch, and in doing so emphasize the reproducibility of such a figure, showing up her contingent and performative character in a poetics attuned to how care work forms part of the reproduction of a social totality. In this way, we could say that feminized poetry enacts a type of critique not all so dissimilar from Marxist feminism's sustained attempt to account for the economic, nonnatural character of femininity, and to highlight its relation to a global system of capital accumulation. As I argue across this book, saying so does nothing to diminish a poem's magic.

Totality Feminism

If feminization is hard to explain within the terms of a critique of bourgeois political economy, Marxist feminism has nevertheless provided some of the most expansive and illuminating analyses to date for understanding just why it is so tricky. The International Wages for Housework Campaign of the early 1970s marked the beginnings of a Marxist-feminist theory and practice that sought to revolutionize "all our family and social relations," in Silvia Federici's words, and her infamous 1975 pamphlet, "Wages Against Housework," pays special attention to the hidden forms of gendered activities that undergird capitalist production while being kept outside of it.[43] Federici's description of housework as "the most pervasive manipulation, the most subtle and mystified violence," attests to the conceptual difficulty of this task,[44] which must reveal the "inner bond (*inneres Band*)" not between wage-labor relations, already set out nicely for us by Marx as the appropriation of surplus value from the laborer's output, but (as we will see shortly) between more ambiguously formed gender relations—relations ironically naturalized by capital when capital determines what counts as "social."[45]

The "hidden abode of production"—which for Marx signified the zone of surplus value production in the factory, away from the "noisy" sphere of exchange—is thus ripe for reappropriation, and the "hidden abode of *reproduction*," in Maya Gonzales's canny phrasing, provides a fitting term for the feminized and feminizing processes that Marx himself missed.[46] Yet if "hidden abode" usefully denotes the illegibility of a substratum of activities and processes that either cannot be rationalized and measured, or are not worth it from capital's viewpoint, it only gets us halfway to explaining their relation to capital accumulation. As we have seen, we must recruit another key concept: value. For Marx, grasping the "inner bond" of capital's forms of development means linking value to its forms of appearance (commodity, money, capital and profit) and the internal laws and tendencies that underwrite their movement. As he demonstrates in the opening chapter of *Capital*, the "substance" of value, abstract labor, is obscured by these forms, which appear to everyday consciousness as natural and presuppositionless things. But once we have established that capitalism's social forms of development, laws, and tendencies include not only production and circulation but another presupposition—the reproduction of labor-power—we discover another "inner bond." Together then, "hidden abode" and "inner bond" mark a methodological commitment to connecting different historical forms by examining the logical categories inherent to capitalism, in Marx's words, "the internal organization of the capitalist mode of production, its ideal average, as it were."[47]

Poststructuralist feminisms, with their emphasis on irreducible difference and particularity, have tended to reject this approach to thinking from the perspective of a totality. And yet Marxist feminisms often share with their linguistic, Foucauldian, and psychoanalytic counterparts—including Judith Butler's theory of performativity—a concern for what's concealed by governing norms, dominant scripts, and fleshy hieroglyphs: a search for what's hidden in the hidden abode. Marxism's critique of the linguistic turn has usually involved a charge that privileging the text or critiquing the modern episteme fails to acknowledge (or even symptomatizes) capital's dominance as the driver of History.[48] The approach I take in this book, however, is intended as a belated reply to the often justified counter-charge brought to Marxism by a variety of linguistic and postcolonial feminisms: a charge that Marxist methodology cannot account for difference; that it is an inherently masculinist mode that centers the white, heterosexual male worker; that its truth claims are economistic.

In the 1988 introduction to her landmark book of 1980, *Women's Oppression Today: The Marxist/Feminist Encounter*, Michèle Barrett commented on the wane of Marxist and socialist feminisms and poststructuralist theory's rise in the academy to put the problem this way:

> Theoretical perspectives using the more flexible vocabulary of subjectivity and discourse have made it possible to explore [ethnicity, race, and racism] without being constrained by the need to assign rank in what is effectively a zero-sum game of structural determination. Hence the proliferation of interesting work on these themes in literary studies and cultural studies generally, and the paucity of advances in sociology and macroeconomic thought.[49]

In the picture painted here, Marxist feminism appears as a method underpinned by the Western Marxism of Althusserian structuralism, a supposedly rigid "zero-sum" mode incapable of taking on additional "intersections" and surpassed (in theoretical sophistication as much as moral and political currency) by the discursive, race-attentive, and implicitly agential realm of literary and cultural studies. Barrett's concessionary tone is worth noting, too. Writing in part to acknowledge the methodological and political shortcomings that resulted from her inattention to race in the Marxist-feminist arguments of *Women's Oppression Today*, Barrett is compelled to agree that the "postmodernist" feminisms of critics such as Rosi Braidotti and Gayatri Spivak—as well as the deconstructive and psychoanalytic turns of what became known as French feminism, and work building on Foucauldian "regimes of truth" or the Deleuzian figure of the rhizome—held out more promising avenues for feminist study than the Marxisms available in the Anglo-American academy at the time, which remained based on Althusserian ideology critique and theories of reified consciousness as "second nature."[50]

But what was the problem with existing Marxist concepts, more precisely? A partial answer to this question can be found in the original text of *Women's Oppression Today*. There, Barrett notes the central role of Louis Althusser's famous 1970 essay, "Ideology and Ideological State Apparatuses," in Marxist theory's shift away from mechanistic models of economic base and ideological superstructure, and toward a "radical reprioritizing of ideology" as a "relatively autonomous element of the social formation."[51] And yet the take-up of ideology critique in Marxist-feminist theory leaves much to be desired, by Barrett's account. Rosalind Coward's argument for a new "materialist theory of signification," for example, "abandon[s] any notion of reality" and erroneously rejects the distinction between knowledge and "the real."[52] Thus, while Althusser's reconceptualization of ideology "appears to rescue sexual politics from their marginality to Marxist analysis" in Marxist-feminist writings of the period, this work lacks an adequate theory of the relationship between "objective reality" and discourse.[53] At the same time, Althusser's model of social reproduction and his account of the way ideological and repressive state apparatuses interpellate subjects is "developed strictly in terms of class," leading to perennial problems for Marxist feminists in their efforts to render it compatible with "a serious consideration of male dominance."[54]

Given this impasse, it is perhaps unfortunate that in Barrett's 1991 book, *The Politics of Truth: From Marx to Foucault*, Georg Lukács's potentially more amenable critique of science as an ideological discourse, and his model of a social totality in which history itself is the objective movement in question, are left unexamined, where Barrett briefly notes instead the charges other critics make against his "anti-scientific" method as a "highly relativist conception of knowledge."[55] Elsewhere, indeed, concepts like "reification," "second nature," and "relative autonomy" have been complexified, reinterpreted, and repurposed in pertinent and enduring ways to think about capital's relation to difference, not least in Hall's pivotal 1980 essay, "Race, Articulation, and Societies Structured in Dominance," and in Kevin Floyd's critique and redeployment of Lukács's concept of reification in his 2009 book, *The Reification of Desire: Toward a Queer Marxism*.[56]

But my own study nevertheless marks something of a departure from these Althusserian and Lukácsian approaches to thinking about ideology. The readings in the following chapters seek to show, rather, that new understandings of the concepts of value and social form provide much more capacious and flexible critical tools for feminist analysis than have previously been admitted, and that Marx's systematic method of thinking totality, far from ignoring unmeasurable particulars, works to draw out those dimensions of capitalist mediation that cannot be thought in the language of structure.

Because critiques of capitalist value emphasize the formal aspects of capital's movement—theorizing value as a *relation* that takes on various forms—they provide a way forward for a Marxist-feminist literary study that need not translate literary texts into fully cognizable concepts. And yet, a feminist literary criticism informed by value theory is distinctly unlike those rooted in Althusserian theories of interpellation, which similarly appeal to the explanatory power of the purely formal when they theorize the production of subjectivity as, in Best's words, the "misrecognised identification with the formal, empty subject position of the narratives and representations that constitute the social."[57] Far from helping us to diagnose a case of "misrecognised identification" with capital's narratives, value theory and Marxist feminism can work in the service of a feminist literary criticism attuned to the highly ambivalent and dialectical ways in which capitalist subjects might "identify." Let us get more specific about this method, then, and attend in particular to what remains an under-recognized strength of the early texts (not to mention slogans) of Marxist-feminist analyses. Indeed, these early interventions suggest how, in experientially informed ways, Marxist feminists understood value's dissimulating movement in both a visceral and dialectical sense.

The International Wages for Housework movement that sprang up in Padua, New York, and London, among other urban centers in 1972, marked the beginning of a period of sustained anti-capitalist feminist activism and Marxist-feminist theory. Mariarosa Dalla Costa's and Selma James's influential 1972 pamphlet, "Women and the Subversion of the Community," drew on the Italian operaist notion of the social factory, first advanced in Mario Tronti's argument that capitalist production had spread beyond the factory floor and into the social field as a whole.[58] Along with others associated with the journals *Quaderni Rossi* and *Classe Operaia*, figures such as Antonio Negri and Raniero Panzieri argued that new forms of self-organized struggle, independent of trade unions and political parties, and including tactics like sabotage and absenteeism, were key to challenging a new post-Fordist regime of accumulation, and in this vein Dalla Costa and James argued that "the 'unreliability' of women within the home and out of it" would put advanced capitalism in crisis. Federici's "Wages Against Housework," meanwhile, sought to underscore the deliberate impossibility of the demand for wages for housework, since unlike the struggles of the waged worker (who in demanding higher wages "challenges his social role but remains within it"), Wages for Housework represented a "struggle to break capital's plan for women":

> When we struggle for wages we struggle unambiguously and directly against our social role.... To say that we want money for housework is the first step towards refusing to do it, because the demand for a wage makes our work visible, which is the most indispensable condition to begin to struggle against it, both in its immediate aspect as housework and its insidious character as femininity.[59]

In making housework appear, Federici is able to point to the gap between forms of appearance—housework's "immediate aspect as housework"—and their real content or *inneres Band*—housework's "insidious character as femininity." Importantly, it is the perpetual disappearance of the process of feminization under capital that makes such a task necessary. It is in this regard, then, that "Wages Against Housework" is at its root concerned with how capital's objective thought-forms thwart our understandings of its real operations, and therefore with the relation between consciousness and action, abstract thought and concrete activities. In other words: *"They say it is love. We say it is unwaged work."*[60]

For Dalla Costa and James, "the myth of female incapacity" implies a relation of dependency between men's consciousness and the figure of the housewife:

> The role of housewife, behind whose isolation is hidden social labor, must be destroyed. But our alternatives are strictly defined. Up to now, the myth of female incapacity, rooted in this isolated woman dependent on someone else's wage and therefore shaped by someone else's consciousness, has been broken by only one action: the woman getting her own wage, breaking the back of personal economic dependence, making her own independent experience.... *The advent of the women's movement is a rejection of this alternative.*[61]

Linking the housewife, "this isolated woman," both directly to hidden social labor and indirectly to "someone else's consciousness"—where the latter relation is mediated by "someone else's wage"—Dalla Costa and James suggest that the idea of the housewife is a powerful fiction, and one that helps to uphold the gendered division of labor. It is not obvious how this relation between "housewife" and "someone else's consciousness" is to be more precisely theorized. Notable, however, is that Marxist feminists suggest an approach that takes neither the wage relation nor reification as its primary basis for a critique of capitalist totality: instead, the hidden abode of reproduction provides a vantage from which to critique gender not as an ideological problem to be solved by consciousness-raising, nor as a static, categorical difference between waged and unwaged labor, but as *social form*. Part of what is so radical about early Marxist-feminist texts, therefore, is that the method they suggest for theorizing the dialectical relationships between concrete activities and the abstraction of gender begins not with the commodity, the wage, nor the laborer, but with the "formless" histories and negative relations obscured by these forms of appearance.[62]

The analytical kernel of the first key texts of Marxist feminism thus signals an important revolution in Marxist thought that was elsewhere and in comparable ways taking place in the New Reading of Marx, which was itself part of a broader revisionary "return to Marx" in Germany, France, Italy, the United States, and the UK. These dissident Marxisms initially emerged in the 1960s at a time of social upheaval and countercultural resistance, and they sought to break with the Stalinist dogmatism of actually existing socialism in the Eastern Bloc in order to recover an "esoteric Marx" using texts that had historically been neglected, including the *Grundrisse* and *A Contribution to the Critique of Political Economy*. Analyzing capital accumulation as a form of impersonal domination, and often reinterpreting Marx's critique of political economy as a social theory, theorists such as Backhaus and Helmut Reichelt—and later, Michael Heinrich, Moishe Postone, Christopher Arthur, and Diane Elson, among others—presented "a Marxism stripped of dogmatic certainties and naturalistic conceptions of society,"[63] in Werner Bonefeld's words, and shared an emphasis on abstraction with Adorno's work as well as that of Alfred Sohn-Rethel. While Sohn-Rethel was never centrally involved in the Frankfurt School, his 1972 study, *Intellectual and Manual Labour: A Critique of Epistemology*, is heavily influenced by its intellectual productions, not least where Sohn-Rethel explains how real abstraction comes about "by force of the action of exchange":

> People become aware of the exchange abstraction only when they come face to face with the result which their own actions have engendered "behind their backs," as Marx says. In money the exchange abstraction achieves concentrated representation, but a mere functional one—embodied in a coin. It is not recognisable in its true identity as abstract form, but disguised as a thing one carries about in one's pocket, hands out to others, or receives from them. Marx says explicitly that the value abstraction never assumes a representation as such, since the only expression it ever finds is the equation of one commodity with the use-value of another.[64]

Sohn-Rethel's account helpfully underscores how value slips beyond people's cognition—"behind their backs"—because it is not an ideal abstraction (which might be imagined or symbolized) but a *real* one, a relational concept expressed only in equations. For Sohn-Rethel, *Capital* explains the logical inversions of a society in which money constitutes "the real community," one in which "abstraction is therefore the effect of the action of men, and not of their thought,"[65] and where the abstraction of exchange-value organizes what he calls the social synthesis: "the network of relations by which society forms a coherent whole."[66]

Yet this attention to the purely categorial aspect of Marx's critique of political economy, which Sohn-Rethel shares with other dissident readers of Marx, risks a concept of capital as a set of free-floating abstractions—a concept that somewhat glosses over the antagonistic human social relations at the heart of capital accumulation. As Bonefeld argues, in their tendency to read *Capital* and surrounding texts as *logical* expositions of capitalist categories, recent value debates often neglect the fact that the production of surplus value depends on a *historical* progression of unequal and antagonistic class relations: relations based on the separation of the laborer from their means of reproduction by a generalized dependence on the wage that must be reestablished at every moment. These relations, Bonefeld notes in nonetheless Adornian tones, are immanent to the "conceptuality of the law of value." Underlining how exchange relations presuppose production and vice versa, he links the law of value to another "constitutive presupposition": that of the system of "permanent primitive accumulation," which develops "on the logic and by the force of" the continual separation of the proletarian from their ability to reproduce themselves otherwise.[67]

Understanding abstraction as the operative mode of the law of value can thus help to explain the relationship of the value abstraction to violent historical processes of dispossession that can be figured now not only as an antagonism between proletarian and capitalist, but as the ongoing imposition of the "differences and divisions" detailed in Federici's well-known work on primitive accumulation in *Caliban and the Witch*:

> Primitive accumulation ... was not simply an accumulation and concentration of exploitable workers and capital. It was also an accumulation of differences and divisions within the working class, whereby hierarchies built upon gender, as well as "race" and age, became constitutive of class rule and the formation of the modern proletariat.[68]

Federici's account helpfully frames class differentials as mediations of the differential values of different labors, performed by different subjects, according to market rates, even or especially when that wage is set at zero. In this important sense, the impersonal and abstract nature of value helps us to see how capital "makes" differentials,[69] because differentials are abstract, dynamic yet objectively existing relations that emerge as social averages—as identity categories dialectically mediated across populations—and that, in turn, impose or develop existing hierarchical relationships between different subjects.

What is so important about these real-but-abstract relations for how we read gender in literary texts? To return to one of my opening claims, I am arguing that a wide array of poets working today are writing about the obscured relations between abstraction and difference, between an entire society and a variety of entirely specific social determinations. Importantly, they are writing both about capitalist abstraction itself as something sensed but not articulated, and from the position of the *underside* of abstraction—what I refer to above as the "formless" and obscured histories that Marxist feminism takes as its starting point. What might be incompletely comprehended as negative affect can thus be understood as a way of structuring form and feeling so as to capture not only an experience of the poet's immediate surround, which would be legible as "sociable," but an experience of the not-quite-here-and-not-only-now: a sensitivity to totality that unfolds beyond the identificatory logic of conceptual thought, perhaps to theorize what Jameson once called the "Real" glimpsed no longer as Nature but as Capital.

Such dialectical unravelings reveal an important point about the difference between difference and differentials. If the production of class differentials (which, if we are being dialectical about it, also means differentials produced as race, gender, sexuality, ability, and more) is a process driven by abstraction, then difference might be conceived as the diversity of capital's phenomenal forms and the reliable failure of "definite individuals" to reduce to the limited shapes of identity categories—a concept that stands in somewhat homologous relation to the textual, Derridean sense of *différance* as a temporal and spatial resistance to conceptual closure.[70] There is of course a deferral of meaning involved here too: and yet this time, difference appears not as a horizon of endless supplementarity or the play of signification but as the potentially infinite number of real and hierarchized ways in which one might exceed or default on an identity category conditioned by capital, a movement that—as we will see in Chapters 1 and 4, especially—ineluctably folds identity's negation into the perception, at a sensory level, of an entire sequential totality of forms and moving contradiction. Indeed, this failure to fully become a subject, to *become an abstraction*, is traced in the work of a number of groundbreaking theorists of difference—from Eve Sedgwick's well-known *Tendencies* (1994) to Lisa Lowe's *The Intimacies of Four Continents* (2015), to name just two—in critiques that suggest (explicitly or not) how capitalism's internal contradictions make such identities impossible.[71] But it is also a failure arising, not unrelatedly, from an everyday kind of dissension. As Best reminds us, capitalism's dominant narratives "can indeed be 'unmasked by a clear-eyed attention' to the real movement of capital," since "such attention is otherwise called analysis (Marx also calls it 'science') and in addition to being the work of theorists, it is frequently also the outcome of comparing one's own life experience against the day's dominant narratives and scrutinising the difference."[72]

Moving in on that dissension, at the center of this project is a claim about what aesthetic experience can do for feminist critique. The question of how such experience is constituted and expressed has become a site of renewed focus in lyric studies, where, in Jonathan Culler's account, a concept of lyric as the mimesis of the poet's experience has been replaced with the simplistic idea that lyric represents the action of a fictional speaker or persona "whose situation and motivation one needs to reconstruct."[73] Yet as Virginia Jackson persuasively argues, Culler's attempt to recover a more variegated tradition of communal lyric speech happens to be one where "*we* all seem to be White," and symptomatizes the persistent disavowal in lyric studies of the nineteenth-century Black poetics that provided the basis for (white) lyric poetry's most highly prized value, "the pathos of impossible speech."74

Indeed, Jackson's reading of "To the First of August" by the Black teenage poet Ann Plato, whose only publication was a barely circulated book of poems and essays in Hartford, Connecticut, in 1841, dramatically stages this tension when it underscores the difficulty of trying to locate an identity, authorial or speakerly, in a lyric poem that at first seems so generic and immediate as to be detached from any discernible subject. Yet there is more: on further study, Jackson argues, a reader might discern how the poem stages a contradiction between its ostensible resolution in the white supremacist figure of Britannia and the "multiple, indistinct figures to whom [Britannia] delivers 'freedom'"—figures who "shade into the background." The "difficult facility" of Plato's work thus informs Jackson's critique of two centuries of racialized lyric reading—from John Stuart Mill to the Southern Agrarian New Critics and even a post-lyric avant-garde—as it proceeded on the very basis of the Black impossible speech it had to repress, in order to privilege what critics and editors wanted to "overhear" in a poem: namely, "the intimate address of the private person."75

The historical development of this bourgeois lyric imaginary, which invented "lyric" in tandem with the rapid invention of new racial categories in the nineteenth century, is further thrown into relief by Sonya Posmentier's account of how Black US critics developed their own lyric theories and reading practices. To this end, Posmentier reads a 1939 grant proposal by Zora Neale Hurston—a bid for funding to make ethnographic recordings in her home state of Florida—as double-sided in its status as, on the one hand, a bureaucratic document, and on the other hand as a literary text that seeks to aesthetically as well as pedagogically guide its reader in non-institutionalized practices of lyric theory and reading so as to provide "a primer for how to read, hear, and understand Floridian culture."76 As Jackson and Posmentier pose the question of what counts as a poem or a reading practice in the first place, then, both point to the twin activities of reading and writing poetry as dialectical experiences that unfold within the larger frame of a global racial capitalism, in this case as it quickly developed over the nineteenth and early twentieth centuries. Their insights return us to a concept of aesthetic experience as a dialectical activity that takes place through—and thereby also registers—the realities of capital and social difference in processual relation.

Aesthetic experience as dialectical activity: nowhere has this concept been more incisively theorized for our current moment of capitalist decline than in Ngai's work to delineate the aesthetic categories that now predominate in the Global North. Drawing our attention to how the "increasing interpenetration of economy and culture" in the postwar decades has led to "a weakening of art's capacity to serve as an image of non-alienated labor," Ngai demonstrates how the decoupling of aesthetic experience from what is conventionally recognized as art—in a society where almost every experience is aestheticized in some way and where the distinction between artworks and commodities is dissolved—requires new aesthetic categories capable of theorizing the different kinds of subjective agency at work in every part of late capitalist social life.

The cute, the zany, the interesting, and the gimmick thus offer conceptual "quilting points" for a more direct theorization of the relationship between art and society than older aesthetic categories such as the beautiful and the sublime, which purportedly transcended ordinary sociality. In this way, "our aesthetic categories" provoke consideration of the central roles of intersubjectivity, ambivalence, and contradiction in our engagements with aesthetic objects—experiences that might feel strong or weak, warm or cool, and may be borne in relation to high art or mass culture—but they also get us to think about the embodied and discursive aesthetic activities that produce late capitalist subjectivities in the first place.[77] And just as important for our study of how feminized poetry registers the mediation of gender within the matrix of capital's perceptual economy, Ngai's categories offer updated ways to grasp the dialectical modes of perception and aesthetic judgment that Theodor Adorno describes in *Aesthetic Theory* and *Notes to Literature*. Writing about the aesthetic concept of interpretive understanding, Adorno maintains that:

> [I]f that concept is meant to indicate something adequate, something appropriate for the matter at hand, then today it needs to be imagined more as a kind of following along afterward [*Nachfahren*]; as the co-execution [*Mitvollzug*] of the tensions sedimented in the work of art, the processes

that have congealed and become objectified in it. One does not understand a work of art when one translates it into concepts—if one simply does that, one misunderstands the work from the outset—but rather when one is immersed in its immanent movement; I should almost say, when it is recomposed by the ear in accordance with its own logic, repainted by the eye, when the linguistic sensorium speaks along with it.[78]

The power of "the 'cognitive yet nonconceptual character' of poetry" to draw the subject into its internal dynamics is particularly important for Ngai, who, building on Shierry Weber Nicholsen's reading of Adorno, underlines that "the enigmatic 'muteness' of poetry is thus linked not just to its refusal of communicative language, but to its turn toward a mimesis that involves the subject, in a 'silent internal tracing of the work's articulations,' assimilating herself to the object's form."[79] Because the poetic works to which I turn in this study attend to experiences of simultaneously abstract and concrete relations, their mimetic action not only registers the formal characteristics of gendering processes as they are lived and felt on both highly personal and all-too-disinterested scales, but does so in a way that allows us extra-conceptual access to that process. Thus, I aim to show how what Vishmidt has called "a rationality premised on sensuous non-knowledge,"[80] or a form of experiential perception that cannot be resolved into concepts, is made possible in these works, as well as how this "non-knowledge" may help to show, often with painful specificity, how gender is inextricably bound up in racial domination and the reproduction of class relations. With this bracing possibility in mind, let us consider some brief and fairly straightforward examples of work by feminist poets who are writing in modes at least tonally if not declaratively aligned with Marxist-feminist political struggles during the postwar boom era of the 1960s and 1970s, the moment just prior to the period of global economic stagnation from which the rest of this book's poetry archive is drawn.

Capital's Categories

The laborious, repetitive character of reproductive activities has been expertly and often humorously explored in twentieth-century feminist poetry, particularly since the advent of second-wave feminism in the early 1960s. Diane Di Prima's 1961 book *Dinners and Nightmares*, for example, captures not only the mundane drudgery of domestic work, but an attendant anxiety emerging at the point where the private oppressions of the kitchen are compounded by images of a male-coded public world, as in "NIGHTMARE 2":

> Having a cleaner house than usual I did the dishes. Gathering those long slime worms, dayold spaghetti, I dropped from the sink into the garbage them whereupon one slithered to the floor and lay there smirking.
>
> Ugh I said but having a cleaner floor than usual I tried to pick it up, whereupon it nudged limply over and again smirked. After ten minutes of chase I with dirtier hands than usual gave up.
>
> O well I said under the water faucet it will be hard as nails tonight the bastard and I'll pick it up stiff as a board.
>
> Whereupon looking down again I saw a line of sleek roaches were marching the worm away and singing Onward Christian Roaches.
>
> The din was unbearable and I remained horrored to the spot until a slightly larger roach, obviously leader, nudged me to see if I too could be carried off.[81]

The smirking, inert piece of spaghetti is cute in the sense that Ngai observes when she comments on the power of supposedly impotent phenomena to elicit a mix of tenderness and aggression in their beholder, who is "frequently overpowered by a second feeling—a sense of manipulation or exploitation."[82] Indeed, within the *mise-en-scène* of this poem, the spaghetti seems to symbolize a more inchoate force, perturbing in its paradoxical elusiveness and all-too-slippery materiality. The grammatical reversal of "I dropped from the sink into the garbage / them," whereby the object unconventionally follows the predicate of the sentence, sets up an antagonism between "I" and "them," a struggle playfully echoed in the second stanza, where the subject is separated from their verb by a rather antiquated use of the subordinate clause: "After ten minutes of chase / I with dirtier hands than usual gave up."

In their comedic and unnerving performance, these rhetorical constructions imbue the feminized figure in the kitchen with an understated stoicism, as their monologue—"Ugh I said," "Oh well I said"—marks the everyday perseverance of women-in-kitchens, where the "usual" (a word repeated twice in this short poem) serves doubly to suggest not only a quotidian cycle of tedium, but a measurable standard from which one of the primary products of reproductive work, a clean house, can be judged as "better" or "worse." But what is really perturbing about this poetry of the household abject is the way it highlights the psychological horror of domestic entrapment as a historical condition. The poem turns a surreal corner at the word "whereupon," and, in a shift that transplants the speaker into a social world just as absurd as the space of the kitchen itself, the image of a uniform line of roaches carrying a "slime worm" suggests a triple nightmare of oppressive religious regimes, militaristic obedience, and creaturely sacrifice.

Ironically granting a banal piece of day-old spaghetti the synecdochal power to stand in for a whole set of social relations suggests power flowing in exactly the reverse direction. As Federici puts it in "Wages Against Housework":

> It is important to recognise that when we speak of housework we are not speaking of a job as other jobs, but we are speaking of the most pervasive manipulation, the most subtle and mystified violence that capitalism has ever perpetrated against any section of the working class.[83]

Pervasive, subtle, mystified: Federici's emphasis on the obscured violence of the gendered division of labor also recalls the perceptual delinking discussed above as an objective movement, one that imposes limits and foreclosures on what may be thought or drawn into representation—limits met with many forms of pushback in feminist poetry of the 1960s and 1970s. June Jordan's 1977 poem for the Mississippi activist and civil rights leader Fannie Lou Hamer, for example, laments the counterinsurgent impedance of housework: "lion spine relaxed/hell / what's the point to courage / when you washin clothes?"[84] Alice Notley's 1973 poem, "But He Says I Misunderstood," on the other hand, tracks the irritated repetitions of a feminized speaker who connects her sense of insignificance to a longer chain of systematic disadvantage:

> . . . he forgot to put my name on our checks
>   However,
> He went to get the checks however
> He had checks to deposit in his name
>   Because
> He's older & successfuller & teaches because[85]

In both of these cases, it is clear that more is at stake than the problem of the toil of laundry or the feeling of inferiority. Federici famously answers her own question—"what difference could some more money make to our lives?"—by insisting that the demand for wages is in fact a demand *against* housework, since it also demands the revolutionizing of "all our family and social relations" and not merely the recognition of housework as necessary to value-production in the waged sphere.[86] Thus, where Marx notes the perfunctory role of the wage-worker who is transformed by industrialization "from his very childhood, into part of a specialized machine,"[87] Federici is equally forthright about the training of girls who must transform into women:

> A lot of us recognise that we marry for money and security; but it is time to make it clear that while the love or money involved is very little, the work which awaits us is enormous. This is why older women always tell us "Enjoy your freedom while you can, buy whatever you want now . . ." But unfortunately it is almost impossible to enjoy any freedom if from the earliest days of life you are trained to be docile, subservient, dependent and most important to sacrifice yourself and even to get pleasure from it. *If you don't like it, it is your problem, your failure, your guilt, your abnormality.*[88]

In the wake of civil rights and decolonization movements, second-wave feminism, Black Power, workers' strikes and anti-nuclear and student protests, many feminist poets *did not like it* and wrote as much—often, it bears noting, to explore feelings of failure, guilt, and abnormality with a pointed sense of humor shared by Marxist-feminist documents of the time. Witness Betsy Warrior's Wages for Housework campaign poster depicting an abandoned iron burning a pair of trousers (Figure 1), or Notley's description of childcare: "Some of it is pretty and useful, like when I say to them / 'Now we will go for a walk in the snow to the store' / and prettily and usefully we go."[89]

Marxist feminism's account of the becoming-concrete of capital's abstractions thereby aids our reading of the non-conceptual aspects of feminized poetry and our understanding of what happens when we are carried along by aesthetic works that convey a sense of capital's various mediations of gender. Rather than unveiling an underlying structure in the kind of "big reveal" that has come to caricature modes of paranoid or diagnostic decoding,[90] these poetries offer us dynamic ways to think about the recompositions of gender as

Figure 1. A campaign poster for the Wages for Housework movement; artist Betsy Warrior.

Source: Yanker Poster Collection at the Library of Congress, c. 1965–80. https://lccn.loc.gov/2015649375

they toggle sensory and intuitive forms of perception to larger rhythms and systems. Nealon's reading of Marx is especially helpful for thinking about these processual aspects of a capitalist totality, particularly as he highlights the denaturalizing work that Marx's analysis performs when it questions the very basis of capital's basic categories:

> To read *Capital* is to see that the framework of thinking from the whole that Marx takes up from Hegel and recontextualizes, that is, the framework of totality, is less like a boiling down of diverse particulars into a

flattening ur-concept ("the wage" or "class conflict") and much more like the unfolding of a concept embedded in a social relation ("the commodity").... Critiques of Marxist thought that derive from Schellingian critiques of Hegel suggest that dialectical thought fails to think outside its categories—to think outside the wage, outside class, outside exploitation. But Marx's emphasis was always to examine how categories come into social being in the first place.[91]

Indeed, in volume 3 of *Capital,* Marx describes three social classes—the capitalist class, the landowning class, and the working class—as social forms of appearance tied by property relations to capital's ostensible sources of revenue: capital, land, and labor (where these latter three categories comprise the Trinity Formula, the three sources of revenue presented by Adam Smith).[92] What we might think of as the three "base" social classes, then, are classes embodied and reproduced by actual people who are either capitalists, landowners, or proletarians.

But as we know, these categories are further differentiated, most obviously along lines of gender and race. This fact, along with our earlier insight regarding the limited shapes of available identity categories and the endless number of ways one could default on these forms of appearance, returns us again to the question: How do *these* categories, and not others, come into social being? Herein lies a crucial connection, I would argue, between Marx's critique of value and recent developments in transfeminism, where we find a renewed focus on gendered categories of identity as social abstractions that in part emerges from queer theory's longstanding critique of identity, and especially from its disarticulating work to reveal how the "richest junctures" in sexual and kinship relations aren't the ones where *"everything means the same thing,"* as Eve Kosofsky Sedgwick resoundingly put it.[93] To be sure, this queer negativity informs Emma Heaney's critique of the ideology of cisgender, which employs the effective tactic of simply redescribing its object:

> We're used to thinking of cisness as an identity. One is cis if one is not trans, one has a cis body if one doesn't have a trans body. But ... cisness is more accurately understood as the ideology that sorts us into these two categories. Cisness is the belief that, for almost everyone, one or another set of qualities adhere to our bodies at birth based on the appearance of our genitals (either at or before birth with imaging technology).[94]

Heaney's refusal of the identitarian vocabulary of cisness relies on the idea of sex and gender as distributional categories, and sex as a mediating technology. We might say that the social classes of capitalist, landowner, and proletarian are helpful analytical concepts here, then, because they represent what Marx might call the "thinnest" social identities: we can tie each of them, respectively, to three corresponding forms of appearance—the supposed revenue sources of capital, land, and labor. The distributional categories of gender and sex, on the other hand, arise from a more complex array of social arrangements, laws, and customs. In *Feminism Against Cisness*, Heaney offers a clarifying example of this fact when she describes how the trans feminist activist Marsha P. Johnson's identification with her mother, a "strong Black woman," provided the ground for her sex identification. Importantly for Heaney, Johnson's account of her identification with womanhood is closely connected to the varieties of feminized labor—washing, ironing, cooking, sewing—that she saw her mother performing. Johnson's account of sex identification thereby offers an example of "one material way in which the abstraction called sex materializes in the consciousness of individuals, both for those whom we call cis and those whom we call trans."[95] What better way to highlight the impersonal, economic dimensions of sexual difference than by pointing to the perpetual and repeated actions that made Johnson's mother into a woman, and subsequently provided a site of affinity for Johnson to develop her own, reflexively social sense of sex identity—"an identity born of skill transmission"?[96]

Conclusion

In the chapters that follow, one of my aims is to explain the payoff of value-critical Marxism for a politicized mode of literary analysis that has been placed on the defense by postcritical trends in literary studies over the last two decades—a shift away from what many experienced as a more high stakes and politically intense moment of theoretical production in the 1990s.[97] Doing so involves showing how the critique of value means practicing Marxist literary criticism differently from the symptomatic and (post)structuralist ways to which Marxists have been accustomed.[98] But such a task is only made possible by what the poetry itself brings to Marxist critique. Crucially, the works I read here are able to do two things at once, as they both express the reality of capitalism's appearances and critically register various levels of dissension from them. Moreover, in folding our reading experience into those points where something feels a little off, maybe deeply wrong, or even pleasurably incorrect or artificial, these poems draw us into the critical work of comparison—comparing what we know versus what appears before us—a dialectical kind of criticism that, as I suggest in Chapter 1, is not simply akin but rather systematically connected to the comparative and deductive aspects of value critique.[99]

Yet bringing what we "know" to our readings always begs the question: What *do* we know, and how? *Behind Our Backs* is less about what poems or poets can or cannot know, and more about how certain poetic strategies record and solicit aesthetic experiences of nonidentity in a way that already enacts a mode of critique and still demands *more* (and different) critique. In this spirit, each of my chapters brings a different but related critical framework into dialogue with feminized poetry to explore, among other things, the problem value's disappearing action poses for feminist consciousness-raising; the abject as the reproductive underside of value; the exemplarity of Indigenous feminist abolitionism; and the negativity and transindividuality of post-lyric writing diasporically attuned both to African American sorrow songs and more recent Black radicalisms. The particular works of poetry presented here have been chosen for the very specific forms of feminized difference they allow us to think about: firstly, in terms of how the poets' positionalities as queer, trans, Punjabi diasporic, Indigenous, and Caribbean diasporic writers come to bear on the motivations of the writing—across political orientations ranging from camp to new materialist, anarchist to abolitionist, for starters—and secondly, and relatedly, in terms of the distinct strategies these poetries model in order to "draw the real into [their] own texture,"[100] to register the ways social forms are shaped by capital's inner logics and tendencies. In bringing these works together, the argument of *Behind Our Backs* does not lead with periodizing claims per se, but it does proceed on the basis of two historical assertions. One is a claim derived primarily from value-critical Marxism, from Jameson's arguments in *The Political Unconscious* and *Valences of the Dialectic*, and from Marx himself, about what history actually is, insofar as my arguments and readings are based on a concept of "History" as the movement of capital propelled by the uncoordinated actions of individuals, what Marx called the moving contradiction of an "upside-down world."[101] As a result, I inevitably make another claim, which is that these recent efforts in feminized poetry to write about the inverted or otherwise thwarted appearances of objective social forms are undertaken in an era of obvious and sharp social contradictions, and *Behind Our Backs* endeavors to read them as such.

Mostly written after the 2007–2008 financial crisis, this poetry is toggled to a period of terminal economic decline, or what macro economists have called "secular stagnation."[102] Indeed, both Marxist and liberal economists have come to regard the capitalist restructuring during the late 1960s and early 1970s as the beginning of the end for so-called healthy capitalism.[103] As Robert Brenner argues, economic slowdown started not with the 1973 oil crisis but with flagging profit rates in the mid-1960s. His analysis of postwar capitalist economies shows how, after the "long boom"—the postwar golden age of high-profit US manufacturing—capital entered a period of extended crisis in which the global economy only continues to stagnate and contract.[104] In the aftermath of the New Left political struggles and economic turmoil of 1968–1973, the various institutions that mediated the relation between capital and labor in the postwar era—not least unions and welfare states—fell into rapid decline. As Sean O'Brien points out, this has instead been an era in which the conservative family form has been consolidated as "a site of risk absorption and asset leverage" in financializing and oil-fueled economies in the Global North.[105]

The 2007–2008 financial crisis and the COVID-19 pandemic have rapidly accelerated this global economic decline, leading an increasing number of critics to examine the re-externalization or *expulsion* of labor. While those who are regularly employed confront capital more directly, with less of the protection of unions or the thirty-five-hour work week, for example, ever more people find themselves locked out of the wage and the formal economy. Recent studies by Jason E. Smith and Phil Neel and analyses by the Endnotes and SIC collectives offer especially clarifying explanations of this transformation. Drawing on Marx's theory of surplus populations, or a reserve army of labor, these theorists show how the tendency to boost productivity by increasing "constant capital" (introducing new machinery and tools, for example) expels a growing mass of people from the cycle of accumulation, meaning that the reproduction of the relationship between capital and labor has itself entered into crisis.[106] Their claims are supported by Marx's argument about a contradiction internal to capital's own logic: technological advances increase productivity by reducing the relative portion of waged (human) labor required for production, but in doing so they squeeze out the only real source of value—abstract labor—thus lowering the value of each commodity produced.[107] We see the results of the disintegration of the "capital-labor relation" and its circuits of reproduction in rising unemployment and underemployment, in the proliferation of precarious work in the service sector, and, as Annie McClanahan has shown, in the reliance of low- and middle-income households on consumer debt.[108] Recent arguments have also cogently tied these economic transformations to the ideological resurgence of ethnonationalisms, right-wing conspiracy theories, Islamophobia, antisemitism, and transphobia: narratives in which the bogeyman figure of a globalist agenda—sometimes called "Cultural Marxism," often simply "Leftism," most recently "wokeness"—functions "to reconcile certain contradictory facts, like crushing inequality in what is supposed to be the world's premier democracy, or declining living standards in the richest country in history."[109]

This contradictory situation, the present threads of a much longer history of uneven development in the global economy, produces the uneven poetics of poets like Mayer, Gabriel, Annharte, Kapil, and Black. What at different points in this book (and drawing on the language of other critics) I refer to as "hidden abodes," "aching gaps," "elsewheres," and "polytemporal pacts" are poets' attempts to write that history and to do so in a way that conveys both its immediate reality and its nonidentity. To riff on Marx's argument in the *Grundrisse*, this poetic critique of capital requires from its readers and writers that they move counterintuitively from the abstract to the concrete—to the many diverse, perceptible particulars arranged by poems—and back again to what might now be grasped as a "rich totality."[110] In this post-2008 regard, Bernadette Mayer's 1970s and 1980s poems are outliers in my archive. But I begin with her older poems because, from a previous dearth of critical attention that some have put down to their idiosyncratic, hard-to-categorize nature,[111] recent critical interest in Mayer's engagements with post-Fordist work patterns serves to underscore the secular, long-term character of our current moment of capitalist decline.[112] Indeed, the surge of interest in her work among poets and critics over the last decade is also clearly tied to its unabashedly anti-capitalist sentiment, which may today seem more urgent and less one-dimensional than it once might have to theorists of Language poetry.[113]

Chapter 1 accordingly argues that because capital is a social modality that paradoxically eludes representation yet assumes objective forms, finding purchase in the "reality of the appearance," to use Hegel's term, it presents a problem for a feminist politics of consciousness-raising reliant on cognition. The chapter begins by highlighting the ways that radical and revolutionary feminist theories have shared with socialist feminisms a tendency to rely on notions of fixed and ontologized social classes (the concept of "sex class" being one egregious example), to suggest that we find a much more robust account of feminization in recent value-critical feminist analyses that understand gender and sex as mediating categories produced by capital's function of abstraction. Turning to Mayer's conceptual projects and serial sonnets, I suggest that value-critical accounts of the mediation of gender help us to see how Mayer's poetry *also* works with a sense of gender as an impersonal and mediating force. Indeed, we can read her poems for the way they track the recompositions of sex and gender, in part through metrical and syntactic maneuvers that connect gendering moments to emphatically capitalist movements of space and time. What *is* feminization at root? Where is it coming from?—they seem to fundamentally ask. This mode of critique, while not analytical in the way of Marx's method, nevertheless shares the totalizing and speculative drive that underwrites *Capital*.

Chapter 1 subsequently discusses a long poem by Kay Gabriel, drawn from her 2022 collection, *A Queen in Bucks County*, to argue that Gabriel is making art that senses determinations by the value-form where they are otherwise at their most illegible. As with Mayer's work, Gabriel's dialectical expressions of identification and disidentification with gendered and sexed identity categories surface in polysemic and surprising ways. There is, therefore, something special about this type of poem and its capacity to gesture beyond itself that might be conceived in terms of its unevenness, its difficulties and antagonisms, in the misalignments between its formal properties and ostensible content, which allow the poem and us to veer away from capital's self-representations and dominant narratives. The result is a poetics that, by way of a series of cunning metaphorical substitutions, shows us how the trans body—like all bodies—is both *real* and *not real*, a phenomenological and capitalist reality perennially reconstituted by capitalism's "heres" and "elsewheres" in the same constitutive moment.[114] The queen in Bucks County is thus not "realized" in any single erotics or identity, but instead unmasks the artifice of all social relations in the world depicted across the collection as a whole, which uncannily resembles ours.

From works that make feminization legible by connecting it to a capitalist totality or by staging a dialectics of (dis)identification with gendered social forms, Chapter 2 considers two further ways in which feminized poets have inventively theorized capitalist abstraction, reading Bhanu Kapil's 2015 collection, *Ban en Banlieue*, which experimentally traces the systematic effects of a globalized capitalist violence, and Alli Warren's 2013 collection, *Here Come the Warm Jets*, which records an intuitive sense of value's spectral qualities and its form-determining movement. The chapter begins, though, by setting out a more general definition of form-determination, firstly by way of a reading of Elson's essay, "The Value Theory of Labour," which itself offers an illuminating reading of Marx's theory of value and a clarifying account of how value socially "fixes" labor. The particular concept of domination theorized here explains how value gains "external independence" in the money form, as if moving all by a force of its own, and as we will see, Elson's account aids our understanding of value's relation to feminizing forms of social reproduction when it describes the formation of labor in capitalism as "a process of social determination that proceeds from the indeterminate to the determinate; from the potential to the actual; from the formless to the formed."[115]

What is formed? What remains unformed? With these questions in mind, the chapter also draws on the systematic analysis put forth in an essay by the Endnotes collective, "The Logic of Gender." Endnotes's concept of the abject, in particular, as a capitalist category highlights the unrealized capaciousness of a dialectical critique of value, particularly for feminist inquiries into the unstructured, unformed, or hidden abodes of a capitalist whole. Taking it up in this manner, I read Kapil's *Ban en Banlieue* as a salient example of a feminized and racialized poetics that traces a process of abjection through a system of global interconnections. For Ban, the Punjabi British subject of *Ban en Banlieue*, the life-shaping violence of white supremacy often figures on an impersonal and totalizing scale. At the same time, the collection's imagery, somatic themes, and diaristic forms establish a connective intimacy with other subjects facing capital's secular tendencies to expel populations from the formal economy. *Ban en Banlieue* thus delineates a gendered "remainder" of activities produced and shaped by capital that must remain outside of market relations. But I also suggest, to some degree in contestation of Kapil's own comments on the resistance of gendered and racialized experience to analysis, that the abject dimension of feminized reproduction can be theorized as a negative dialectic and constitutes a *doubly* dissimulated excrescence of violence traced in our experience of reading this diasporic feminized poetry. Indeed, Kapil's work suggests we could expand the category of the abject to account for an even less discernible (and significantly racialized) dimension of capitalist abjection beyond the set of abject feminized reproductive activities that Endnotes re-theorizes as an economic category.

Further pursuing the question of what can and cannot be discerned in capitalism, Chapter 2 concludes by reading Alli Warren's contrasting poem, "Acting Out," as a *writing* of the abstract that attempts to actually enter the space of mediation itself. Inevitably, the poem fails in this task. But it complicates Alberto Toscano's observation that figuration is a requirement for thinking the abstract, because the affective and rhythmic dimensions of the poem bypass figuration altogether. While "Acting Out" is self-confessedly confined to the realm of its own humanist temporality and mediated perceptions, it nevertheless seems to describe the active process of form-determination, implicitly acknowledging how time and history are organized by abstractions that cannot be cognized even as they are propelled by the actions of individuals "as they *really* are," in Elson's words; that is to say, "as they operate, produce materially, and hence as they work under definite material limits, pre-suppositions and conditions independent of their will."[102]

The poetry and theory I examine in the second half of this book reminds us that a world locked to the rhythms of capital accumulation is not the only possible world. Chapter 3 shows how Marie Annharte Baker's poetry is grounded in Anishinaabeg concepts, subjectivities, and relationships that, for Annharte as well as this reader, strongly resonate with Marxian (and we might say, small-c communist) understandings of how our social world is made and remade. Leanne Betasamosake Simpson's delineation of the concept of "*kwe*," the Ojibwe word approximating "woman," is especially significant here for the way it encapsulates a method of generating both one's own identity and one's material world through physical, personal, and spiritual relationships. Kwe as such creates a meaningful and intentional social world that we can pointedly contrast to a history made behind the backs of the producers. Moreover, and perhaps most pertinently for the argument of this book, it is a way of doing theory: indeed, Simpson's image of *kwe-as-theorist* emphasizes both "kwe" and "theory" as the result of daily practices. This form of knowledge, she insists, is "not just experiential knowledge or embodied knowledge," but "theoretically anchored to and generated through Nishnaabeg intelligence."[116]

And it is hard to overstate the theoretical drive of Annharte's 2012 collection, *Indigena Awry*. My readings seek to highlight the range and extent of conceptual production undertaken in her poetry at the level of poetic form and linguistic invention, not only as it works to critique the fictions of Indigenous authenticity prescribed by a liberal politics of recognition that props up the ongoing dispossession of First Nations in Canada, but also as it generates new Indigenized concepts. As such, "coyote," "grandmother voice," "medicine line," "squaw," or "plain old kokum" become, in Annharte's hands, intentionally bastardized ideas that are all the more rhetorically persuasive for the humor and pleasure they bring to the task of marking out the contradictions of settler-colonial societies. In this vein, Chapter 3 proceeds to read Annharte's work as, among other things, a critique of racializing settler conceptions of Indigeneity. I argue that her poems are aligned with an abolitionist politics that understands "race" as an array of ascriptive procedures, and racial categories as "indices of structural subordination," to use Christopher Chen's incisive terms.

Yet the precise meaning of abolition is very much at stake here because Indigenous cultural identities are based in cultures and traditions that predate European colonization, and thus they are not reducible to the hierarchical racial categories that Chen theorizes as "race." Addressing the question of what it means to abolish an abstract identity category, I note how the appearance of this political horizon from within the waves of militant struggle propelled by the New Left in the 1960s finds a corollary in the under-recognized abolitionist sentiments of late twentieth-century Anglo-American poetry. While we can periodize these political and cultural shifts in advanced capitalist countries by connecting them to cycles of accumulation and crisis, the meaning of a politics and poetics of abolition is fundamentally recast in Indigenous contexts, which require that we dialectically account for other temporal orders and striations of history—a practice Harry Harootunian calls "deprovincializing Marx."[117] Reading Annharte's poetry as an abolitionist poetics emerging from a historical temporality that is conjunctural to (but crucially not the same as) the dominant model of cycles of accumulation specific to the (settler) Global North, I argue, allows us to better read Annharte's poems for their specifically Anishinaabe critique of capital's production of a liberal-settler version of "Indigeneity." And as with the figure of "Gynegran" who, like a coyote, "is flexible and inconsistent. Adaptable contradiction,"[118] such an approach enables us to grasp the deep theoretical work of her vernacular lyrics as they deliberately meld significations of race, gender, and class to suggest their immanent co-constitution, challenging intersectional models and Marxist-feminist methods alike.

The question of incommensurable temporalities is the central focus of Chapter 4, which reads the British, US-based artist Hannah Black's 2022 novella, *Tuesday or September or The End* as a lyric work, as well as a book of speculative fiction that resonates thematically with Black's recent sculpture and video works. Black's characters dramatize the opposition between a socialist electoral politics and an abolitionist pursuit of insurrectionary revolution, but it is the role of speculative thought that dominates the plot, as Black links "faith in the infinite possibility" and a hermeneutic based on the language of astrology and chance to the capacity to imagine other social arrangements.[119]

While we can note Jameson's longstanding preference for narrative as the literary genre that possesses a "unique capacity to hold multiple temporalities together"—a capacity that allows narrative works "to make time and history appear," as he puts it in *Valences of the Dialectic*[120]—I argue in this chapter that the holistic method he offers for reading the interferences and incommensurabilities of distinct historical temporalities is wholly apt for reading post-lyric works that do the same. Jameson's method is a dialectical reworking of Paul Ricoeur's attempt to accommodate incommensurable concepts of time offered by linguistic critics—the notion that grammatical tenses reflect our experience of time, for instance, versus the notion that language in fact *produces* temporal experiences. Ricoeur's "third way" solution of an existentialist notion of time is one that Jameson finds obviously unsatisfying, but he nevertheless discovers in this argument "a new methodological key"—one in which the "reality" of time and temporality can be figured in "the intersection between several incommensurable representations." This insight, I argue, taps into what is unique about a Marxist dialectical method, a method whose very basis in material history is what makes it perpetually open to its own negation and reconstitution. And it can also highlight a strategic disloyalty to categories of literary genres and conventions in work such as Black's, especially where the clash of narrative and lyric services to theorize the relation between totality and difference, or subject and system.

On this basis, I read *Tuesday or September or The End* as an example of a literary strategy that Fred Moten calls the "not-in-between": a lyric tradition of Black radicalism in which speech-based strategies such as anacrusis, arrhythmia, dialect, and accent gesture to the difference—the "not-in-between"—between the real movement of history and its representations. Reading C. L. R. James's *The Black Jacobins*, Moten thus finds "a serrated lyricism," a linguistic innovation that ushers in "a complex recasting of the dialectic."[121] The in-betweenness of this literary concept itself bears noting, inflected as it is by both Marxist dialectics and a deconstructive notion of *différance*. But perhaps what is most compelling here for Marxist readers is the way Moten's Black radicalism insists on its emergence from an incommensurable yet "irruptive" striation of historical time that cannot be separated from the colonial and imperialist progression of European Enlightenment. In this regard, I argue that his view of dialectics not only resonates with Jameson's theory of the violent intersections of multiple temporalities but shares its basic conceptual contours.

Moten's lyric reading of James's prose informs this chapter's lyric reading of *Tuesday or September or The End*, which emphasizes the speculative dimensions of both dialectical theory and reading. For Black's protagonist Bird, the spatial history of Caribbean diaspora structures an ability "to perceive movements in the general mood" in the hair salon where she works.[122] Yet for Bird, cosmological forces offer not an escapist anti-politics but an insurrectionary energy guided by an image of a world unbounded by abstract capitalist time, and importantly one in which meaning might be restored. In Jamesonian fashion, dialectical interpretation thus requires "extending the very frame of time" beyond the history of capitalism,[123] expanding outwards to geological and even cosmological (read: utopian) time, to dramatize a series of dialectical reversals that point to the contradiction at the heart of capital's meaningless logic. Yet as this chapter also argues, the eventual break of *Tuesday or September or The End* takes lyric rather than narrative form, where Black encourages us to understand moments of recognition—of self, of others, of the space of a relation—as incomplete moments in a textured and moving system that is not only situated in historical (capitalist) time but in the deep time of human history, geological formations, and planetary movements. These incommensurable temporalities not only allow Black to lyrically evoke what Sedgwick poignantly called transindividuality, the concept of identity as a state of dispossession, but also to suggest how subjectivities and political imaginaries are socially bound to larger systems—our current one of which is dependent on the perpetual dispossession of our means of reproduction, which is also to say it is dependent on us.

# Consciousness-Raising and the Problem of Value

Bernadette Mayer and Kay Gabriel

IN HER 1978 ESSAY "CONSCIOUSNESS," Vivian Gornick traces the emergence of the feminist practice of consciousness-raising, taking the women's groups and radical organizations of New York City as her example.[1] The simplicity of the practice is key to its success, Gornick observes: in the shared act of recounting, women's privatized experiences are transformed into legitimate subject matter for cultural analysis. Radical feminists soon sensed that the result was "political dynamite."[2] The discovery of similarities among women's experiences was explosive not only because it opened affirmative avenues for empathy and collective action among members of women's groups, but because it prompted recognition of structural causes and new practices of interpretation. Charting the meeting of a consciousness-raising group in Greenwich Village, Gornick records the words of one member, Roberta, who rejects the idea of a monolithic woman's experience—"whatever on earth that is"—but exclaims: "oh God! The samenesses we have found, and the way in which these meetings have changed our lives!" The discovery of sameness is accompanied by the familiar recognition of a discrepancy. On being told to smile by a stranger while walking down Fifth Avenue, another contributor to the group, Lucie, observes, "I had just an ordinary, sort of thoughtful expression on my face. And he thought I was *depressed*. And I couldn't help it, I said to myself, Would he have said that to you if you were a man? And I answered myself immediately: No!"[3]

Consciousness is raised, writes Gornick, when women come "under the spell of a wholly new interpretation" and remain there.[4] But the coordinates of these new interpretations were famously multiple and often opposed. Lucie's expression of negative solidarity is made powerful by the absurdity of its gendered inversion, and yet this scenario depends on a subjunctive grammatical formulation—"if you were a man"—to conjure an imaginary man into a scene that would never take place, for its meaning would be different. The blank negativity of this impossible scene leaves open all kinds of interpretive possibilities. Thus, while Lucie's recollected experience registers the way women are called into existence through antagonistic moments of gendered ascription, her insight is predominantly defined not by a sense of gender variation but by its stark political claim to a binary inequality—one that produces a collective identity in its movement from a particular experience to the categorical social group "not-men," yet highlights this shared experience of feminization only in its most normative and static form.[5]

Recognizing consciousness-raising as a brilliantly collectivizing and genuinely liberating strategy does not foreclose a critique of its limits, however. Reading poems by Bernadette Mayer and Kay Gabriel, this chapter argues that the problem with articulating feminized experiences—in other words, doing consciousness-raising—is that they often bring more to the table than can be conceptualized in conscious thought. This has presented a special problem for Marxist feminism. In seeking to connect women's experiences to an understanding of a global, imperialist capitalism, Marxist feminists have tended to rely on a distinction between reproduction and production that posits the former's externalization—its naturalized, unpaid, or disavowed character—as the basis for ethical and positivist claims about reproduction as a site of plenitudinous resistance to capitalist forces, and which, in the same conceptual movement, have enabled gendered identities to be conceived in straightforwardly positive terms. In the discussion that follows, an analysis of capital's function of real abstraction—what I will characterize as its emptying-out movement—can help us to instead understand reproduction and its corollary, feminization, not as a logically required "outside" to capital, but as elements of a contradictory, mediated social whole.

As established in the Introduction, Marx's critique of value demonstrates how it moves through the world in relational ways that may be analyzed but never directly represented, and this insight helps to explain an important limit to consciousness-raising. Relative and equivalent, literal and abstract, the value-form imparts an abstract quality to the concrete in a direct mode when it appears as money, commodities, or labor, and an indirect mode as it emerges from and takes social form in a differentiated and hierarchized concrete world of bodies, subjectivities, geographies, and logistics, to name just a few of those forms. This means that there is no "uncovering" of ideology per se, since ideology can now be understood "not as a modality of subjectivity but rather as a radically historical modality of capital itself."[6] As we will see, Mayer and Gabriel employ a range of formal and often vernacular poetic strategies that, albeit not always intentionally, work to trace this historical modality—the "real" of capital—through its inverted appearances and phenomenological forms.

This type of inquiry leads us away from epistemological questions of what poems or poets might "know" and towards direct observations about how both Mayer and Gabriel record and solicit aesthetic experiences of nonidentity in their work: the sense, for example, of how an experience unfolding in a present, socially locatable moment is at the same time formed by its constitutive relations to elsewheres both known and unknown. The possibility of coming into (feminist or class) consciousness is implicitly acknowledged, in these works, as something of a misnomer, and not only because it is not possible to cognitively map a capitalist totality, to recall Fredric Jameson's well-known argument, but because the reality we perceive is, in fact, objectively real.[7] As Werner Bonefeld puts it:

> There is only one world, and that is the world of appearance. However, what is appearance an appearance of, and what appears in appearance? Social objectivity "does not lead a life of its own." The relationship between coins is a socially constituted relationship of economic objectivity—the social relations vanish in their economic appearance as a relationship between coined metals, and this appearance is real—it imposes itself over the social individuals because it prevails in and through them. What appears in the appearance of society as a "stone," or a "coin," is thus a definite social relationship between individuals subsisting as a relationship between "coins."[8]

Bonefeld characterizes this objectivizing process—in which economic relations are realized in our daily activities—as the assertion of the "irrational rationality" of economic forms, alluding to the strange way in which capital's thoroughly rational aim of producing more capital is also the absurd pursuit of its own self-expansion. But, as he notes, what is really at issue is the *social* constitution of economic forms. As he puts it simply: "why does this content of human social reproduction take that fateful economic form?"[9]

The ultimate wager of this chapter is that feminized poetry fulfills an important critical function in helping us to answer this question. In reading these poems as always more than themselves, we restore our function as effective feminist critics alert to the work's solicitation of a "felt sense" of subjectivation—to adapt Gayle Salamon's term—that may not necessarily be cognized or represented but is nonetheless based on a shared historicity.[10] This is akin to what Jonathan Flatley evokes when, drawing on Theodor Adorno's notion of the shudder as "radically opposed to the conventional idea of experience,"[11] he describes literary texts as "machines of self-estrangement" that use affect as the "shuttle" through which to insert history into aesthetic experience:

> The affect that one has in the space of the artwork (which hovers alongside the cognitive experience as what Adorno calls a "trans-aesthetic subject") links one back to the world like a rubber band or the bungee on a bungee jumper, pulling one back from the artwork into the world, but pulling one back through a strange parabola which has altered one's view of the world and unsettled one's relation to it.[12]

The return from the artwork, in which "one has the sensation that one has just been temporarily dislocated from one's subjectivity," entails that we register the historical constitution of our individual experiences: in other words, that we register an abstract dimension of our own subjectivity. And yet, Flatley notes, describing his own sense of this movement, "I have that feeling of inexplicable familiarity."[13]

There is a striking resonance to be drawn between this experience and the "unparticularized" and everyday perception Sianne Ngai describes in judgments of the capitalist gimmick: "notice how the appraisals of labor, time, and value that our judgment of the gimmick conjoins are left unparticularized, as if implicitly grasped as historically relative and moving."[14] What kind of feminist insight results from the sense of self-estrangement instigated by the artwork and this implicit grasping, also, of the "historically relative and moving" character of labor, time, and value? More specifically, in the case of feminized poetry, what does this tell us about the abstract and negative dimensions of feminization in capitalism as they are perceived, registered, and interpreted by both poet and reader?

It is not unlikely that when Mayer catalogues a set of reproductive tasks in *Midwinter Day*, or when Gabriel associates sexual difference with the polymers of a fake fur coat in *A Queen in Bucks County*, that at least part of the denotative work of the poem aims to mark capital's function of real abstraction, and in particular the ways in which feminized individuals are antagonistically mediated by this moving contradiction. At the same time, these works trace a dialectics of identification with the feminine—what Denise Riley framed in 1985 as a negotiation of the "quicksands" of "women" as a category—and offer a way to link individual experiences to a systematic critique of feminization.[15] What's more, the strategies these poets employ to make connections between the singular and the general very often gesture to those connections at the most fundamental level imaginable, linking capitalist abstraction to feminization to not only point to the "irrational rationality" of this shifting and contradictory social abstraction but to expand on Marx's crucial question about *why* labor takes the form of the value of its product in order to ask: Why is feminization linked to degradation?

Before turning to what recent poetry has to say about this question, however, we should consider some of the telling ways in which radical and revolutionary feminist models of causality have attempted to explain forms of feminizing subordination—in part by divorcing feminist critique from economic critique—as well as the Marxist- and socialist-feminist question of feminization's function within a social totality: is gendered difference internal to capital's logic, or a necessary consequence of it? From the analytical category of "reproductive labor" to the ontologizing concept of "sex class," what is striking about these divergent accounts, often articulated in opposition by their proponents, is that they share a tendency to rely on static and positivist concepts to explain gendered and sexed difference.

"Sex Class"

Distinct tendencies of socialist feminism and radical feminism were present from the inception of the women's liberation movement in the 1960s; yet as it gained strength in urban centers and university cities like New York, Chicago, Berkeley, London, and Cambridge, a split between socialist feminism and what, by 1977, had emerged as a new stream of revolutionary feminism not only arose from disagreements about movement strategy and objectives, but analytical divergences concerning the root causes of sexism, misogyny, and the sex-gender binary itself. Even before it was eclipsed by cultural feminism's focus on "personal rather than social transformation,"[16] earlier versions of radical feminism in the United States and UK leaned toward what Gornick calls "a new psychology of the self—a political psychology."[17] In her meticulous work on the history of women's liberation in Britain, for example, Jeska Rees describes the British feminist Lynn Alderson's recollections in order to highlight an approach that centered lifestyle decisions as a mode of agency, one where radical feminism "encompassed every choice that [Alderson] made, from her sexuality, to who she lived with, to how her household was organised."[18] These anti-traditional practices were accompanied by a preference for grassroots, non-hierarchical ways of organizing over socialist models of a central committee or program. Radical feminists were also less invested in housework struggles: "many were lesbians who had very different priorities to those identified within the socialist feminist critique of 'the family'; for them, feminism was about learning how to live without men."[19]

But the emergence of revolutionary feminism in the late 1970s marked a more pointed rejection of socialist feminism. Revolutionary (and transphobic) feminists like Sheila Jeffreys and Susan Brownmiller sought to theorize the types of misogynist violence that socialist feminism, with its focus on reproductive work and equal pay, had failed to explain. In particular, the concept of sex class, along with male supremacy, was revived to posit male violence and sexuality as the primary modes of social control and subordination. Ironically, despite being introduced by Shulamith Firestone's Marxist-inspired "flawed masterpiece,"[20] *The Dialectic of Sex: The Case for Feminist Revolution*, sex class was conceived in remarkably undialectical terms as a foundationalist concept that posited biological difference between the sexes as the ultimate root of all oppressions. Yet even as it rejected Marxist analysis as an adequate framework for explaining women's oppression, revolutionary feminism nonetheless contorted Marxist terminology to posit a set of discrete and ontologized classes: it is hard to miss how, at a rhetorical level in papers by Jeffreys, Sandra McNeil and others, the concept of sex class is produced when the binary categories of "male" and "female" supplant "capitalist" and "proletariat," and in doing so replicate a sociological understanding of class as a set of structurally defined social groups.[21]

Revolutionary feminists were right to reject twentieth-century orthodox Marxism's deterministic and teleological "worldview" of a historical unfolding that would eventually result in socialism as the "providential mission of the proletariat."[22] But it is worth underscoring the extent of what is lost, for Marxists and for proponents of the term "sex class," as the phrase evacuated these Marxist concepts of their relational, negative, and historically variable dimensions, whereby the ongoing dispossession and continually renewed propertyless-ness of proletarians is both the condition and necessary outcome of capital's valorization. Despite its critique of traditional Marxism, moreover, revolutionary feminism also replicated the orthodox Marxist tendency to frame the overcoming of "false consciousness" as a step that would inevitably lead to liberation. As Caroline Sheldon put it in a 1978 paper, the "class consciousness of women" would lead them to "rise up in revolutionary fervour," but it would only be achieved, Rees notes, when women recognized the "true nature" of male sexuality and heterosexuality as modes of domination.[23]

Revolutionary feminism's record in Britain is thus especially curious for the way its radical demands rested on a dangerously simplistic structural binary. In the course of arguing that the socialist-influenced "six demands of the women's liberation movement" (for equal pay, equal opportunity, free contraception and abortion, twenty-four hour nurseries, the right to self-defined sexuality, and legal and financial independence) were reformist demands that acceded to a patriarchal state and should therefore be abolished in favor of total revolution,[24] revolutionary feminist theory oversimplified the class antagonism revealed by Marx's critique of "things and their men"[25]—a world of social relations mediated by commodity fetishism—to argue for the primacy of a different antagonism, this time framed as a male-female dichotomy structured by male supremacy and based in biological determinism.[26] Its abolitionist rejection of reformist demands for things like pay equality and equal job opportunity was thus strangely divorced from economic analysis. Socialist feminism, on the other hand, was still shaped by the vestiges of the programmatist party structure of twentieth-century socialism and communism and, as Samuel Solomon notes, frequently charged with an economic determinism and an assumption that patriarchal dominance was an epiphenomenal problem that would inevitably recede in the course of proletarian revolution.[27]

In this regard, the debates that led up to the sex wars of the 1980s were marked by acrimonious divisions in the women's liberation movement over questions of causality. And yet, both in the UK and United States, consciousness-raising was common across these divisions and beyond the largest organizations of women's liberation: consciousness-raising "coming out groups" were an integral part of the work of the Gay Liberation Front in the late 1960s and early 1970s; they were a feature of the New York meetings of the Street Transvestite Action Revolutionaries (STAR), where Sylvia Rivera and Marsha P. Johnson defended street queens in opposition to "respectable queers";[28] and they provided the initial basis for meetings of the autonomous, Philadelphia-based trans group the Radical Queens.[29] Most enduringly, perhaps, the figure of the consciousness-raising group is immortalized in the "Statement of the Combahee River Collective," who describe the need for it with startling clarity:

> [W]e had no way of conceptualizing what was so apparent to us, what we knew was really happening. Black feminists often talk about their feelings of craziness before becoming conscious of the concepts of sexual politics, patriarchal rule, and most importantly, feminism, the political analysis and practice that we women use to struggle against our oppression.[30]

In marking the gap between "knowing" systematic violence and "becoming conscious" of systematizing concepts, the statement underscores the importance of being able to name specific and shared oppressions.

But consciousness-raising does not alone amount to a critique of the relationship between capital and feminization, since we are talking about a historical modality that cannot be brought into consciousness and cannot be overcome through thought. If capitalism's record of assimilating second-wave feminist critique to its own ends has politically neutralized this once-dissident organizational and critical practice, as Michaele Ferguson and Nancy Fraser among others have argued, then how might feminist critique transcend those limits and strategies of containment?[31]

Abstraction and Difference

The movement of value slips beyond people's cognition, behind their backs, because it is not an ideal abstraction but a real abstraction—a relational concept expressed only in equations. We might ask, then, whether the gap between *knowing* and *becoming conscious* can ever be bridged in capitalism. Yet if we critique feminization not as a production of difference understood solely in positive terms—much less in terms of a concrete "reality" of sex or race—but as a function of abstraction that empties out singularities (as embodied, psychic, experiential living activities) in the process of creating other abstractions (categorical particulars such as "women," "men," "children," "families"), the dialectical and dynamic relation between capitalist accumulation and gender constitution becomes available for analysis. As recent Marxist-feminist critiques of value suggest, the sex-gender binary emerges from capital's mediation of the dynamic threshold between waged and unwaged labor, a boundary that (as we will see in a moment) itself results from the contradictions of capital's own idealist logic. So let us consider precisely what is abstract about femininity, which is also to say "social" about it, in Marx's sense of the fetishistic objectification of social relations.

The 1970s and early 1980s work of Italian feminists like Silvia Federici, Leopoldina Fortunati, and Mariarosa Dalla Costa sought to undo the idea of unpaid domestic work and childrearing as the natural role of women, and instead to demonstrate that such activities undergird capitalist production. But while this emphasis on the capitalist production of gendered subjects enabled a critique that was not dependent on an ontologizing concept of sex class, Marxist feminism has struggled to adequately theorize the relation of gender and sex to the general law of capital accumulation, particularly as it bears on the question of historical "outsides." As the *Endnotes* collective observes:

> Clearly, all activities taking place in the capitalist mode of production are social, but certain reproductive activities are rejected by its laws as non-social, as they form *an outside within the inside of the totality of the capitalist mode of production*. This is why we use the social/unsocial binary, sometimes found in feminist accounts, with caution. A problem with the term [non-social] is that it can imply that "reproductive labour" occurs in a "non-social sphere" outside of the capitalist mode of production ... or as a vestige of a previous mode of production.[32]

In the newly established field of social reproduction theory, the notion of a reproductive sphere of anti-capitalist potentiality located outside of waged production has led feminists to advocate for commonizing practices perhaps best exemplified by Federici's praise for the kitchen commons as the place where women may "reclaim the house as a center of collective life."³³ Yet while any feminist would be hard-pressed to disparage the practices of mutual aid, care, and solidarity that, especially in times of mass underemployment and global pandemics, attempt to fill the gaps left by the absence of state welfare support, it is precisely because we are living in an era of waning profitability and declining demand for labor that it seems important to trouble what Marina Vishmidt calls the affirmative valorization of "something called 'women's labour,'" which "risks re-naturalizing and re-gendering it by describing it as 'reproductive.'" Even as it acknowledges the many ways in which feminized reproductive activities are integrated into the reproduction of capitalist social relations, when social reproduction theory asserts that reproductive work generates relations of "resistance and communities in struggle" and "counter-capitalist values of care and solidarity,"³⁴ it tends not to examine the fact that the social forms and perceptual economies these activities reproduce nevertheless remain tethered to a capitalist social modality. Thus:

> [T]he desire to separate reproductive labour as a political matrix from its position in the reproduction of capital is a common telos of the feminist politics of social reproduction, and one which can generate unwelcome effects such as the moralisation of care work, the self-evident necessity of crisis management, and the undergirding of gender roles, none of which diverge in any radical way from capitalism's perennial strategies for extracting profit from those least able to sustain it.³⁵

This contradiction, as Vishmidt argues with Zoe Sutherland, arises in part because social reproduction feminism's concept of social totality is rooted in an "integrative ontology of labour": what Moishe Postone and others have critiqued as traditional Marxism's transhistorical conception of labor as an activity common to all societies and one to be liberated and socialized.³⁶

The problem with this model of social totality is that reproduction is erroneously conceptualized according to a twentieth-century Marxism that simultaneously dehistoricizes the category of labor *and* centers it as the potential site of revolutionary change, rather than grasping the often concurrent activities of productive labor and reproductive work as specifically capitalist social forms. Labor is conceived as the "stuff of life" rather than as a social form produced and shaped by capital in its concrete as well as its abstract dimensions. To what extent does this error overlap with a wider swath of understandings of what "good" reproduction is and what it means, both in feminist theory and more vernacular contexts? And what are the repercussions for our understandings of gender and sex as mediated social forms? If the feminizing work of childrearing, washing, cooking, cleaning, sex, and emotional care has, as some Marxist feminists persuasively argue, actually produced the category "women,"[37] then one of the best ways to grasp the historical nature of this subjectivizing process is through careful attention to the way feminized poetry has registered demurrals from and outright refusals of that category.

One of our other best tools, of course, is Marxist critique itself. As discussed in the Introduction, the new readings of Marx enable a more radical understanding of capitalism as a total system when they allow us to link the hidden abodes of social reproduction to the inner bonds of capital's logic. Because dispossession is "internal to capital's concept," as Bonefeld argues, it is possible to argue that capital's inner bonds antagonistically shape its historically gendered hidden abodes. This claim is distinct from the idea that gender is internal to capital's logic, which implies that hidden abodes must inevitably take the form of feminized reproduction as opposed to some other socially devalued form. Indeed, it offers a chance to move beyond the Marxist-feminist "logic or history" debate—the question of whether gender is inherent to the logic of capital, or a historical contingency, and therefore not logically necessary to capital's accumulation—by showing how capital is an impersonal force that reproduces social differentials in order to manage its own internal antagonisms, opportunistically torquing pre-capitalist forms of difference beyond recognition in the process. Capitalism can be understood, rather, as a moving contradiction that subsumes non-capitalist reproduction into value-producing processes wherever it can, and at the same time—thanks to its contradictory need to exploit as much labor as possible while driving down total labor costs—produces "outsides" to value-production that, in addition to the work of unpaid reproduction, have been widely theorized in terms of surplus populations, wageless life, and core-periphery models, to name just a few analytical frameworks.[38]

The point that gender and sex are mediating categories produced by an *impersonal* force is therefore a theoretically and politically powerful insight. Not only does it avoid the re-naturalizing and re-gendering of reproductive activities and the social category "women" to more accurately insist on the historical contingency of that subordinate category and the possibility of its abolition as we know it; it also suggests new ways of understanding feminized experiences and the way they are registered, particularly in their negative dimensions.

Indeed, Beverley Best's recent critique of reproduction and its relationship to gender offers a remarkably precise account of this impersonal movement. In "Wages for Housework Redux: Social Reproduction and the Dialectic of the Value-Form," Best argues that gender differentials arise not because capital necessarily excludes social reproduction from the value-form, but because its compulsion to subsume all life processes according to its logic—toward "the full socialization of labour"—is impeded when capital meets its own limitations in the marketplace; there, inter-capitalist competition, with its need to expel labor-power from production, among other cost-cutting measures, prevents unfettered growth. To argue that the value-form logically requires a non-abstracted outside as its precondition would therefore be to ignore the "the utopian movement of the value-form itself":

> [W]hat is historically specific about capital is precisely that it emerges as the *necessary evacuation* of all concrete specificity of laboring subjects—in other words, it is logically, categorially, a function of abstraction—even as it emerges from concretely specific modes of oppression (including gender) and takes social form in them.[39]

From the standpoint of capital, there is nothing about social reproductive activities that structurally necessitates their exclusion from the value-form. The production of gender differentials thus arises not from any *logical* need for an outside to value-production, but from a "terminal contradiction": the way capital's totalizing movement towards continuous expansion is always compromised by its inability to make individual capitalists "subvert their own immediate interests" and act in the interests of the system as a whole.[40]

Attempting to subsume as many reproductive activities as possible into value-productive forms of labor, as Best emphasizes, is "the only thing that capital *can and could do*." But, as Marx explains in chapter 25 of *Capital I*,

"The General Law of Capitalist Accumulation," technological advances allow capitalists to increase their profit margins by paying fewer workers. While this increases the capitalist's advantage in the market for a limited time, shedding labor also means squeezing out the only real source of value, abstracted human labor-power, and thereby lowering the value of each commodity produced. Eventually, intra-capitalist competition evens out, and a new business cycle entails the hiring of new workers—except this time, on less favorable terms. Noting that "all social reproductive activity is financially supported exclusively, if indirectly, by the wage," Best rejects Nancy Fraser's term "boundary struggles"—which Fraser uses to distinguish class struggle from (more properly feminist) "struggles over how social life is reproduced." It is rather, Best argues, that boundary struggles cohere around "the same points of conflict that have catalyzed class struggle all along: the diminishing of the average wage, rising rates of unemployment and precarious employment, the consequent growth of both gendered and racialized surplus populations that cannot be absorbed by the formal economy."[41] The always-shifting boundary between waged and unwaged labor therefore functions as a lever of sorts: a mediating, moving contradiction that produces social forms of hierarchy and difference.

Best's account thus helps to explain how gender differentials emerge as a historical consequence of capital's abstracting movement even though they are not internal to its logic. Crucially, her analysis proceeds at the most abstract analytical level because it is a critique leveled at capital's logic considered from the standpoint of capital itself, and in this way Best seeks to correct feminist accounts of the production of social difference that are nonetheless understandably animated by what she characterizes as a political desire:

> What is the appeal for placing a critique of gender oppression at the very core of capitalist accumulation? I would argue that the formulation articulates not a critical deduction or logical analysis, but rather a political premise, even a political desire of sorts, and one that I wholeheartedly share . . . [And yet] years of debating whether, as modes of oppression, class drives gender, or vice versa, in patriarchal capitalism, or whether class struggle is logically internal to capital, while feminist struggle is historically contingent, and so on, hasn't gotten us very far, not in forging an imaginary of anti-capitalist struggle, nor in the utopian project of the abolition of gender.[42]

In departing from the Marxist-feminist "dissociation thesis"—the claim that capitalism logically requires an outside to value-production (and sometimes, also, that this outside is necessarily gendered)[43]—Best's analysis "seeks to instrumentalize capital's immaterial but objective indifference to the gender of the workers it exploits, an indifference that lies as a virtual but unrealized opportunity at the abstract core of capital itself."[44] Capital's contradictory movement—its perpetual failure to indefinitely expand by abstracting increasing portions of our social world—points, in other words, to its own dialectical reversal and the abolition of gender. It is what really and in practice testifies to the fact that "not the thinnest crack of light separates feminist and anti-capitalist struggle."[45]

Critiquing value, as did Marx, as a moving contradiction that pushes forward independently of conscious thought, acquiring and shedding social forms of expression, is therefore a practice analytically distinct from the practice of consciousness-raising, simply because value cannot be brought into consciousness. It can only be discovered through the "cold" analytical critique of political economy, since value is only expressed relatively, through comparing one commodity with another. And a commodity is a mysterious thing, as Marx has it:

> [B]ecause in it the social character of men's labour appears to them as an objective character stamped upon the product of that labour; because the relation of the producers to the sum total of their own labour is presented to them as a social relation, existing not between themselves, but between the products of their labour. This is the reason why the products of labour become commodities, social things whose qualities are at the same time perceptible and imperceptible by the senses.[46]

The perceptible and imperceptible double character of the commodity extends, Marx argues, to our entire "bewitched, distorted and upside-down world" (though the gendered language in this case is perhaps more the translator's, David Fernbach's).[47] Hence, in an exemplary demonstration of the comparative practice needed to grasp this double character, Roberta from the consciousness-raising group exclaims, "oh God! The samenesses we have found!" But interpreting such correlations is another matter:

> [T]he subject of economic analysis is the inverted world of "Monsieur le Capital and Madame la Terre" that Marx talks about in his chapter on the

Trinity Formula: a definite form of sensuous human practice asserts itself in the movement of "perverted" economic forms, and this appearance is real inasmuch as the social relations of production assume the form of a relationship between things that objectivize themselves in the person.[48]

The insight that the reality of capitalism is not concealed by commodity fetishism but in fact perversely *expressed* by it can help to explain why subjective experiences of this system can be so difficult to interpret. The task of the critic, we find, is not to disabuse readers of false consciousness, as the teleological Marxism of a socialism-to-come might have it, but nor is it to uncover what Lukács theorized as "second nature," to understand capital's self-expanding movement as the ontological priority of its economic laws.[49] Nor, it turns out—and as we discovered in the Introduction—is it enough to analyze subjectivity under capitalism using Althusser's concept of interpellation and in terms of the subject's misrecognized identification with capital's concepts and representations. So what should literary critics be doing if they want to critique capitalism's social forms and subjectivizing powers?

To say that this "inverted world" of appearances is objectively real is not to say that the truth of capital lies obviously before us. Rather, it is to point out that a different mode of (literary) interpretation is required—one that grasps the double character of social forms themselves. Consciousness-raising and the critique of value are both, in their own ways, comparative practices: the former offers a way to connect shared experiences by identifying a common enemy or structure, and the latter compares commodities as they are exchanged on the market to reveal that their quantitative relation is not accidental but regulated by the magnitude of their value.[50] Yet what seems key for anti-capitalist feminisms is that the latter analysis can complete the former because it enables us to grasp the nonconceptual but constitutive relations that undergird and organize social forms of appearance, and thus to understand those forms dialectically, in their positive and negative aspects.

As becomes clear in the readings to follow, the critique to be found in feminized poetry suggests a similar understanding of what we might call the concrete and abstract double character of social forms. This poetry is bound to capital's totalizing force of abstraction and its terminal contradiction, which takes social form in differential (gendered and sexed) categories when it is expressed in the general division between waged and unwaged labor. And if the methodological frameworks offered by new interpretations of Marx tend to operate at a highly abstract level to theorize capitalist totality, then one of the questions that feminized poetry is poised to answer is how this plays out at the level of identity formation, where, as we will see, forms of identification and *dis*identification with gendered and sexed identity categories surface in polysemic and surprising expressions of pleasure and doubt, comedy and suspicion, and often as the record of an ironized—though no less real—occupation of the feminized pole of the sex/gender binary. The following sections of this chapter accordingly suggest how, in addition to a more obvious register of activities, imagery, and objects that Mayer and Gabriel use to explore and critique experiences of femininity, their poems also perpetually expose feminization's unnatural-ness; posing fundamental questions about the forces that make the feminine what it is in any given moment. It is with that radicalism in mind that I mean to highlight a few of the ways that feminized writing responds to what Best has elsewhere called "the perceptual economy" of capital; the "phenomenal forms produced by the objective movement of capital, capital's 'objective thought forms,'" which are not identical with capital but, rather, systematic inversions of its real movement.[51]

Manly Things

Feminist critics have so far focused on the expressive, demotic, and pragmatic dimensions of Mayer's writing projects and her community work, but such portraits can foreclose our sense of the totalizing and speculative critique advanced in her poems. Indeed, for post-2008 feminists satisfied neither with a transcendent politics of the agential body nor the earthy moralism of the kitchen commons, Mayer's work provides another form of totality-thinking: one that traces the dialectical binds of social reproduction suturing the abstract and the concrete.

For Mayer writes "manly" poetry of epic proportions precisely because she's a signal poet of social reproduction. From *Memory* to *Sonnets* to *The Desires of Mothers to Please Others in Letters*, she not only records the processual and monotonous patterns of reproductive activities themselves but tracks the production of gender as a constant movement of recompositions in order to document what feminization actually involves. Her encyclopedic impulse does not mark a philosophical attitude of equanimity, but a way of questioning categorial ordering and hierarchizations. Mayer hints as much herself in a conversation with Juliana Spahr, who records:

> I once jokingly asked her if she identified as heteronormative, and she seriously replied that she hoped no one identified as heteronormative. Then she said she hoped no one would ask her to identify in any way, but if she had to, she would identify as bisexual. Her work owes much to 1970s gender bending and bisexuality. It is celebrative of sexuality's possibilities.... Yet I say 1970s gender bending and bisexuality and not 1960s polyamory or "free love" because the work is often focused on unequal power relations in intimate relationships. It is not naïve in its utopian pursuits (Mayer is well aware that 60s free love was not necessarily liberatory for women).[52]

We might say, indeed, that the sense that there is an objective reality to the world, and that reading and writing poems is not an "abdication of reality"[53] but a way to register what's wrong about it, undergirds the often-breathtaking beauty of Mayer's work.

Yet with a couple of notable exceptions,[54] the reluctance of critics to read feminized poets as critics of a capitalist totality can in part be explained by the banal sexism of a twentieth-century anti-capitalist poetics that—even when influenced by the idea of the "feminine" as a central category in the antihumanisms of Derrida and Deleuze—found in poems by actual women the wrong kind of "particulars" and "detail."[55] One result of this *horror feminae* is that feminist attempts to defend the value of "particulars" in Mayer's work (but not only Mayer's) have tended to re-entrench a gynocentric gender binary that Mayer herself often works to undermine. Reading Mayer as a poet reclaiming the "filthy and female," for example, Maggie Nelson emphasizes the mystical aspects and excess verbiage of her projects as forms of sexed abundance. She compares Mayer's depictions of dirt with the matteral, earthy artwork of Robert Smithson, noting the idea that "female matter (mater) is different from other matter—female dirt is different from other dirt."[56] Nelson evokes this essentialist notion to contest "the obsession with controlling women's bodies" and to aver that "female matter" is a powerful, threatening surplus: "in short, women leak: their filth—inaugurated by Eve's disobedience in the garden—is punitive, dangerous, and redundant."[57]

This dated idea of feminine matter finds expression today in the host of feminist new materialisms that pose, if not traditionally essentialist, a still very much feminized concept of plenitude against the idea of gender as a social abstraction.[58] While Nelson notes Mayer's obsession with "economy" in *Desires of Mothers*, she means domestic economy in the sense of the oikos as it merges with "the economy of language production." It is as if, in talking openly about capitalism's rhythms, one runs the risk of acknowledging the fetters of their abstract reality: indeed, abstract Newtonian time is purportedly overcome in Nelson's reading, as she underlines how the textual and productive desire of Mayer's work resists the economy of (socially necessary) time measurement and "reminds us that humans also take great pleasure in experiencing time, money, bodily sensations and/or words that also feel somehow impermeable to measurement."[59] When Nelson describes Mayer's logorrhea—addiction to talk—as "the hallmark of contemporary discourse,"[60] there is no mention of the increasing demand on women to chatter and smile in the postwar era.

Ann Vickery's Foucauldian study of feminist Language writing takes a different approach to defending Mayer and her contemporaries, situating Mayer in "a genealogy [that] interrogates the cultural space of poetry by approaching it horizontally in time (poetry as practice) rather than vertically (poetry as canonical tradition)."[61] Yet the opposition of "practice" and "tradition" arguably risks framing feminist poets as the pragmatic, sensible opposite of their modernist male forebears: Marxist poets like Charles Olson, George Oppen, and William Carlos Williams; masters of the long poem known for their speculative claims, totality-thinking, and appeal to abstraction.[62] The contrast between a diagnostic and masculinized theory-poetry and an "experimental feminine" that was altogether more grounded (in expression, in "the body," in ephemeral forms of "practice") is especially prominent in appraisals of Mayer's work, which seemed to occupy both and neither of these camps. Indeed, this is an anxiety Gillian White identifies as "lyric shame" in her account of Mayer's uncertain relation to the anti-expressive tenets of Language writing in the late 1970s: highlighting paternalistic remarks from male Language writers about the need for marginal groups to "have their stories told," as well as feminist worries about the egocentric heroics of "the self" and the use of "the domestic present" as material for poetry, White tracks Mayer's anxieties about choosing speech *and* writing, Lyric as well as Language, "with full knowledge of the avant-garde critique."[63]

White is sensitive to Mayer's understanding that expressive speech is not identical to itself. It is both communicative and mute, as Adorno might say, and as White also suggests when she notes how "the admonishment against expression produces an expressive anxiety" in *The Golden Book of Words* (1978).[64] On this point, White underscores Libbie Rifkin's take on *Unnatural Acts*, Mayer's collaborative publication at St. Mark's Poetry Project:

> "In its desire to take on the 'unnatural' as its primary model for producing artworks" and in "Mayer's near-invisible self-positioning," *Unnatural Acts* and the workshops that informed it "deviate radically from . . . fantasies of self-legitimation and organicism."[65]

To be sure, "our poems aren't our appearances," reads the cover of issue 2 of *Unnatural Acts*.[66] This view of Mayer as a poet recoiling from subjectivation, preferring the "unnatural" over the compulsion to identify with a gender or a poem, could not be more opposed to Nelson's positivist emphasis on the textual pleasures of Mayer's work, which Nelson likens to Mayer's pleasure in the "excess" of having more children.

Mayer's ability to divide critics, but also to incite ambivalence,[67] seems due at least in part to the relative imperviousness of her poetry both to textual ideas of the feminine and to the linguistic Marxism of Language writing. Might we—despite Mayer's call to "work your ass off to change the language"[68]—put this down to a lack of faith in the insistence that it'll be language that brings about change? Or might readers today more readily perceive a deliberate ambivalence in Mayer's work in the wake of Alicia Silverstone's anti-hero Cher Horowitz in *Clueless*, the broad appeal of *RuPaul's Drag Race*, Grace Jones's "over-coded persona,"[69] or the rise of Riot Grrrl–inspired glitter femme—performances of hyper- or queer femininity both sincere and ironic that help us to appreciate the negative critique of books like *Midwinter Day* and *Desires of Mothers*? Here, feminized excess appears not in the guise of a productive body—a figure Marina Vishmidt diagnoses as a symptom of "abstraction-phobia"[70]—but as a buoyant assertion of the thoroughly social constitution of a feminized "nature."

In his Marxian reading of *Memory*, Jasper Bernes argues that Mayer anticipates the proliferation of feminized labor through the service sector and white-collar technological work. Observing how Mayer's transcription of the freneticism and "manic intensity" of the "double day" marks the merging of "productive" clerical and information work with "unproductive" reproductive tasks in *Memory*, he suggests that the "subsumption of leisure by labor" in the postwar era can be theorized as a Hegelian logic of moments made apparent in her poetry as "an automatic process gone haywire."[71] Dialectical totality-thinking thus guides our interpretations of the meaning of the poem's formal features—its mix of verse and prose forms, use of meter and parataxis—and enables large, ambitious claims.[72]

Yet the "logic of moments" that structures *Memory* also matters because it allows us to consider the process of feminization as so many categorial moments of a synchronic whole. The concept of the feminization of labor tends to take the category of the feminine for granted—deceptively imputing it with static meaning—and Bernes's focus on the technological sublime likewise leads us away from the question of how the becoming-alike of reproduction and production produces gender in the first place, resonating instead with something like Tiqqun's image of capital as a global cybernetic matrix, or what Gavin Walker has recently figured as an uncontrollable "spinning torus."[73]

In a more recent essay, Bernes underscores this very problem: "we need to *know* what capitalism is, but not in order to wonder at it and enumerate its sublimities."[74] Indeed, when we are stupefied by that sublime—whether we feel it as some primordial uncaptured (perhaps "feminine") energy, or understand it in Jamesonian fashion as the incomprehensible web of capitalist abstraction—we can too easily lose a sense of how the experiments and ambiguities of contemporary feminized writing offer us tools for feminist critique. Mayer's early "Incidents Report" sonnets, for example, place the speaker's active body, and the bodies of others, in awkward spatial and temporal relation to an object world seemingly moving to its own electronic, mechanical, and capitalist rhythms:

> but then on the boatride my hand
> got caught in the elevator door
> by the firecracker tossed in
> by a child who was a woman as missing
> as the coffee money, anyway I

lost balance and, falling, woke up
jerking off through the chair,
another chair, was still falling
on my foot, sorry.[75]

What this "Incidents Report Sonnet" actually reports is an ambiguous mix of disorientation, accident, embarrassment, and guilt, where soporific "jerking off" marks the climax of a series of linguistic and grammatical blockages: "my hand got caught," or "I lost balance and, falling," and "another chair, was still falling / on my foot"—situations in which a speaker pushed around by the world of capitalist objects can only apologize for being in the way in the first place. The production of gender seems caught—frozen for a moment so that we might see it—in Mayer's distorted syntactical units, temporally confused grammar, and self-consciously halting rhythms: "but then on the boat ride," and "anyway I," and "the chair, another chair," and the final, superfluous, "sorry." As the speaker's body slips out of step with the workplace implied by the poem's title, line breaks arrive mid-clause, and a dissatisfying ending gives way to a sense that something is both deeply and familiarly wrong—thus just beyond the speaker's comprehension but possibly not out of her (awkward) hands.

"Incidents Report" sonnets appear in Mayer's 1989 book *Sonnets*, written between 1965 and 1989. While *Sonnets* lacks the kind of project-oriented, thematically explicit meditations on reproductive activities found in *Memory*, *The Desires of Mothers to Please Others in Letters*, and her recession-era long poem *Midwinter Day*, the collection usefully marks how Mayer's attempt to document processes of feminization is not only to be found in her "encyclopedic impulse," her cataloguing strategies, and her "radiating and run-on sentence, with its seemingly infinite capacity for digression,"[76] but also in the way she registers the double character of social forms and experiences through what we might call her lyric negativity: the way, for example, casual diction, often intimate and home-based, is undercut by unexpected grammatical invention, as in the example above, or by the way sexual and domestic intimacy is always "bound with social concerns," as Spahr observes.[77] The gristly, somewhat hard-to-digest literality of Mayer's language and grammatical choices in the *Sonnets* is unlike the simple syntax of the descriptive and observational statements that often characterize her conceptual projects. While her linguistic invention has led some critics to characterize her work as Language writing—a categorization that her body of work as a whole implicitly troubles[78]—there is an interesting way in which the awkward syntax and ordinary language employed here work in concert with the loose, tumbling musicality of the lines to enact a different kind of critique when they convey a sense of feminization unfolding in real time and in relation to forces unseen.

"Incidents Report Sonnet" is unusually resigned for Mayer, for whom the delimited autonomy of a subject weighed down by financial, familial, and other social obligations is often asserted through humor, irony, and nonchalance towards social—and especially sexual—regulations. The second in this short series, "Incidents Report Sonnet #2," for instance, gently ridicules conventional modes of speaking about the event of masturbating for the first time. As Mayer opens the poem, "I was not yet married when / at age 2, a female other, I / put my finger into the forms of address,"[79] she mocks the kind of rhetorical formalities designed to cushion social taboos like masturbation, sex before marriage, and childhood sexuality. The coded secrecy surrounding such topics comes to seem prudish and silly, a form of intimate speech unnecessarily constrained by socially sanctioned norms for talking about sex—the "forms of address" that Mayer also puts her finger into. The whole stanza reads:

> I was not yet married when
> at age 2, a female other, I
> put my finger into the forms of address
> of the most blue night early in the morning
> and said to my sister Rosemary, "Well,
> what do you think of this!"[80]

The exclamation here is full of irony. The exaggerated description of a two-year-old who is not yet married but discovering her own sexual desires is met by a convivial and camp expression—"Well, what do you think of this!"—where everyday vernacular is reflexively employed to highlight its status as a preconstructed speech pattern. Pathos in this instance, then, manages to avoid the fantasy of self-expression of which lyric poetry is so often accused, since linguistic freedom is acknowledged contextually as an ideological fallacy.

In the second stanza, Mayer conflates sexual discovery and housework with characteristic coyness:

> At the time we were both
> sitting on the floor before the balls
> of blue glass we were to clean
> so often in the future and by the window
> Rosemary once fell out of, who agreed
> our exploration was fascinating[81]

Wry humor sharpens Mayer's critique as it converges with the sonnet's warped temporal dimensions. The section above plays with grammatical time—an odd progression from past perfect continuous (lines 1–2), to the conditional (line 3), to the future continuous (line 4), to the past perfect (line 5), to the simple past tense (lines 5–6); and while the retrospective casting of these lines implies a certain fateful inevitability regarding the result of feminized and feminizing domestic tasks, the alternative temporalities set in motion by Mayer's counterintuitive switching of tenses simultaneously suggests (especially when put next to her experimental investigations of time in *Memory* and *Midwinter Day*) a type of temporal antagonism: a straining against the clock-time that, even beyond the sphere of wage-labor, arranges feminized bodies, their desires, and their unpaid work as it accumulates into history in the larger sense. This sonnet ends with the couplet, "Only trouble is / Our mother hit the ceiling," a closing gesture that evokes the ways sex and gender are continually naturalized and reproduced intergenerationally.

Mayer's sonnets float in and out of traditional sonnet forms, and "Incidents Report Sonnet #2" clearly gestures towards Petrarchan and Shakespearean traditions. Despite some slight formal differences—this sonnet is made up of two sestets followed by a couplet, not exactly following Petrarchan or Shakespearean rules of three quatrains before the couplet—the poem does follow the general structure of a traditional sonnet, first by setting out a "proposition" or "problem"—what do you think of this masturbation activity?—then moving to a "resolution" in which Mayer confirms that yes, sexuality is fascinating! Finally, the Shakespearean-style volta, traditionally the point of the sonnet's thematic turn, arrives: the only problem, these lines reveal, is that our mother is not happy about our sexual explorations. This undoing of form by way of content—in which Mayer substitutes recognizably poetic language for chatty colloquialisms, form-appropriate themes for idle talk about masturbation—is undergirded by comic relief. Her humor sidesteps the sexist charge of "feminist killjoy" while maintaining an antagonism towards sequestering gender norms, showing up the historically masculine sonnet as a malleable vessel after all—less in the interests of reclaiming the sonnet in the name of the feminine and more as a means of dialectically negating it.

Scenes of domestic intimacy, everyday tasks, and sexual play do not testify to the supposed immediacy of quotidian experience, then. Rather, they register the thoroughly mediated nature of these sensory and cognitive experiences, pointing to the constitutive forces that shape and delimit them. Mayer's gangly, almost matteral prosody thus insists on the awkward reality of a gendering time, showing us not only that duration is real but that abstract social relations are too.

If such formal gestures amount to a feminist critique of feminization itself, an essay by Timothy Kreiner helps to further underscore how readers might best apprehend that critique. Linking Federici's concept of the "patriarchy of the wage"[82] to Mayer's record of reproductive activities in *Midwinter Day*, Kreiner points out that "not unlike Marx's notion of value, gender is, for Mayer, less a static marker of individual identity than the result of dynamics negotiated between people subject to forces not of their own making."[83] *Midwinter Day* was for the most part composed on a single day in December 1978, but Kreiner reads the book in relation to a tidal shift in the conditions of women's work during the 1970s and early 1980s, a transformation characterized most directly by Mayer's complaint about the unpaid domestic work she performs, and by her lament of the end of a time when bringing up children on the "margins of the counterculture," without resorting to regular paid work, was possible. As Kreiner notes, a declining manufacturing sector and the squeezing of the traditionally male, blue-collar, Fordist family wage gave rise to the postwar "double day" for women, as record numbers of previously unemployed mothers secured waged work in order to make ends meet. Thus, "the situation of women writing in the postwar era cannot be grasped apart from the protean relationship between gender and economic forces re-shaping many women's lives."[84]

Commenting on Mayer's switching between verse and prose in *Midwinter Day*, Kreiner observes:

Time is, of course, the poem's principal thematic and formal preoccupation. The prima facie equation here of prose with housework further equates day with necessity and night with labors of love. Sex, poetry, and dreaming comprise a kind of creative, nocturnal "work" opposed to the day's laborious "tedium of uncondensed routine." It is tempting, therefore, to wager that the poem's formal logic reproduces the familiar sexual division of labor between the prosaic, domestic tasks typically performed by women and the artistic, characteristically masculine heroics that give the stuff of lyric epic proportions.[85]

Indeed, Nelson and Vickery similarly emphasize Mayer's anxiety about the perceptions of the domestic and the artistic as mutually exclusive domains. But as Kreiner underscores, *Midwinter Day* actually complicates "conventional notions of aesthetic theory opposing art to labor, freedom to necessity." Quoting Mayer, he observes:

> [T]he necessary acts of caring for children give rise to ruminative, well-nigh lyric (albeit prose) reflections on modes of life and desire in Part Two: "What an associative way to live this is, dreams of hearts beating like sudden mountain peaks. . . . Everybody wanting something or nothing to be done to them, then one of the shoes falls off again."[86]

A closer look at these lines reveals how, even as they present an idealized vision of the nuclear family model with its cozy and excluding busyness—as Vickery notes, "the joyous celebration of her heterosexuality made [Mayer] a difficult subject for feminist critics wanting to expound on the constraints of sexual ideology"[87]—they also dismantle the supposed split between the domestic and the poetic, provoking more general linkages. "Hearts beating like sudden mountain peaks" evokes the arm-numbing task of beating whipping cream until it suddenly begins to form peaks as much as it does the Romantic sublime of actual mountains. In the quote above, Kreiner omits the clause that follows—"I can see in my chest like other breasts"[88]—that brings all of this ambivalently towards the poet's own body, whose breasts are both attached to this speaking subject but also now the lyrical "mountain peaks," and *also*, and at the same time, "other" breasts not her own. In this chain of quick similitudes, the weight of the lyrical metaphor breaks down, homoerotically linking this speaker's breasts to other breasts elsewhere, beyond the bounds of *this* family home, though possibly contained within another one.

While Mayer's encompassing familiarity points us away from spellbound visions of a capitalist cosmos, her work also avoids the moralizing pragmatism that can characterize both affirmative, ethically coded versions of social reproduction theory[89] and the post–9/11 turn to the body as ground for analysis of political subjectivation—the latter of which, Vishmidt argues, "presents us with the possibility of a pseudo-concreteness that often accompanies theoretical projects intolerant of the (real) abstraction that organizes contemporary social life." This is another form of mystification: one where "the body" provides a "jargon of authenticity" because it is productive, vital, foundational even; it is "something which produces but is itself not produced."[90]

Because the fact that reproductive activities often escape measurement as socially necessary labor time is no good thing. Indeed, as Best is not the only one to argue, this resistance marks the root of the production of gender.[91] And in reading Mayer as a conceptual poet of everyday action, a poet of real abstraction even,[92] we find a more sharply politicized—yet still totalizing and speculative—mode of cognitive mapping. Take the following section from an early point in *Memory*:

> . . . like
> holidays in the city, we must've done some wash either last
> night or this morning & hung it out on the fire escape to dry &
> I remember being really tired the night before this. There wasnt
> much recording to do this day though because everything was
> closed or empty. Ed was still asleep when I got up. I washed at
> least 3 blue shirts to take to massachusetts & overexposed them
> on the fire escape. Tom said the underexposed ones look like a
> casket. Then I washed our blue hockey shirt, my 30's outfit, a
> lot of t-shirts including anne's tye-dyed one, two pairs of army
> green socks, ed's pants & hannah's green & white shirt. Put
> them out to dry. It was sunny. We went out.[93]

The washing gets done in the interstices of the day, when others are asleep, and before "we went out," while Tom comments dryly on Mayer's work but does not seem to assist with it. Mayer's speaker is caught between the kinds of feminized clerical work tracked elsewhere in *Memory* and the reproductive tasks that do not disappear on holiday. It is left to her to deal with the persistent, conflictual fact that many reproductive activities either cannot be sped up—since "you cannot look after children more quickly: they have to be attended to 24 hours a day"[94]—or are not worth the outlay of capital that would require.

Mayer's inventive recalibrations of form and content simultaneously record (and indeed produce) feelings of anxiety, a recurrent feature of her "autobiographical turn" in the late 1970s.[95] White frames this tendency as a type of "lyric shame," to note how Mayer's subversion of lyric voice in *Midwinter Day* involves an "admonishment against expressivity [that] produces an expressive anxiety." Quoting the lines, "Some say / This place is too pretty or too clean, not Marxist / Or Leninist or Maoist enough," White argues that Mayer's lyric shame arises in part as a response to the oft-tacit agreement, within the contemporary avant-garde culture of Language poetics, that expressive lyric poetry signals a failure to pursue any "revolutionary ethical, social agenda."[96] Yet as the reading of "Incidents Report Sonnet" above suggests, Mayer's gendered shame may not have an "agenda" as such (much less an ethical one), but it certainly has a critique, since it registers gender by intuiting the social as capitalist. Putting aside the most baldly essentializing claims of poststructuralist feminisms—that the female body is a site of temporal alterity, for example, or that there is such a thing as a nonconsecutive, nonlinear "women's time"[97]—we might therefore think of the linguistic and temporal awkwardnesses of a poem like "Incidents Report Sonnet" as a determinate poetic technique that makes palpable a set of otherwise ungraspable social relations.

Read this way, the uneven, intra-historical, epic bathos of Mayer's poems—in all their moments of clerical work, reproductive activities, dreams, translation, allusion, and violence—offer an active and painful transcription of the production of gender itself. If doing (Marxian) theory means advancing forms of knowledge that we cannot empirically prove, reading Mayer's poetry asks us to attempt precisely that task. And it is because they are internal to a hidden abode of feminization, reminding us that capital is the product of human social practice, that the antagonisms of her work amount to a rather august theory of capitalist totality, and one that places feminism at the ground zero of critique.

The Activity of Sex

That feminized poetry's critique of capital's movements and mediations has received minimal scholarly attention is symptomatic of a more comprehensive omission in late twentieth-century literary criticism. As Christopher Nealon has underlined, writing about the economic turbulence that came after the 1973 oil shock, "[economic] developments are keenly felt in the poetry of the period... but they are felt and dismissed, or felt and shunted to the side, in the criticism, with the intellectual cost that critics have had nothing other than a cursory account of the history of the twentieth century." Poetic criticism of the 1970s and 1980s thus "tended to name, then draw back from... the crises and the triumphs of global capitalism from about 1973 on," which as Nealon points out are precisely "the conditions that arguably made it urgent to restore to the study of poetry a sense of high intellectual stakes."[98] Indeed, while it is true that Mayer along with many of her contemporaries (including Alice Notley, Anne Waldman, Joanne Kyger and others) wrote about and practiced spiritual and mystical rituals, these poets also wrote about laundry, money, jobs to make ends meet, and gendered violence. Yet Nealon notes "a powerful structure of feeling in American political life" during this period:

> One that has always posed problems for the left, which congeals in the idea that it is a betrayal to think against the system—a betrayal against one's friends, one's community, one's art. Distantly behind this idea lies the real material threat against workers who choose to strike—the possibility that striking would threaten their family's security, or bring down violence on them. Transposed into an academic setting, the idea seems to be that, in developing a critical analysis of capitalism, the critic forsakes daily life, the small beauties; he becomes arrogant, unable to see what's right in front of his nose; or she becomes preachy, solipsistic, hypnotized by abstractions. If one is a critic of poetry, the too-critical critic loses the ability to perform subtle close readings.[99]

If economic conditions today render such ideas patently absurd, they nevertheless persist (as Chapter 4 elaborates). But what if a poet makes it feel remiss to *not* read the movements of capital in their work? In the reading that follows, I will offer a second, more recent example of poetry attentive to both the non-conceptual dimensions of a lived experience and the really abstract forces through which it is shaped. Indeed, the New York-based poet Kay Gabriel—whose work inherits many of Mayer's inventions and is emblematic of a broader compelling tendency in contemporary feminized poetry of the last decade—has developed her own critical analysis of capitalism, which appears in her work both literally and metaphorically as a dialectic of form and formlessness.[100] Yet it is precisely because it provokes incredibly general (which is to say, fundamental) questions about what "gender" and "sex" are that Gabriel's recent book, a serial poem entitled *A Queen in Bucks County*,[101] requires reading dialectically, for what the poet can only intuit, and for the way she grapples with the impossibility, in capitalism, of coming fully into sexual and class consciousness.

A Queen in Bucks County entails a buoyant *dérive* through what Gabriel has called the "gay and trans coded spaces of social reproduction"[102]—and yet, not too buoyant, in part because the book's surreal scripts are set in a moment of post–Me Too TERF and SWERF-ism, rising fascism, and ethnonationalism. But the hedonist proclivities of Gabriel's deliberate excesses and surreal scripts nonetheless imbue her work with a dynamism resembling what Louis Cabri, writing about the Canadian poet Nancy Shaw, calls "the erotics of concealment and disclosure."[103] At the same time, the formal abstractions of Gabriel's poems draw attention to the abstract character of social interactions in order to theorize gender in relation to a number of declarative "contents": consumerism, academia, aesthetics, transphobia, homophobia, and the feminized figure of the "wife," most obviously. Strategies of recitation, transcription, lyric apostrophe, and epistolary forms provide the book's formal architectures, and these frameworks are embellished with derisory idioms, thespian high affect, and paratextual reference in a poetics both expressive yet sardonically infused with what today reads as a kind of wistful "LangPo"-inspired play with unstable semantics and textual surfaces.

As we will see, Gabriel's interest in such artifice marks an interest in the dialectics of feminization, and particularly sexual difference. Artifice, in this constellation, is informed by a queer politics that has for a long time linked high-femme aesthetics, among other supposed or intended excesses, to a revolutionary politics that knows capital as the enemy.[104] In *A Queen in Bucks County*, a politics of style is thus geared toward the repeated implication that the reproduction of gender in capitalism is at root the reproduction of delimited conceptual categories, meaning that "we can construct a thing called women's history, but we cannot presume to know the biological reality of people living inside and outside of it," in Holly Lewis's useful formulation.[105]

This point is memorably underscored in one of the book's more vulnerable moments, where Gabriel alludes to the experience of a trans teenager living in the satellite cities adjacent to Toronto, which she equates here with the New Jersey suburbs of Bergen County:

> Here's a fable: a girl grows a wolfish tail in the subdivisions. It's probably Brampton, Mississauga, Etobicoke, but why not Bergen County? Horny teens frot it up with pork swords, get periods and check out on screen like library books. The tail wiggles on its own, wired into a cultural nervous system from which it receives its tense and intermittent pulses. It wants to see the world, and grows and grows, wobbling under Target panties, taped to a hairy teenaged leg. Finally it develops its talents and dashes to the high school, dragging its snarling occupant along: *bump, bump.*[106]

The taped-down penis, a "wolfish tail" in the suburbs, has a life of its own: its "occupant" cannot restrain it with tape and Target panties—the meager tools at her disposal—and it threateningly grows. Daily mediocrities serve a critical function here, as Gabriel locates this penis in a world of mid-size North American cities and box-store chains—an environment of common denominators that has the effect of suggesting the particular and the general at once, linking the specificity of an individual's sex to a social totality in a manner that allows us to think about how bodies are both abstract and concrete in the same moment. Indeed, we could even say that this personified penis-tail is made representative of a social relation called sexual difference. It drags its occupant along to high school in a stark antagonistic drama that suggests how capitalist abstractions become "real."

Thus, as the book proceeds through a series of letters—some addressed to names identifiable as those of the poet's friends in the Acknowledgments, others more ambiguously addressed to or signed off by "Kay," or most often, "Turner"—ready-made character parts serve an important function in *A Queen in Bucks County* as categories to be inhabited only partially or incompletely. Kay and Turner, especially, are proper names weighted with multiple significations and never appear as straightforward sites of identification. Turner is both the actress and pin-up model Lana Turner, the Romantic painter J. M. W. Turner, but also the poet Kay Gabriel, as well as a flirtation device:

> . . . Last night I dreamt of myself, Lana Turner, a milky sentence, lumps in my mouth. I tell Jo *Turner is a way to seduce my friends without having to deal with the consequences.* I tell Stephen *Turner is a heteronym of the author.* Shiv calls me "boyish, girlish." Dear Connie. What'll I call you? Come back tomorrow, I'll be more specific.[107]

As is evident here, it is not so much that names and character parts serve as empty vessels to be transiently inhabited, but rather that they always figure in relation, taking form through the book's sustained and multiple modes of apostrophe. Often, the recipients of Turner's letters receive florid, pornographic descriptions of Turner's sexual adventures, delivered in touchingly conversational style and couched in the intimacy of shared queer experience, as in a letter to Stephen:

> What happened since my last letter? I traveled, cried, fucked. I lost my bag in transit, I broke up with lineation—that's a lie. . . . A punk ate my ass between the urinals and the piss tub. I didn't remember we'd fucked before until I rode his face like teenagers in a playground encounter stiff old swings, the seat's too small so you stand. Then your fingers get stuck in the chains. He chewed my taint, he smacked at my hole, a week's stubble irritated my ass and the base of my nut sack, then it was midnight. Men screwed up their bodies to squeeze past us and pee.[108]

In this account of semi-public fucking, Gabriel conjures a moving image made sexy and slapstick at once—not least with the term "nut sack." The ironic double character of the sex scene is undergirded by the poem's temporal shuttling between past, present, and past perfect tense, in a recursive strategy that points to the gap between the description of sex and the activity itself. We are repeatedly reminded of this gap throughout *A Queen in Bucks County*. In a later passage, for example, Gabriel plays on the erotic trope of abstracted body parts to suggest what is unrepresentable about having sex: "Have you ever wanted to get fucked by an abdomen, an armpit, a couple of peddling legs? My preferred position with Cam for instance letting him piledrive my face from above."[109]

By drawing our attention to these twin activities, description and sex, the poem points to the insufficiency of its own concepts. But Gabriel also acknowledges the importance of the discursive formation of sex—precisely by discursively forming varied and multiple concepts of sex for her readers—at the same time as she draws our attention to sex as an act that is specifically *not* discursive. In an early poem-letter, "I Do My Best To Cheat," for example, we find the speaker's delightfully revengeful description of sex with a jock, who is initially "doing laps around you as if about to score the latest in a line of trophies," yet ends up as the submissive bottom and source of the speaker's own sexual pleasure as the poem nears its close: "I pumped him into a flowerbed. I pumped him into a ditch, and now I'm telling you."[110] Compare this with a later, sweeter scene of sex with a recurring figure, Cam, who:

> . . . knows it better than maybe anyone, so when I purr at him to fuck my face he obliges with enthusiasm and a little ceremony. *What an obliging man* Liam agreed *what a handsome cock!* It's visually delighting: long enough to impress without discomfort, a perfect smooth head coquettishly uncut, attractive low-hanging balls that drape his perineum when he reclines louche in the sun amid complaints of feral cats from the yard. I say he's used to it but there go the muscles in his face—now tense, now relaxed, and expressive enough for two.[111]

The warm humor of this description is pleasurably underwritten by the approving presence of a third party. It paints a handsome picture, but more importantly, perhaps, reminds us that "penetrability is an act; it can be beckoned,"[112] as Emma Heaney puts it. The activity of sex is in fact understood in *both* of these records of sexual encounters as a dynamic, relational, and changeable practice. Indeed, Gabriel avoids the moralizing economy that would oppose them as good (connective) and bad (antagonistic) forms of sex. Of more interest here is the uneven social field highlighted by the comparison between straight and queer sexual desire, as *A Queen in Bucks County* foregrounds how the form of the activity of sex mediates sexual difference itself, forming and re-forming feminized subjects in the process.

Reading dialectically can thus help us to apprehend the non-conceptual aspects of poetry such as this, and perhaps to better understand what happens when we are pulled along by a poetry able to feel or sense the way capital mediates the reproduction of sex and gender in dynamic and contradictory ways. To demonstrate this point more fully, let us turn finally to "You Say Wife," a poem that appears towards the end of *A Queen in Bucks County*. Like much of the book, "You Say Wife" takes the anachronistic—and here, deliberately gauche—form of a letter. It is a poem that figures sex both as an act and a category, an activity and a structure. The poem satirizes the misogyny and homophobia of an anti-capitalist politics that blames consumerism on women and gays; it conjures grad students, campus cops, and tenured profs as they populate the now-familiar and recurring formations of campus politics in the US university; and it sings rhapsodically about literal sex too.

"You Say Wife"

"You Say Wife" is introduced as "a letter in seven arguments." The first, "On Lies," comprises three neat paragraphs in which the speaker diaristically asks herself, "Do I care about straight men? The question is maybe misplaced. // Anyways they care about me."[113] These opening musings present a conceptual problem tied both to the perceived threat that trans women pose to men's "hetero protestations," and relatedly, to the speaker's ambiguous relation to another figure, an implied friend: "I don't even believe them, culprits of their own desire, though as Cam says I think they believe themselves." Perhaps this is a grammatical joke: Is what Cam says what I believe, or does Cam say I believe this? As the poem shuttles between what "they" believe, what "I" believe, what "Cam" believes, and what "Cam says" "I" believe, the friendly solidarity of the expression is made fragile.[114]

The surprise of the third paragraph, then, is a shift in register, as the poem exits its intimate conversational mode and addresses its reader to make a statement:

> This thing is multiform, contingent, ambivalent and I call her my sex. Even if I make choices I still like everything. I like myself and you, but the hole we share accuses us both. I'll call it autofiction; on its head it accuses the world.[115]

These lines reply unambiguously to the typical complaint—shared by TERFs, incels, and general homophobes and misogynists—that the "choice" to be woman or man, gay or straight, is an agreement into which people enter gladly, rather than a result of the limited categories available for viable subjecthood, or in Gabriel's rendering, "the hole we share" that "accuses us both." "I still like everything," then, is not an indiscriminate embrace but a political assertion. Gabriel returns to this theme in a later line with firm resolution: "Say it's the same old sex bent double. It's mine now, and goes between me like a stent."[116] The glottal stop of the word "stent," as it corrals the consonants and vowels of the previous sentence, juts up semantically against a stent's function as a tube typically inserted in the heart to restore the flow of blood. But its abruptness is strategic, for it outmaneuvers another accusation hovering in the background: this time that an unsurgically modified male-to-female body is not *really* female and only appears feminine when a penis is tucked away, or "bent double." In a dizzying bait and switch, the speaker reclaims her sex, which, bent double, is "mine now," before conjuring the act of penetrating herself with this penis as it catachrestically "goes between me" to suggest a new, unlocalizable subject, unmoored from whatever is understood to be "me" in the perceptual economy of capital.

The campness of this moment is the source of its power, a dynamic in keeping with the rest of this poem. Take the following lines, from Argument 3, "On Being a Wife":

> You say wife like style or you say wife like rifled through someone else's stocks or you say wife like wages. Wearing only animal print and plump in the right places. Dear Kay. Suspicious, you delayed wifery. Now you wear it like a polymer mink. Anybody can be a wife in the country like everybody's a piece in town.[117]

Gabriel does not abstract "wife" here so much as trace the ways "wife" is already an abstraction: in the first sentence, "wife" appears like that famously ambiguous aesthetic category "style," and subsequently as a kind of panicked duplicity in the image of a wife (or wife-owner?) rifling through stocks—a scene that suggests wagers on future profit as much as it conjures the more bathetic image of a sock drawer, complete with hidden items and their adulterous secrets. In another catachresis, wife is "like" wages, since as Gabriel well knows, wife is obscured by wages when, as Marx famously presumed, wages—not wives—are all that's necessary for the laborer to procure the means of subsistence.

If "wife" is a sequence of appearances that can never be directly represented, however, the poem posits not an absent cause but an accusation: "you say" things are this way. Yet if this "you" at first appears as an other, and a logic to reject, it soon *turns into* and *on* "Dear Kay," who is not yet a wife—whose "delayed wifery" is "suspicious"—but who is nevertheless "wearing" wife in a polymer mink. As the distance between "you" and "Kay" collapses, so does that between wife and non-wife, country and city, which here melodically suggest monogamy and promiscuity: "Anybody can be a wife in the country like everybody's a piece in town." Rather than read this staged collapse as a merely nostalgic trip to the land of postmodern fragmentation—a veneer it nevertheless retains—we might consider how the conceptual neatness, assonance, and playful off-rhymes of these sentences seem delicately designed to arouse suspicion. Indeed, their structure recalls Gertrude Stein's entry for "Custard" in *Tender Buttons*, which, in a pleasant twist for students and teachers alike, comments on its own sentences as units of contracting and then expanding measure to observe that, "This makes a whole little hill."[118] Yet if the crest of the hill in "You Say Wife" is our "Dear Kay," there is nothing value-neutral about her. In contrast to Stein's high abstraction—which, as Natalia Cecire has pointed out, has been an opportunity for critics to depoliticize her poems as unreadable nonsense best approached with automatized or distant readings[119]—Gabriel's poem seeks to historicize itself as it moves from the abstract idea of a wife to the concrete, overtly feminized image of a wife, "plump in the right places," to Kay, the author-poet-speaker who interrupts this thought to wear "wife" for herself. The second half of the paragraph then reads as a comment on Kay's relation to this objectively existing abstraction, "wife." Kay's wifery is delayed, yet she wears it still "like a polymer mink," a metaphor that synesthetically suggests both the classed connotations of faux fur and by extension what Ngai has called "the *socially binding* or *plasticizing action of capitalist abstractions.*"[120]

"You Say Wife" thus triumphantly declares its own staged character, as Gabriel's recombinative strategies draw attention to the artifice—the foreclosures, obligations, wants, and recalcitrances—of *all* social interactions in capitalism. Her work moves dialectically between constraint and excessive overflow, fixity and unknowable freedom, because she is interested in the contradiction between the private individual who appears to be an agent, who enters gladly into a form of appearance, that "exclusive realm of Freedom, Equality, Property and Bentham," and on the other hand the *truth of the matter*, again in Marx's words, "the physiognomy of our *dramatis personae.*"[121] As such the poem not only gives concrete shape to the feminist adage that "the only way out is through," but also speaks to Gayle Salamon's notion of a "felt sense" of a body: a concept Salamon figures in psychoanalytic and phenomenological terms to explain how "the body one feels oneself to have is not necessarily the same body that is delimited by its exterior contours, and . . . this is the case even for any normatively gendered subject."[122] The felt sense of a body is tied to the felt sense of the objective movements of capital in "You Say Wife," in a shared acknowledgment that, as Salamon puts it in Butlerian terms, "this felt sense is a product of, and also subject to, cultural interpretations."[123] Hence the sadness of a late line in the poem that reads, "it's a shame for words to be more vibrant than sex—and sexier, too, says my enthusiastic boyfriend,"[124] marking a longing for whatever life it is that an abstract linguistic system both suggests and outlaws, and a letdown made devastating by the uncontroversial obviousness of the sentiment.

In a surprising way, critiques of value share a common aspiration with Gabriel's poem in their efforts to "overcome the fragmentation of the experience of . . . exploitation," as Diane Elson claims for value theory.[125] This poem is admittedly predisposed to being read in such a way: indeed, I am arguing that, alongside the recent work of (Marxist) poets such as Amy Ching-Yan Lam, Verity Spott, Anne Boyer, and Eric Sneathen, Gabriel's work attempts to "think" abstract relations, to bring them into figuration despite the knowledge that such a feat is impossible. But it is precisely for this reason that work like Gabriel's might helpfully inform how we approach reading *anything* produced in capitalism. We may on this point note the deep historical reservoir of formal techniques and problems on which poets can draw to stage the *agon* of what Marx called "domination by abstraction": in subjective terms, the sense that one's life is intimately shaped by forces that somehow always feel elsewhere. Reading Gabriel's poem dialectically, with a theory of gender as social form in our arsenal, it becomes possible to return to abstraction its referent; or in other words, to read in Gabriel's writing a form of totality-thinking that understands the constitution of gendered subjects as not merely cultural after all—nor simply a ripple effect of reification, commodification, or ideology—but rather as a formal and form-determining relation driven by capitalism's fundamental inner laws.

"You Say Wife" thus gestures to the presuppositional character of a capitalist totality, including its mediations of hidden abodes. In Gabriel's hands, the trans body theorizes an alienation whose abolition cannot happen in any one place—neither in town nor in the country, at one comical point—and especially not in any one part of the speaker's body. Just as value is a relation and not a thing in itself, this speaker is not "realized" in any single erotics, even if she is grounded in a particular femme body. Indeed, the phrase "between me" astoundingly conceptualizes an inner bond that is internal to an antagonistically socialized, still-transforming body. It registers the ways this gendered and sexed body is both real and abstract, here and elsewhere in the same constitutive moment. Read in this way, the poem gives us the tools to think capitalist abstraction not as sublime other, but as the social synthesis of an *exchange in toto* that gathers, institutes, and deploys difference wherever it goes—one that is, in this specific and hopeful sense, entirely dependent on what we do.

Two Senses of Abstraction
Bhanu Kapil and Alli Warren

FOR DIANE ELSON, AN ACCURATE grasp of Marx's analytical categories reveals a historical process of value "forming what is intrinsically unformed."[1] Here we find a pointed similarity: feminized poetry uses poetic abstractions in a manner not homologous, but certainly comparable to how a critique of value uses analytical abstractions to tell us something of the social whole. Indeed, just as Marx uses abstract categories like "labor" and "exchange-value" to unmask capitalist abstractions for what they *really* are—real abstractions that could "never exist other than as an abstract one-sided relation within an already given concrete living whole"[2]—feminized poetry draws on a range of rhetorical techniques, formal strategies, and other poetic devices to grasp capitalist abstractions as one-sided relations that presuppose an entire social modality—a modality (why not put it polemically?) that is otherwise wrongly perceived in a "religion of everyday life."[3]

As Chapter 1 has already suggested, this comparison has special purchase for a feminist method. Bernadette Mayer's and Kay Gabriel's poems both record and solicit experiences of the nonidentical, conveying a sense of capitalist social forms—including bodies and subjectivities—as dialectical moments within a social totality, real in appearance though never simply "themselves." But our focus here is a little different. Rather than showing up the obstinate reality of capital's social forms, the British Punjabi, US-based poet Bhanu Kapil, and the Californian Bay Area poet Alli Warren draw our attention to the abject underside of value in a global economic system (Kapil) and to the strange operation of the value abstraction itself (Warren). Later in this chapter, I therefore read what Marina Vishmidt calls a "counter-reproductive neg-

79

ativity" in Kapil's 2015 book, *Ban en Banlieue: a critical poetics of the global banlieue* attuned to a doubly illegible and systematic violence produced by value's dissimulating movement—the process through which it casts off that "concrete living whole" (to stay with Marx's term). The final section then turns to explore how a sensory understanding of value's form-determining movement is notated in a poem by Alli Warren, which can be read as an attempt to bring into figuration what the poem simultaneously suggests is the essentially *non-figurative* force of capital's abstracting movement.

Indeed, the poetry studied in this chapter confirms the political stakes of value-critical accounts of gender by encouraging a more holistic sense of doing theory, one in which aesthetic works do what value theory cannot, and make capital's abstracting movement differently "knowable" when they trace the obscured lineaments of its formal determinations. With this goal in mind, the following section begins with a reading of Elson's landmark, recently republished 1979 essay, "The Value Theory of Labour," not only because it dramatically foregrounds the representational challenges posed by value itself, but because it consolidates *Behind Our Backs*'s understanding of (a) how value is both real and not real, in the sense discussed in the Introduction as the semblance of independence through which value acquires a real force, and following this, (b) how Marx's argument about abstract labor is not an economistic one but rather an analysis that explains how, in socially fixing the activities of life, forming what is intrinsically unformed, value comes to dominate an entire society. As it demonstrates how value's apparently natural, self-moving qualities conceal its internal connections to the human activities of production and reproduction, Elson's approach also helps us to see why concrete forms are never simply reflections or instances of the logic of capital itself—an insight that, in many and various ways, permeates discourse about identity and difference.

"The Value Theory of Labour"

The title of Elson's essay cleverly foregrounds the way it overturns received ideas about a "labour theory of value," and her analysis instead resonates with the efforts of *Wertkritik* (value critique) authors such as Norbert Trenkle and Robert Kurz, as well as British Marxists including Christopher Arthur, who set out to "reconstruct" Marx's analysis in order to re-evaluate the object of his critique and the procession of his method across the three volumes of *Capital*.⁴ As Ingo Elbe summarizes this critical turn in readings of Marx's work:

> A reinterpretation of Marx's critique was envisioned from the methodological perspective of social theory: the question as to the original object of *Capital* (economic form-determination), the particularity of scientific presentation (the dialectic of the forms of value), as well as the connection between the three volumes ("capital in general—many capitals") are posed anew, as distinct from quantitative approaches, and with a particular emphasis upon the significance of the *Grundrisse*.⁵

Such re-readings have strongly rebutted the classical view, left unquestioned by traditional and orthodox Marxisms, that labor is the substance of value, and that value is embodied by the commodity. As Norbert Trenkle, one of *Wertkritik*'s key advocates, introduces his inquiry: "is 'labor' an anthropological constant? Can we use it as such to make it unproblematically into a point of departure for an analysis of commodity society? My answer is an unambiguous 'no.'"⁶ Indeed, value-theoretical accounts involve what Elbe describes as a threefold abandonment of traditional Marxism: a move away from substantialist theories that understood value to be the labor congealed in commodities; away from reformist conceptions of the state in favor of a view of the state as an integral component of capitalist domination; and away from "labor-movement-centric" interpretations of the critique of political economy, or the idea of a "'labor-ontological' revolutionary theory" that failed to distinguish the form labor takes in capitalism from labor in other kinds of society.⁷

From within the heat of such debates, which (for a moment at least) repoliticized the task of reinterpreting Marx, Elson's intervention points out that the object of Marx's theory of value is not price—as various theorists of the "transformation problem" would contend⁸—but labor. In re-reading Marx this way, we arrive at "an understanding of why labor takes the forms it does, and what the political consequences are."⁹ It is a mistake, she explains, to misread "value" as "exchange value" or "price," and to posit a relation between a dependent and an independent variable in a labor theory of value. She therefore rejects the tendency she identifies in Paul Sweezy's and I. I. Rubin's theories of value, as well as in Louis Althusser's "technicist" reading of Marx, to posit the production process as a pre-given structure across which individuals are distributed and assigned to "pre-given places or functions." In these interpretations:

> Not only is labour-time seen as the determinant of exchange value; exchange-value is also seen as the determinant of labour-time. That is, exchange-values are in equilibrium equal to socially-necessary labour time embodied in commodities; and the distribution of total labour-time between different commodities is regulated by the difference between market-price and relative labour-time requirements of different commodities.[10]

There is no need to reiterate the various wrong turns Elson attributes to Sweezy, Rubin, and Althusser (among others), however, to grasp the key import of her critique: these thinkers make an analytical error when they reduce three discrete categories offered by Marx—labor-time, value, and exchange-value—to two. Sweezy and others posit value and labor-time as identical, reinscribing traditional Marxism's claim that the commodity's value is simply equivalent to the socially necessary labor time needed to produce it.[11] Rubin, on the other hand, reverses this argument by arguing that "value"—by which he means exchange-value—determines the distribution of labor across various branches of production. But he cannot account for the *form* that the labor process takes, Elson stresses, because his reduction of value to exchange-value means that his critique unfolds at the level of the *circulation* of value, and therefore presupposes a set of already existing variables brought together in production: labor power, the means of production, the owners of production, and the commodity.

Elson turns all of these interpretations on their heads. Her reading of Marx insists on a vital distinction between, on the one hand, the value-form, which in its dual character as value and use value lacks independence, and on the other hand, the value-form's *appearance* as exchange value, which gives it an illusory independence—as the key to understanding how value *form-determines* the structure of the labor process. In the course of this reading, Elson demonstrates that the object of Marx's theory of value is not value, nor exchange value, but the *labor process*—or as she puts it, noting the clunkiness of the formulation, "the determination of the structure of production *as well as* the distribution of labor in that structure." To this end, she cites Marx's famous description of labor, in the *Grundrisse*, as "the living form-giving fire; ... the transitoriness of things, their temporality, as their formation by living time," before offering the following elaboration:

> [Labour] is a fluidity, a potential, which in any society has to be socially "fixed" or objectified in the production of particular goods, by particular people in particular ways. Human beings are not pre-programmed biologically to perform particular tasks. Unlike ants or bees, there is a potentially vast range in the tasks that any human being can undertake.[12]

Elson calls this the indeterminateness of human labor: a fluidity common to all states of society. While she leaves the category of concrete labor intact (controversially granting it a transhistorical legitimacy[13]), her question about abstract labor remains paramount: *How does human labor come to be determined and fixed as objectified abstract labor?*

Marx's concept of determination is thus not "deterministic"—not a concept of a regulative law—as Elson highlights by reference to a key passage in *The German Ideology*, where Marx asserts that "the social structure and the state are continually evolving out of the life process of definite individuals," but "of individuals, not as they may appear in their own or other people's imagination, but as they *really* are; i.e. as they operate, produce materially, and hence as they work under definite material limits, pre-suppositions and conditions independent of their will."[14] In a reminder of what is at stake in this sober observation, Elson notes:

> [T]o speak of "determination" here does not, of course, mean the denial of *any* choice on the part of individuals about their work. Rather, it is to point to the fact that individuals can't just choose *anything*, are unable to re-invent the world from scratch, but must choose from the alternatives presented to them.[15]

Individuals *must choose from the alternatives presented to them*. But why? After a brief exposition of Marx's categories of relative, equivalent, and universal forms of value, in the important chapters at the beginning of volume 1 of *Capital*,[16] Elson works up to a crucial question: If the objectification of abstract labor—value—requires an expression in a universal equivalent, the determinate form of the money commodity, and thus has an independent expression of its own, does this not undermine Marx's claim that value is not an absolute entity—that it is not an independent, freestanding convention? Not at all, we learn, if we take heed of "a little-noticed distinction drawn by Marx, that between 'internal independence' and 'external independence'":

> Value lacks the "internal independence" necessary for it to be an entity because it is always one side of a unity of value and use-value, i.e. the commodity. But the value side of the commodity can be given "external independence" if the commodity is bought into a relation with another commodity which serves only to reflect value. *This produces the illusory appearance that value in its money form is an independent entity*; but the autonomy it confers on value is only relative. It is this externally independent expression, in objectified form, of a one-sided abstraction, the abstract aspect of labour, which is the fetishism of commodities.[17]

Value, as a one-sided, "externally independent" abstraction, appears only in exchange.

For Elson, two key observations follow from this insight. First, that "in the form of the universal equivalent, abstract labour is not only objectified: it is established as *the dominant aspect of labour*."[18] As such, the concrete dimension of labor is subservient to the abstract, because its purpose is to "[make] a physical object which we at once recognise as value."[19] In a similar way, Elson notes how the *private* aspect of labor ("the isolated processes of production operating independently of one another") ultimately serves its *social* aspect, through the social mode of recognition known as commodity exchange. She is careful to note that this does not mean that the private, concrete, and social dimensions of labor are obliterated; rather, it means that they are *subsumed as expressions of abstract labor*:

> The argument of *Capital*, I, goes on to show the dominance of the universal equivalent, the money form of value, over other commodities, and how this domination is expressed in the *self-expansion* of the money form of value i.e. in the capital form of value. Further it shows that the domination of the capital form of value is not confined to labour "fixed" in products, *it extends to the immediate process of production itself, and to the reproduction of that process*.[20]

Let us summarize: Abstract labor is the dominant aspect of labor because it is the *only* form of labor reflected in money; therefore the private aspect of labor serves its social aspect; therefore the money form of value dominates (or form-determines) processes of production and reproduction. Importantly, in Elson's account, the domination of the value-form begins with the universal equivalent—the money form of value—and moves inward to the labor process, underscoring the way the abstract dominates the concrete. Indeed, as Elson points out, "Marx's argument is not that the abstract aspect of labour is the product of capitalist social relations, but that the latter are characterised by the dominance of the abstract aspect over other aspects of labour."[21]

Following all this, we might reasonably ask what Elson means when she refers to "the reproduction of that process" in the passage quoted above, and it might be fair to assume that she simply intends to invoke a broader notion of the reproduction of a total society (in an Althusserian sense, for example). Despite this ambiguity, a value theory of labor provides us with two key insights relevant to the question of gender: first, that real abstractions arise from the life process of individuals "as they *really* are; i.e. as they operate, produce materially, and hence as they work under definite material limits, presuppositions and conditions independent of their will"; and second, that the capital form of value *appears* to take on a life of its own in its external independence, and this fetishistic result allows for the domination of value to extend beyond the commodity, to the production process and to the sphere of social reproduction. But these observations do not quite capture the ingenuity of Elson's method as it highlights the central importance of abstraction to capital's self-moving expansion, primarily conceived not in terms of replication, reification, or commodification, but as a processual account of social "fixing" that not only brings the Marxist-feminist dialectic of (formless) hidden abodes and social form into sharper analytical focus, but also explains what is definitively impersonal about capital's domination.

The Logic of Gender

What does a value theory of the representation of labor in capitalism tell us about other orders of representation, and how might that inform the feminist reading practice this book wants to develop? And to pose a different but related question: How does the domination of value—as an abstract, apparently independent form—propel feminization itself? One of the more influential Marxist accounts of capital's relation to the "merely cultural" reconfigures Marx's concept of real subsumption to explain how capital enfolds the social into its logic, suggesting that the life process itself, as the "general intellect," has become productive of capitalist value.[22] But if we adhere—as Elson does—to Marx's definition of real subsumption as the social reorganization of the labor process and its reproduction in anticipation of increased relative surplus value, this argument begins to look like a category error: while real subsumption gives rise to a number of effects, "real subsumption" is not necessarily the name of those effects.[23]

Elson's reading, on the other hand, enables an understanding of how value dominates as a one-sided, "externally independent," fetishistic abstraction able to obscure its immanent structural relationships: an insight that also underscores why value theory might be important to anyone interested in the politics and aesthetics of representation. Up to this point, we have considered this process as the serial movement of value through its social forms, wherein social relations based on human activity take on objectivized and apparently natural forms of appearance that mystify capital's internal logics. We have seen in Chapter 1 how the Marxist-feminist argument that capitalism logically requires an outside to value production is less convincing than a Marxist-feminist account of how the always-shifting boundary between waged and unwaged labor is the result of capital's own moving contradiction—an impersonal force that produces social forms of hierarchy and difference (and another way of thinking about capitalism's historical "outsides"). But much more could be said about how exactly this leads to "the production of gender," particularly with an eye toward the question of what feminized poetry can tell us about that mediation.

With this question in mind, let us turn to one last intervention to aid our practice of reading feminized social forms, this time in the systematic analysis put forth in an essay by members of the communist collective Endnotes.[24] "The Logic of Gender," part of a post-2008 turn to communization theory that we will further touch on in Chapter 3, is one of a small but consequential set of value-critical advances in Marxist-feminist theory. Crucially for this chapter's methodological concerns, "The Logic of Gender" explains how the social cost of biological reproduction, which is a hindrance to value-production despite being absolutely necessary to it, is reflected back onto the population through the organization of bodies as a *gendered average*, an abstraction:

> What the female gender signifies—that which is socially inscribed upon "naturalised," "sexuated" bodies—is not only an array of "feminine" or gendered characteristics, but essentially a price tag. Biological reproduction has a social cost which is *exceptional* to average (male) labour-power; it becomes the burden of those whose cost it is assigned to—regardless of whether they can or will have children. It is in this sense that an abstraction, a *gendered average*, is reflected back upon the organisation of bodies in the same way that exchange-value, a blind market average, is projected back upon production, molding and transforming the organisation of the character of social production and the division of labour. In this sense, the transformation of the condition of gender relations goes on behind the backs of those whom it defines. And in this sense, gender is constantly reimposed and *re-naturalised*.[25]

Note the parallel drawn here between the abstraction gender, "a gendered average," and the abstraction exchange value, "a blind market average." In theorizing gender as a price tag, Endnotes demonstrates how, at its most abstract level, gender can be analyzed in relation to value, which appears in its inverted social form as price. Yet this is not an isomorphic or homologous comparison between gender and price: rather, a price tag solves a problem for capital in that it provides a way to compare and differentially remunerate labors in the interests of profit margins, and the capitalist concept of price itself provides the measure for this operation. It is therefore not that one abstraction "leads" to another, even if we might in theory follow capitalist abstractions from their simplest to their most complex and particular forms. Rather, categorical abstractions like gender and race are dialectical moments of appearance mediated by other categories—the price of labor being one of them—in the architectonic movement of a totality ultimately guided by the relation between capital and labor.[26]

"The Logic of Gender" thus marks a distinctly new line of inquiry in Marxist-feminist critique and offers a compelling alternative to what its authors argue is an inadequate binary framework of productive and reproductive labor often mobilized in Marxist-feminist theory. In place of these categories,

Endnotes proposes two overlapping spheres—the directly market-mediated (DMM) sphere and the indirectly market-mediated (IMM) sphere—which serve as useful categories for understanding the types of domination required to quantify and enforce different kinds of productive and reproductive activities (Figure 2). While abstract, value-productive (including reproductive) labor is socially determined by "direct market-mediation" and hence requires "no structural necessity toward direct violence," activities belonging to the indirectly market-mediated sphere of "non-labour," including paid, non-value-producing work such as care work, are compelled by other mechanisms, "from direct domination and violence to hierarchical forms of cooperation, or planned allocation at best." It is not possible to "objectively quantify, enforce or equalize 'rationally' the time and energy spent in these activities or to whom they are allocated."[27] Central here is the relation of any activity to the market and to valorization.

Within this framework, Endnotes introduces an economic concept of the abject to describe a particular type of indirectly market-mediated activity: a set of unpaid reproductive tasks that, having in the past become waged, "can now be seen as a constraint, that is, as something outside oneself that it is possible to abolish."[28] Such tasks no longer necessarily appear as the "natural" task of women—and thus when they become unwaged again in times of capitalist crisis and state-imposed austerity measures, an economic category of abjection is *experienced* of a kind of abjection too:

> Indeed, we can say that, if many of our mothers and grandmothers were caught in the sphere of IMM activities, the problem we face today is different. It is not that we will have to "go back to the kitchen," if only because *we cannot afford it*. Our fate, rather, is *having to deal with the abject*. Contrary to the IMM activities of the past, this abject has already been to a large extent denaturalised. It does not appear to those performing it as some unfortunate natural fate, but more like an extra burden that one must deal with alongside wage-labour.[29]

State-subsidized childcare services being withdrawn, for instance, means that the previously paid work of daycare workers has been returned to parents, and disproportionately to women. Yet what is most striking here is the way abjection, for Endnotes, describes a moment when the boundary between waged

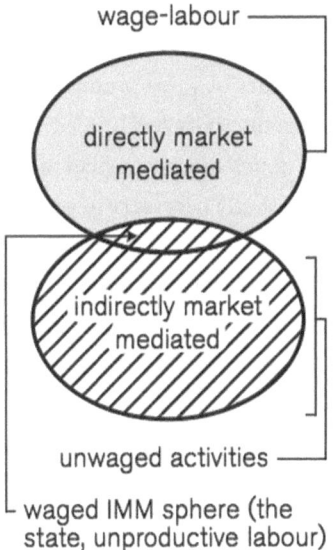

Figure 2. The Venn diagram represents directly market-mediated (DMM) activities and indirectly market-mediated (IMM) activities. The overlapping portion shows the category of waged activities that are unproductive of capitalist value (such as those paid for by the state), and that are therefore indirectly market-mediated.

Source: Endnotes, "The Logic of Gender: On the Separation of Spheres and the Process of Abjection," *Endnotes* 3 (2013): 69.

and unwaged work is felt *as* gender, if not in an immediate way, then in at least in a way that makes gender's abstract, intangible social form seem tangibly close: indeed, "the abject sticks to one's skin."[30]

Invoking the abject in this way of course summons Julia Kristeva's concept of abjection in *Powers of Horror: An Essay on Abjection*. For Kristeva, the abject "lies there, quite close, but it cannot be assimilated." Abjection is that "twisted braid of affects and thoughts" with no definable object, and it draws us "toward the place where meaning collapses."[31] While Endnotes's rendering of the abject shares key characteristics with Kristeva's definition—describing the abject as "that which is cast off, thrown away, but *from something that it is part of*"³²—the significations of Kristeva's term are largely transposed into political-economic categories to connect everyday concretizing processes of feminization to the vicissitudes of value production in capital accumulation. When capital's faltering productivity levels need remediating, not only does the technology of gender—much like race—help to provide the flexible, cheap, relative surplus labor increasingly necessary to capital's survival; it also serves up feminized people as a sector of the population upon whom, to varying degrees, abjected reproductive processes may be imposed.³³

Yet Kristeva's psychoanalytic concept of the site "where meaning collapses" points toward another dimension of abject social reproduction. This gendered abjection is of a different order even to the experiential aspect Endnotes vividly describes: in Kristeva's framing, "the abject is not an ob-ject facing me, which I name or imagine"; rather, "the abject has only one quality of the object—that of being opposed to I."³⁴ Some common feminized symptoms of it may spring to mind: depression, anxiety, the sudden intrusions of trauma. More than a little like capital, the abject is oppositional, but simultaneously everywhere and nowhere.³⁵ Might we read the poetic strategies of feminized poetry as attempts to register these repressed, non-representational, and meaningless aspects of the gendered "remainder" of reproduction as they stand in relation to the *repressed, non-representational, and meaningless* movement of value? If, as Endnotes contends, "the indirectly market-mediated sphere has a different temporal character,"³⁶ the arguments to follow suggest that in different ways, a value-critical feminist reading of Bhanu Kapil's and Alli Warren's work tells us something of that temporality's political character in an era of economic stagnation and surplus populations—which is to say, what the poetry itself, rather than "seek[ing] desperately to repress,"³⁷ now seems to want to try to unmask.

More than a question of what's missing in a Marxist literary criticism traditionally focused on the relationship between labor and literature, or production and literature, social reproduction's relationship to the aesthetic—and poetic language in particular—challenges the tricky, opaque divide between poststructuralism and Marxism. As the reading to follow suggests, indeed, *Ban en Banlieue* seeks to formally limn the movement of the value relation itself. In a medical register, Kapil calls this "an epidemiology of violence"; in a Freudian one, "organ-speech."³⁸ Yet we can also theorize this negativity—

socially bound to capital's internal logics on the one hand, formalized in poetry on the other—in terms of a Marxian reconceptualization of the abject: a category of experience both cast off from, yet still a part of, a racializing and feminizing system of social reproduction.

L(a)ying Down in the Abject

In *Ban en Banlieue*, Kapil describes the scene of her childhood, the outskirts of London in the 1970s, as *"les banlieues,"* in a pun both on her own name and on the 2005 Paris race riots. "Ban," whose actions and feelings are often described in the third person, is the book's protagonist and is solidified as a kind of outskirt too: "she's both dead and never living: the part, that is, of life that is never given: an existence."[39] Ban, a British Indian "immigrant," who we are invited to understand both is and is not Bhanu Kapil, records her daily life sporadically, shifting between discursive registers and making associative logical leaps. Often, the speaker's mode is omniscient and philosophical—observing, for example, that "(*Ban.*)" is also "To be: 'banned from the city' and thus: *en banlieues*: a part of the perimeter," or making brief remarks on the suburban landscape, noting, "A puff of diesel fumes on an orbital road," or "'The country outside London, with its old parks and labyrinths of rhododendron or azalea."[40] But this speaker perennially loses her opacity, becoming a more clearly defined, first-person subject: "Perhaps I should say that I grew up partly in Ruislip," "I analyze my glimpse on the asphalt," "In April 1979, I was ten years old,"[41] Ban tells us, and the appearance of a lyric "I" seems almost a surprise. Then come more explicit and complex desires and refusals: "I wanted to write a book about lying on the floor of England," or "I hate white people. // That is another sentence."[42]

For Ban, the Punjabi-British subject of *Ban en Banlieue*, never-English despite being born in England,[43] the life-shaping violence of white supremacy resounds somewhat paradoxically in nebulous yet definitively historical tones, played out on a global and totalizing scale. This is achieved, in part, through the pragmatic and observational mode Kapil frequently employs, bolstered by factual elements such as dates, childhood ages, and geographical locations, but also through her references to other subjects whose lives are touched (though the writing does not explicitly note it) by capital's secular tendencies toward structural unemployment and the production of surplus populations, and by the ascriptive processes that produce race. The book is dedicated, for example, to Blair Peach, an anti-racism campaigner who in 1979 was knocked unconscious and killed by the Metropolitan Police while protesting the white supremacist National Front in Southall, an immigrant suburb of West London. Later, Kapil describes a girl in New Delhi who was raped and left to die one night in December 2012, "about 10 minutes from the Indira Ghandi airport—the girl lay dying on the ground."[44]

Sometimes, subjects are introduced not as agents but via records of what has been done to them, as "our Gujarati and Kenyan neighbors" appear only as the victims of National Front youth league member Stephen Whitby's racist morning pranks: "with regularity, he'd empty out the milk bottles . . . filling them with an unrelenting supply of urine before putting them back on the step."[45] And yet, while the anecdote directs sympathy towards the recipients of Whitby's bottled piss, Kapil preempts the potential condescension of (white) sympathy for these unknown-but-racialized victims by subsequently providing another painful anecdote:

> Once, a man was beating his wife. Stephen Whitby climbed over the wall and banged his head on the window. He spat at the window then thumped it with his hand, screaming "You fucking Paki!" He screamed: "Go back home, you bleeding animal!" The man stopped beating his wife, then resumed.[46]

In her fragmentary notation of punctuated assaults and droning background noise, and in metaleptic reversals of images of victimhood, Kapil spells out the ways in which the violence of a system produces—and is experientially absorbed by—racialized and feminized individuals, and just as Ban of the *banlieue* seems to reach across to other surplussed subjects, she is grammatically and syntactically produced as surplus voice herself. The unstable removes between author, speaker, and subject mean that Ban frequently refers to herself in the third person, rhetorically separating her present subjectivity from what usually appears as her younger self. Often, these moments take on an air of childhood simplicity, as "Ban has tickets from the West End, and playbills" or "Ban is lying in the dirt, all sticky from her ice."[47] But the speaker increasingly resembles an onlooker re-watching an inevitable tragedy unfold—"Ban is nine. Ban is seven. Ban is ten. Ban is a girl walking home from school just as a protest starts to escalate"⁴⁸—especially because we learn of the affective frequencies of Ban's marginalization *before* we learn many of the facts of her life.

In a pivotal early moment of the book, Ban, "a brown [black] girl," is walking home from school when a race riot breaks out:

> She orients to the sound of breaking glass, and understands the coming violence has begun. Is it coming from the far-off street or is it coming from her home? Knowing that either way she's done for—she lies down to die. A novel is thus an account of a person who has already died, in advance of the death they are powerless. To prevent.⁴⁹

Contrary to the fateful death imagined in these lines, the recurring motif of the book—the act of lying down—generally implies something other than passive victimhood: indeed, even in this scene, the liberal ideal of individual agency is thrown out, and perhaps along with it the lie of meritocratic progressivism, which never accounts for the ways gendered, racial, and class violence undermine its bootstraps logic. Kapil's reminder of this fact surfaces as another register of knowledge and a politicized reserve close to what Fred Moten—in his Black optimist torquing of what Fanon calls the "impurity," "flaw," or deathly dimension of the colonized—characterizes as an epistemology shaped by "a certain reticence at the ongoing advent of the age of the world picture."⁵⁰ Or as Ban puts it: "I am a mixture of dead and living things" and "Almost but never quite dead."⁵¹

Most often, the speaker mentions that Ban is "lying down," but sometimes—usually in what seems like the present, or recent past—it is "I lay down." Lying (passively?) or laying (actively?) on the ground makes for an antagonism and refusal, especially given its place in the history of political protest and the still-recent significance of die-ins to protest the Iraq war, or the police killing of Black people in the United States. But lying down is also a feminized gesture, near-ubiquitous as a sign of feminine sexual passivity.⁵² In particular, the motif reflects Kapil's longstanding concern with the normalization of rape in India, a pervasive problem deeply rooted in the country's national history and exacerbated by colonialism. In 2013, writing of "another gang rape, on the outskirts of Gwalior" on her blog (a poetic work in progress in its own right, and into which most of *Ban en Banlieue* was written before it was published in book form), Kapil describes:

> An epidemiology of violence. That I have written about elsewhere. The incidence of domestic/sexual violence within—communities—and not just: from the outside—as race events—violence that comes from people you do not know—for me—was the thing I wanted to think about for Ban. Though lately—the violence that comes—from nowhere—from everywhere—seems like the most frightening thing of all.
>
> I wanted to write about the body—that perceives—the coming violence and responds to it—before it has ever happened—because it's going to happen—and nothing can prevent that.
>
> Ban lies down in the opening minutes of a riot.[53]

Kapil's figurations of lying or laying down, in their broad overtones of coincident meanings, begin to emerge as an affective counter-position to capital's equally multivalent systems of misogyny and racism: in Kapil's words, "the violence that comes—from nowhere—from everywhere," the type of subjectivizing violence that is always-already in motion, resulting in "the body—that perceives—the coming violence and responds to it—before it has ever happened."[54] In the same movement, Ban's l(a)ying down, as I will call it, seems to signal a desire to be close to the world, or get to know it, both in the matteral sense of land and landscape—the solid earth and its historicity—and in terms of the abstractions of global capital (which, we ultimately find, are part and parcel of the same whole). Because it can be all these things at once, l(a)ying down is a refusal and more: it is a powerful gesture of solidarity with the horizontal figures of abused and murdered women, with Blair Peach, with the child known as Ban, and with all those who bear the weight of (to quote another pointed metaphor) "the strength of the British pound."[55] The figure's holistic remit is further underscored when laying down is itself the act refused, as "to lie down" becomes a euphemism for sex, and the speaker asserts, "These are notes, so I don't have to go there. I don't have to lie down with you. And I don't."[56]

Because Kapil situates the intimacies of patriarchal violence on a global scale, configured through the image of an act of l(a)ying down and the scene of the *banlieue*, the aesthetic experience of reading this work might move us toward an impersonal, de-individualized concept of colonial-patriarchal violence as an excretion of capital's self-expanding motion,[57] without losing sight of the very personal points at which racialized and feminized people are subjected to that violence. Such reading, it is worth underlining, unfolds through a dialectic of form and content. Adorno's arguments in *Aesthetic Theory* are instructive on this question, particularly where he highlights art's attempt to represent what he calls "nature," or "what is not human":

> With human means art wants to realize the language of what is not human.... Art attempts to imitate an expression that would not be interpolated human intention. The latter is exclusively art's vehicle. The more perfect the artwork, the more it forsakes intentions. Mediate nature, the truth content of art, takes shape, immediately, as the opposite of nature.[58]

For Adorno, "what is not human" cannot be represented by human means since there is no escaping capitalist mediation. Yet some momentary form of "disenchantment" *is* possible in aesthetic works, as in his example of Brecht's poetry. Here, disenchantment and aesthetic transcendence are both immanent to the poem's "muteness," a quality both attached to and disengaged from expression:

> In Brecht's disenchanted poetry what is fundamentally distinct from what is simplistically stated constitutes the works' eminent rank.... Aesthetic transcendence and disenchantment converge in the moment of falling mute: in Beckett's oeuvre. A language remote from all meaning is not a speaking language and this is its affinity to muteness. Perhaps all expression, which is most akin to transcendence, is as close to falling mute as in great new music nothing is so full of expression as what flickers out—that tone that disengages itself starkly from the dense musical texture—where art by virtue of its own movement converges with its natural element.[59]

If artworks have no unmediated access to their "natural element," their movement might nonetheless converge with it. In *Notes to Literature*, Adorno similarly asserts that "one does not understand a work of art when one translates it into concepts.... But rather when one is immersed in its immanent movement."[60]

Movement and muteness, then, are abstract forms that converge with the truth content of the social, what Adorno also calls "mediate nature" in the first quote above. If we accept some version of the dialectics of aesthetic understanding that Adorno puts forward, might the silences, refusals, and recalcitrances that emerge from *Ban en Banlieue*'s unfinished note-form; from its gestures of l(a)ying down; from its delineations of deathliness provide an aesthetic corollary for Marxist feminism's economic concept of the abject? Or to try another angle on the same question: recalling Jameson's depiction, in his infamous 1984 essay, "Postmodernism: Or, the Cultural Logic of Late Capitalism,"[61] of the postmodernist viewer who catches a glimpse not of Nature in the Romantic sense, but of Capital full-blown, might we replace that postmodernist image of a sublime capitalist matrix with the somewhat more devastating purview of the capitalist abject, rendered here by Kapil's work both as a social form excreted by the meaningless movement of value, and as a set of experiential concrete determinations?

On this note, it is worth highlighting that *Ban en Banlieue* and Kapil's writing more broadly suggests no immediate affinity with Marxist critique. On the contrary, among the theorists named and pointedly scattered throughout the book—Henri Bergson, Elizabeth Grosz, and Melanie Klein appear prominently—Adorno is the only Marxist referenced, and then only in doubtful tones, and by allusion to his work at its most abstractly philosophical, where he expounds upon ethical systems, domination, consciousness, and ontology through the trope of animals. As Kapil writes: "Adorno substituted people for animals; I feel cautious and sad reading / his words in the middle of the night, studying the body for Ban. / Why? / 'To reduce the living body.' [E. Grosz]."[62] Indeed, while Kapil's gestural renderings of "matter" deliberately avoid any fully formed conceptualization, her references to Grosz's *Becoming Undone* (2011) imply not the matter of historical materialism but of vitalist new materialism—"Here a person might BECOME not just through acts of descent or alliance (to read India through Grosz) but through the volume and scope of matter itself"[63]—where matter is a vital, evolutionary, transhistorical force whose agency extends beyond human subjects.

Reading literary texts in political distinction from, or in opposition to, the inferred politics of their author is not necessarily a mode of reading "against the grain," as Timothy Bewes has adroitly pointed out.[64] Yet the political and theoretical shortcomings of many feminist new materialisms still seem worthy of note, especially since their anti-dialectical accounts of the productive capacity of particulate matter risk making invisible the gendered subject of reproductive labor, the subject who most obviously produces matter in the form of cooked food, sex, babies, and so on.[65] Kapil's citation of Grosz's work might thus be noted alongside the marked absence of Marxist discourse in a book so concerned with the relation between systemic violence and the experiential sites through which it is felt. We could speculate, however, that if the theoretical language of *Ban en Banlieue* seems at odds with the value-critical approach this chapter makes a case for, it is because Marxist-feminist thought has until recently failed to provide a more satisfying systematic account of how and why feminized and racialized subjects are disproportionately regulated, disciplined, and murdered. The poles of antagonism and passivity, matter and abstraction, victim and aggressor, first- and third-person, spectacular and quotidian violence that *Ban en Banlieue* conflates so tellingly are dialectical tensions that Marxist feminism needs to better understand. Could the dialectical concept of the abject, as it dramatizes the abstract-concrete double character of all social forms, make some headway here?

In any event, Kapil's poetry does—particularly where it suggests a concept of the abject component of social reproduction as a form of immaterial "nonlabor" that must be made *doubly* invisible in order for the production of value to continue in the waged sphere. Indeed, the abject is cut off from the social in a double dissimulation: not only is it deprived of social validation as waged labor, but it is also cast off from what is socially validated as *non-labor*: the mundane goings on of reproductive life—the time supposedly spent cooking, cleaning, washing, exercising, for example—that enable people to turn up at work each day. In honing our definition of the abject as a Marxist-feminist category, we might thus include that which is not talked about openly: activities relegated to a feminized and/or racialized realm of secrecy, or otherwise casually framed as an illegitimate or irrational response to a social sphere of official "equality" in what Angela McRobbie calls "a privatization of grievances."[66] While Endnotes considers abject reproduction as a gendering technology, Kapil's writing points to why the category seems crucial for thinking about the lives and work of women of color in particular.

Consider the following lines:

> This is the snow: I think often about low-levels of racism, the very parts of a social system or institution that are hard to address, precisely because they are non-verbal—a greater trigger for schizophrenia in immigrant populations: in women, that is, than larger events, the race riot, for example, with its capacity: to be analyzed.[67]

The non-verbal, as these lines imply, is a register that goes hand in hand not with the event, "the race riot, for example," but with the recursive, oft-unremarked, and illegible experiences of those forced to endure a volatile quotidian mix of racism and misogyny: a systematic form of violence originating not, ultimately, from the emasculated poverty of a white dispossessed population and deindustrialized social landscape—though it may be meted out at this level—but from the movements of capital itself as it seeks more profitable locations in the global economy and produces a precarious global labor reserve in the process.[68]

Counter-Reproductive Labor

"A girl stops walking and lies down on a street in the opening scene of a riot. Why?"[69] Why, indeed? Ban is figured in lateral relation to the race riot, we might aver, not only because she is feminized (though to be sure, women who riot are often subject to discursive erasure too) but because she is Brown in a world where race is often conceived in oppositional terms of Black and white. But it is less that Kapil's metaphors mark the potential for the metamorphical cultural change advanced by postcolonial theory's interstitial concept of liminality,[70] and more that they suggest *acts*, and with them, notably abstract yet actually existing limit points: Ban cleans the street in Hayes "until all that's left is a ring of oily foam," then, "Looping the city, Ban is a warp of smoke."[71] In an adjacent moment, the speaker wants to lie down, "As I did, on the border of Pakistan and India: the two Punjabs. Nobody sees someone do this. I want to feel it in my body—the root cause."[72] If "the root cause" might be felt but not seen, Kapil's grammatical inversions stage the problem by turning a lyric "I" into an unseen object, "someone," and back again into a speaker with a body that can feel things. Not only this, but the nature of the relation between acts and concepts itself is brought into focus as the riot is ambiguously figured at the (now personified) site of its boundary: "the mouth of the riot is a stretch of road."⁷³ Might the riot spill into the road, or is the stretch of road its mouth, a boundary of sorts? As the metaphorical and the phenomenological jut up against each other, they muddy our sense of what is at risk, and what poses the risk—of who or what is doing the acting—in a way that emulates the everyday, popular difficulty of identifying suffering's root cause.

This ambiguity is significant because acts become objects, as Beverley Best puts it, highlighting the way capital's movement as a social relation also means it must take form in the world.⁷⁴ In this regard, Kapil's strategy of imbuing liminal metaphors with action helps to give conceptual form to a social process that seems to have none. Reading them this way, moreover, helps to extend the concept of the abject in order to stretch its extant meaning beyond a political-economic mapping of the binary categories of naturalized and denaturalized labor, and press it into the service of the more dynamic image denoted by Endnotes's description of the abject, from the standpoint of capital, as "that which cannot be subsumed or is not worth subsuming":⁷⁵ here, abjection also helps to describe capital's production of (and dependence on) surplus populations and reserve armies of labor.

We might dialecticize this economic concept of the abject even further, too, since as Marina Vishmidt has suggested, abject and feminizing forms of reproduction inhere in the negativity of the value-form itself.⁷⁶ Far from the overly esoteric analysis such a phrase implies, Vishmidt's concept of value's negativity expands on Christopher Arthur's rather practical argument about *practice*: namely, that Marx's category of labor might be conceived not only as "productive labour" but also as "counterproductive labour," given that workers are "actually or potentially recalcitrant to capital's efforts to compel their labour."⁷⁷ In Arthur's account, wage-labor is the only "contestable" factor in capitalist production, since unlike land, machinery, and raw materials, it does not enter the production process with a given productive potential:

> In its endeavour to organise production, and to maximise output, capital finds that it is confronted with a special difficulty: the residual "subjectivity" of the worker poses unique problems because it gives rise to a definite recalcitrance to being "exploited" which the other factors do not possess.⁷⁸

Inconveniently for capital, wage-workers with their thoughts and feelings are unlike land, machinery, and raw materials. Thus, for Arthur, value is not simply a positive outcome of the production process, but the result of a process of negation whereby "capital can [only] produce value by winning the class struggle at the point of production," or in other words, defeating workers and any subjective recalcitrance they might have to the abstraction (which is to say, the making value-productive) of their labor. This negation (by capital) of a negation (by the worker) turns Marx's theory of value into a dialectic of negativity and renders value contradictory, both positive and negative at once. In Arthur's Hegelian terms, "value is constituted through the dialectical overcoming ('sublation') of living labour, which is both negated and preserved ('dead labour') as its substance."[79]

"But what happens," asks Vishmidt, "if we think reproduction with or inside the social character of production which renders value contradictory, put reproduction into the term 'counterproductive labour'"?[80] In other words, what happens when we conceive of reproduction not as an "outside" to a waged portion of a social world form-determined by value (as Federici and Peter Linebaugh optimistically frame some forms of feminized reproduction, and as Roswitha Scholz's theory of gendered value-dissociation would hold[81]), but as a negative dialectic internal to abstract labor, and thus simultaneously conceptual and real? In this case, would the abject constitute a counter-reproductive negativity traced in our experience of reading certain feminist poetry?[82] Given *Ban en Banlieue*'s resistance to conventionally expressive forms of syntactic relation, Vishmidt's concept offers another lens through which we might read a work like this with an account of how abjection persists as a counter-*reproductive* negativity: indeed, this is a different way of grasping what the Introduction framed as the pairing of hidden abode and inner bond, the internal connection between feminized reproduction and the capitalist form of value.

As Vishmidt has also pointed out, the commodification of domestic labor in recent decades displaces this genre of exploitation to a racialized and illegalized class of low-waged women.[83] The processual nature of capital's recompositions of gender and race thereby takes form in a series of contradictions, as Kumkum Sangari explains:

> The market is not, after all, an unambiguous anti-traditional force that loosens familial patriarchal practices—it can also sustain, alter or resus-

citate them; it may dissolve familial patriarchal practices to an extent but maintain or reinstate caste, ethnic and racial hierarchies that in turn depend on gendered subordination. The market and market-led states may not only have a stake in familial patriarchal regimes, but the market emancipation of some women may depend on the *continuation* of familial regimes elsewhere. Thus the question of location does not rest on an imperious world map of more or less patriarchal regions; rather, it is a material question of *differential and shifting patriarchal distributions*.[84]

Moving the analysis to a global scale, Sangari's argument underscores the way gender is mediated at the level of averages, through "patriarchal distributions." But it also serves as a reminder that reproduction is inherently an affirmative process: it is the reproduction of the subject to be exploited or cast off by capital, the reproduction of gender, indeed, of the capital-labor relation in all its misery.

Perhaps this is why Ban's refusal, situated as it is at the level of a global *banlieue*, seems such a powerful gesture of dialectical negation as it delineates the movement of capital itself through feminizing forms of reproduction. Sangari further figures that movement in the following incisive terms: "as the material base of patriarchies is patchily eroded or recomposed by state or market interventions, there is a concurrent mobilization *and* immobilization of women's labor, a simultaneous move to defamilialize *and* refamilialize."[85] As I have been arguing, the category of the abject might therefore be put to more challenging dialectical work to offer a value-critical account of the forms of affective, embodied, and intellectual activities that take place in the indirectly market-mediated sphere. At the same time, the concept of the abject is centrally about regimes and horizons of representation insofar as the question of *what* looks like a capitalist social form is intrinsically bound to the question of *who* counts as a viable gendered "reproductive" subject. It thus suggests ways to reconfigure the racist, cis-sexist, and heteronormative categories that Marxist-feminist critique has too often reinscribed.

Sensuous Metamorphoses

From a poetics that primarily traces capitalist abstractions by way of their violent results, let us move finally to consider a 2013 poem by the Bay Area poet Alli Warren that tries to sense the movement of value itself, in an approach that notably diverges from the Althusserian idea, as Alberto Toscano frames it, that "figuration, as a modality of representation," is "a *conditio sine qua non* for 'alluding' to or 'indicating' relations which are intangible."[86] Attempts to figure capital's absent presence run through much twentieth-century US poetry: as Christopher Nealon notes, for example, John Ashbery's attention to capital, that "invisible form in the air," is nonetheless figured through "things," both concrete matter and attitudinal, rhetorical forms.[87] But even as Warren's feminist poem, "Acting Out," similarly seeks to bring the force of capitalist mediation into our perception in what we might loosely term both "concrete" and rhetorical ways, it is also a poem interested in the inadequacy of poetry to this task.

Confronting the difficulty of representing capitalist abstractions, Toscano characterizes the "artistic register" as a kind of "non-specular reflection"—non-specular because, to put it briefly, a painting is the product of a painter who lives within capitalism's own "phantasmagoric" forms.[88] Louis Althusser's 1966 review of the Italian painter Leonardo Cremonini's exhibition at the Venice Biennale provides an exemplary sample for his inquiry in a 2014 essay, "Materialism Without Matter: Abstraction, Absence and Social Form": here is Toscano reading Althusser reading Cremonini:

> [T]he Italian artist's work comes to represent not just a sectoral materialism but a kind of allegory for the materialist method as such. For Cremonini's painting tackles, in the artistic register, *the* problem of a materialism without matter; in Althusser's evocative words:
>
>> Cremonini "paints" the *relations* which bind the objects, places and times. Cremonini is a *painter of abstraction*. Not an abstract painter, "painting" an absent, pure possibility, but a painter of the real *abstract*, "painting" in a sense we have to define, real relations (as relations they are necessarily *abstract*) between "men" and their "things," or rather, to give the term its stronger sense, between "things" and *their* "men."[89]

"'Things' and *their* 'men,'" of course, evokes Marx's assertion, in his section on the fetishism of the commodity in chapter 1, volume 1 of *Capital*, that "it is nothing but the definite social relation between men themselves which assumes here, for them, the fantastic form of a relation between things."[90] Next to this, Toscano notes Gilles Deleuze's caution, in his book on Francis Bacon, that "if force is the condition of sensation, it is nonetheless not the force that is sensed, since the sensation 'gives' something completely different from the forces that condition it."[91]

Knowing the difference between a force itself on the one hand and the sensation it induces on the other is key to the reading practice this book seeks to outline, where poems call forth dialectical readers, and where reader and poet meet as dialecticians. Indeed, Toscano underscores this distinction—and the relation it marks between artwork and viewer/reader—when he notes how, in Althusser's dialectical reading of Cremonini, it is not so much that Cremonini's painting itself represents a "dialectic of the abstract and the concrete": on the contrary, Cremonini seems to "unfold his plastic project in terms of an ascension, a chain of being, moving from the mineral, to the vegetable, to the animal (and the human)," thereby tracing not a force but a series of sensations. It is *Althusser*, rather, who reads in Cremonini's work the force of real abstractions, what he calls a "determinate absence." As Althusser explains:

> In their "finite" world which dominates them, Cremonini thus "paints" ... the history of men as a history *marked* ... by the *abstraction* of their sites, spaces, objects, i.e. *in the last instance* by the *real abstraction* which determines and sums up these first abstractions: the relations which constitute their *living conditions*.[92]

It is here, writes Toscano, that Cremonini's aesthetic problem becomes "nigh-on indistinguishable" from the aesthetic problem of "a Marxist theoretical practice of a materialism without matter."[93] Emphasizing a shift in Althusser's view of art's capacity to represent capital, from what he earlier saw as a practice of "making visible, but not making known,"[94] to what he reads in Cremonini's paintings as an aesthetic practice of actually painting capitalist relations, Toscano explains via Althusser:

> We move, at the figural level, across "the armatures and articulations, consolidated by weight and by history, of the passive body of an island,

dormant in the heavy oblivion of the rocks, at the edge of an empty sea, a matter-less horizon" to "the sharp growth of a bulb, the long shriek of dumb stems" and at last . . . to "dismembered animals scattered among men collecting bony carcases, men like the carcases they bear on their emaciated shoulders." Yet the focus is elsewhere, off-screen, off-canvas—the rocks' "difference," which makes them the "ground" of men; the absences in the presences of the flowers, the invisible "time of their growth."[95]

Of great significance here is how Toscano's account of this painting and its (re)viewer repeatedly highlights the role of Althusser's interpretive practice, allowing us to see how his transposition of the formal qualities of Cremonini's paintings into language provides a compelling record of the dialectics of aesthetic experience—a critical mediation further redoubled by Toscano's *own* reading of Althusser's review. As a result, the questions that conclude "Materialism Without Matter" foreground problems of reading that remain fundamental to Marxist literary criticism: "how are we to tell apart the negative from the positive absences, ideology from the structure of capital? How are we to posit that [real abstraction] which the effects of this absence presuppose?"[96] But they also helpfully underscore how part of the difficulty for any good Marxist reading method—one that Althusser could perhaps not acknowledge in his time—is that capital is not an "absent structure" but a relationship that perpetually moves through a series of social forms. Thus, as Toscano puts it, "the problem of representing capital is much better framed as a problem about the representation of a metamorphosis, the sequence and syncopation of value forms."[97]

Of course, language is a very different "material" to paint, and on this point we might compare Warren's poetry to a couple of its precursors in a recent history of anti-capitalist American poetry, in the materialist poetics of the Black Mountain school and the postmodern strategies of Language poetry. But in both cases, the comparison would point to Warren's difference. While Black Mountain poetics, influenced by Charles Olson's muscular (and undeniably macho) essay, "Projective Verse," developed an improvised "open field" of composition in which the breath composes the line kinetically, an "energy exchange where self and world meet, before the encounter is translated into the irreconcilable terms of subject and object,"[98] certain formulations of Language poetry purported to subvert the "very order of sign production,"[99] which, as Ruth Jennison notes, "indexed a valiant denial of language as a brutal mediation of other systems and darker orders."[100] Warren's attempt to critique capital itself instead takes on an air of feminized pragmatism perhaps emerging from a more recent sense that a revolution of the word does not, in the end, mean a revolution in the world.[101]

Indeed, "Acting Out," the opening poem of Warren's 2013 book *Here Come the Warm Jets*, often seems to describe value's form-determining action in visceral, imaginative, and affective—in short, feminized—lyric.[102] Consider the following lines, which comprise approximately the first quarter of the poem:

> You begin from economic fact
> You enter in overalls, a tart talisman
> > distinguished by what you do and how you go about doing it
> You are a perceptible, finite and particular
> > part of the scaffolding
> Your personal qualities should ideally be completely irrelevant
> > chains of forgetting
> You arise therefore from your stomach and your imagination
> You invite the little lady onstage
> > And run along the nerve from the base to its point in a flat arc
> You are whatever you can afford and arrange,
> > Wherever you can imagine to appear
> You are this third thing
> > fixed only in the variety of your manifestations
> > a universe of meaning, value and practice[103]

Perhaps most arrestingly, "Acting Out" gestures to the split between a masculinized tradition of Marxist analysis and a feminized concept of embodied experience in the allusive resemblance of its "argument" to Marx's own in volume 1 of *Capital*. The poem's second-person object "begin[s] from economic fact," where the preposition "from" suggests a direction as well as a starting point, before the following lines launch into what in this context reads as a sarcastic imitation of the individualism of the contemporary liberal subject, "distinguished by what you do and how you go about doing it." Notably, the following lines are separated mid-clause (and in the middle of a noun phrase) by a line break placing the words, "You are a perceptible, finite and particular" on a line of their own, making for some neatly mirrored scansion that, in shifting "a perceptible" from adjective to noun, suggests that the "you" of the poem actually *is* an isolable particular. But the poem subsequently folds back into normative syntax with flat disappointment, as its unusual linguistic operation collapses into a more familiar semantic progression where form and content seem to align again as "part of the scaffolding."

This movement from a moment of estrangement to one of resolution is underscored by the doublespeak of an easy sarcasm in the following line—"Your personal qualities should ideally be completely irrelevant / chains of forgetting"—where line breaks suggest a distance between essence and appearance. In this poem about value, then, a sense of an individual subject as a (mere) perceptible—combined with the grammatical riff on a *lack* of perceptibility, of simultaneously being "a-perceptible"—resonates with the Hegelian logic of moments that Marx both retained and adjusted.[104] Indeed, the image of a spatial dialectic and its movement is not hard to imagine in Warren's idea of "irrelevant" personal qualities placed along "chains of forgetting" as so many a-perceptible moments of a dialectic, or the movement of capital perpetually renewing itself.

In a certain respect, "Acting Out" thus works to counterintuitively highlight the strong relation between sensuous experience and the "science" of a project like value-form theory: the weird asynchrony, for example, between the laboring connotations of "overalls" on the one hand, and the magical properties of a "talisman" charm on the other, may bring to mind Marx's many satirical invocations of the magical qualities of the commodity, its "metaphysical subtleties and theological niceties"[105]—a characterization that itself plays on the Baroque idea of poetry as an art of fantastic conceits, elevated beauty, and hyperbole. And to further insist on this way of reading the poem: other moments suggest that the conceit of "Acting Out" is its attempt to name both value *and* its social forms ("manifestations"), as in:

> You are whatever you can afford and arrange,
>   Wherever you can imagine to appear
> You are this third thing
>   fixed only in the variety of your manifestations

Effects and sensations are exchangeables here: they are reduced to superfluous "third" things, appearances, a variety of manifestations, circumscribed only by the limits of the individual's purchasing power and the limits of their imagination, different powers tellingly conflated in the lines above. Note how the "third thing" of the final phrase in this excerpt not only alludes to Marx's description—repeated from his *Economic and Philosophic Manuscripts of 1844* in the *Grundrisse* and *Capital*—of value or abstract labor as a "third thing," but to his method, too, which proceeds by deduction to establish that our empirically observable material world of capital, land, and labor must be governed by the law of value. In a triple allusion, "third thing" may also invoke the Quaker idea of shared experiences or activities as mediating objects that facilitate emotional connection.

In this manner, the lyric strategy of "Acting Out" marks an attempt to grasp the process of form-determination—"a universe of meaning, value, and practice"—by poetically naming it, describing its workings, and identifying its violence. The poem is indeed a case of acting out, then, if in that phrase we can hear its common usage as an allegation of socially unacceptable behavior that carries with it feminizing and infantilizing powers. This is additionally why Warren's "you" strikes such an ontologizing and accusatory note:

> You are the clause built into the law
>   significant, fungible and durable
> . . .
> You are the amalgamation of your conceptions
>   and their consequences
> You are the structures you live by
>   and act unfettered against anything
>   detrimental to your interests
> You are the bean eaters
>   couched in productive forces
> You are the humming cycle of land under your feet[106]

The law of value, the primacy of action, the amalgamation of "conceptions." This Marxian conceptual triad of value, activity, and representation continues to guide the poem's thematic progression. And unlike Lisa Robertson's startling 2009 poem "Wooden Houses"—to which "Acting Out" bears an obvious likeness insofar as many of its melodic lines are also composed as repetitious statements about an unnamed "You"[107]—Warren's "you" is not aimed at the figure of a lover, nor even a real or imagined subject, necessarily. Rather, this "you" is always exchangeable. Warren's reference to "the bean eaters," for instance, recalls Gwendolyn Brooks's poem, from the 1960 book of the same name, about an old, poignantly ordinary (and from capital's point of view, replaceable) couple, in their modest rented home and monotonous daily routine. In a later line, "Your desire is elemental and abundant," invokes the psychoanalytic idea of *jouissance* at the same time as it acerbically renders this disorderly experience as just another moment of appearance in the reproduction of capital. Even as the poet appears to turn on herself, writing, "You are accused of being a lyric poet," the chastisement is limited in its power because it has already been rendered absurd: if this lyric poet is exchangeable for any other "you" named here, then so is her accuser. As Warren assures us, when the poem folds to a close, "You are not so different as a mastiff is from a greyhound / a spaniel from a shepherd's dog"; the larger allegorical point being that these dogs may be very different, but they are all categorized as dogs, just as women often are too.[108]

In rhythmically describing the metamorphosis of value, "Acting Out" seeks to feel it as well as systematize it. In this way Warren's poem attempts to bypass figuration and shift the idea of what counts as knowledge to include poetic form in that category. As such, "Acting Out" offers a theory of a theory of how meaning collapses, in an effort to expose the non-human culprit of our unevenly shared misery by rhetorically indexing categorial moments of a synchronic whole. Impressively, the poem strikes a careful balance between a sense of the rolling inevitability of capital's self-expanding movement—the "durable" "clause built into the law"—and the radical contingency implicit in the proposition that the individual "you," while enclosed by value, is in fact only an "amalgamation" of thought and the concrete *effects* of thought ("conceptions / and their consequences"). Rather than a fatalistic sense of historical determinism, this naming act seems to imply that capitalism was never the natural, inevitable form of human relations that neoliberals would have us believe. And yet: under capital, mediation never falls away. If "Acting Out" seems to hang suspended in this deadpan dilemma, then, it might be prudent to read the poem less as an attempt to represent capital than an attempt to show why its representation is impossible. That is to say, if capital functions on the basis of real abstractions, through the life process of individuals "as they *really* are; i.e. as they operate, produce materially . . . independent of their will," then the poem cannot *see* capital from outside of capital, nor from a better viewpoint, and not only because capital's abstracting movement is unrepresentable, but because the consciousness required to really know (and collectively, intentionally make) one's world could only ever come about through revolution.

The impasse depicted in Warren's closing line, however—"Your engine went by at 6 o'clock, your cab went by at 9"—is a *mise-en-scène* of blocked agency. Perhaps, in this way, the poem's taciturn repetitions index the tension between capital's impersonality on the one hand and its compulsion to impose differentials on the other. But the collection of poems in *Here Come the Warm Jets* is far from joyless. From peppy lines like "I see that Finnish motherfucker / Shoeless Big Country / shameless in a tree hut," to the poker-faced sarcasm (or is it?) of "Astrology is real,"[109] its many playful, humorous moments are negatively bound up with the variegated particulars of US American life, where poems with titles like "Hide the Poor," "Can I Prevent My Wages from Being Garnished," and "My Factless Autobiography" feature a speaker both weighed down by her part in this world and willing to make a joke of it.

We might find hopeful promise, too, in the ostentatiously mediated pastoral that imbues several poems in the collection. In "Sensorium," "the cesspool cleaner and the ceruse-maker" go to "market their bodies and call the return":

They get for it their wages

They produce corn, wine, clothes and shoes,
    and build themselves houses

. . .

For food they serve splendid cakes and loaves and sit down to feast
    with their children
And they have wine to drink too

So they lead a peaceful healthy life, and die at a ripe old age
    bequeathing a similar way of life to their children

And repeat the process often in the hour of the sun[110]

Ceruse, an Elizabethan cosmetic used as a skin whitener, famously turned out to contain poisonous white lead. Both poisoned figures then, the cerusemaker stands anachronistically next to the cesspool cleaner, before the poem proceeds to again move through the collection's undergirding themes of the market, commodities, production, and reproduction. Yet this time the embers of feudalism seem not to have quite faded, and biblical undertones emerge from the poem's prayer-like rhythms, its breath lines, its "loaves," "feast," "wine," and its "hour of the sun." Terms like "splendid" and "ripe old age" nostalgically evoke the affective customs of a bygone era, and as the poem combines a sense of old-fashioned (and suspiciously "innocent") commodity production with pastoral settings, it introduces multiple temporalities whose interferences resonate across the collection. "Sensorium" begins with an image of the ideal postindustrial white-collar worker, for instance, as "The figure must be a professional at the call of his job," but a few lines later we encounter less obedient and more sensual kinds of work: "a variety of delicacies, scents, perfumes, call-girls, / and confectionary."

If this collagic technique marks Warren's attempt to capture the long arc of capitalism, what ultimately emerges is a humanist temporality, the kind of subjective and existential historical time that Jameson theorizes as the old-fashioned "narrative history" of events and anthropomorphic characters, which as he explains, is "how human beings will periodize . . . and transform these multitudinous realities into a narrative they can remember, a narrative on the scale of their own temporal existences."[111] Yet Warren's work appears to mark the limits of its own periodizing too, not only in the frustrated undertaking of "Acting Out" but at the ending of "Sensorium," where this faux-pastoral poem notes its own subjective and existential limits to suggest the parameters of a humanist purview:

> And repeat the process often in the hour of the sun
>
> And various country dishes
>
> And what sorts of things are to be feared
>
> To carry arms and ride[112]

Inward/Outward

Like most of the works considered in *Behind Our Backs*, *Here Come the Warm Jets* is not a declaratively feminist book. Its most dramatically gendered moments arrive unceremoniously, as in a poem titled "A Practice Known as Churning," where Warren writes:

> There in the alley we converse
> Idris his love of fresh skin
> Ted his disdain for women
> Their lack of banking
> Terrence and Will their concern
> for purity of pussy[113]

Yet the sardonic understatement of these lines is perhaps in keeping with the political trajectory of a book whose feminism emerges more as part of a comprehensive and integrated effort to arrive at an enlarged historical consciousness, one able to conceive of a heterogeneous, unknowable totality; the effort, as Jameson puts it (and as Chapter 4 will discuss at length), to grasp a former non-reflexive self as itself an object—a "you"—within a larger history.[114]

We could on this score point to an important commonality between Warren's and Kapil's poetry, since it is possible to consider both *Here Come the Warm Jets* and *Ban en Banlieue* as efforts to overcome the limit point encountered by any attempt to situate oneself within a system only knowable through its effects.[115] Whether that means gesturally moving "inward" toward the internal negativity of the abject (Kapil), or "outward" towards capital's abstractions (Warren), these deeply theoretical movements are dialectically bound to each other; indeed, Kapil's writing also radiates "outwards," towards other persons who find themselves placed somewhere along the scale of the socially mediated category of relative surplus population; and Warren's attempt to render capitalist abstraction falters at the border of its own hermeneutic limits, collapsing into a more familiar lyric mode.

The meeting point of Kapil's and Warren's poetry, then, is the capitalist value-form. Kapil's focus at the level of abject reproduction involves an anti-representational, messy poetics of the global *banlieue*. This is a poetics that indexes the doubly dissimulated, counter-reproductive underside of value: a counter-reproductive negativity within the value-form itself, the negativity

Elson acknowledges when she notes that abstract labor is the *only* form of labor reflected in the universal equivalent. Warren's attunement to a Marxian theory of form-determination results in a poetics that takes aim, instead, at what it intuitively knows to be value's illusory independence.

My claim in this chapter is not therefore that poems perform an analysis of capital's function of abstraction, but that they suggest both the existence and something of the character of these internal, systematic contradictions. Consider this effort next to Elbe's description of the project of value-form theory, summarized here as a theoretical practice of "form development":

> Form-analysis develops these forms (such as value, money, capital, but also law and the state) from the contradictory conditions of the social constitution of labor, "clarifies them, grasps their essence and necessity." Form *development* is not to be understood as the retracing of the historical development of the object, but rather the conceptual deciphering of the immanent structural relationships of the capitalist mode of production. It unscrambles the apparently independent, apparently objectively grounded forms of social wealth and the political compulsion of the capitalist mode of production as *historically specific* and therefore—albeit in no way arbitrarily or in a piecemeal manner—as *changeable* forms of praxis.[116]

Kapil and Warren arguably pursue what Elbe calls a "conceptual deciphering"—an unscrambling of sorts—of capital's "immanent structural relationships," moving toward a sense of how those relationships serve to indirectly form-determine much more than the readily categorizable capitalist forms of "value, money, capital, but also law and the state." Reading this poetry together with value-critical feminism thus discloses a widely shared (indeed, popular) awareness of the essential illusion of capitalist forms of social wealth, for in this work, too, capitalism's onward trundle is understood to be anything but "independent."

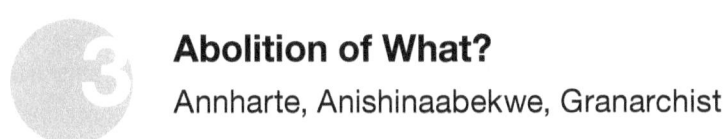

Abolition of What?
Annharte, Anishinaabekwe, Granarchist

"**YOU AUDIENCE / ME SQUAW**," begins Anishinaabe poet Marie Annharte Baker's "Squaw Guide," and with these words Annharte sets out an explicit antagonism between an audience figured as settler and the Indigenous speaker of the poem.[1] Importantly, the opposing terms "Audience" and "Squaw" imply incommunicability, a coerced performance rather than a conversation, not least because the speaker names herself through the racist and racializing language of white settler culture. But these short lines are as much a *détournement* of this relation of domination as they are a commentary on the ways Indigenous subjects have been required to perform acceptable versions of Indigeneity in return for legal and cultural recognition in colonial settler states. In a double twist, Annharte's syntax and line break parody the racist trope, popularized by American Westerns, of the broken English spoken by Indigenous people. While Annharte's satire semantically depends on a structure of colonial oppression in order to make sense, the joke is on the settler, figured here as both ignorant and speechless—now more stupefied than judgmental—in the opening of "Squaw Guide." Her antagonism and humor open onto a different register of knowledge and perception, one where the colonial relation no longer gets to determine what is obvious and what is not.

We can usefully situate Annharte's poetry within a history of decolonizing practice that has often turned to humor as a mode of resistance to what historian Marcia Crosby calls the "produced authenticity" of the figure of the "Imaginary Indian."[2] In this regard her work contests the "Native trickster" archetype that appeared repeatedly in Indigenous literary texts and became the convenient focus of an emerging field of Indigenous studies in the 1990s: as Kristina Fagan demonstrates, this persona often functioned in predominantly white academic discourse on Indigenous literature as a dehistoricizing and commodifying celebration of difference, one in which humor was a creative, idealized, spiritual attribute inherent to the postmodernist and genderqueer trickster figure rather than a social strategy rooted in Indigenous political struggles.[3]

But as I want to suggest in this chapter, the comedy at work here is just one part of a much more holistic abolitionist sensibility we can trace across Annharte's poetry and prose of the last three decades. The mesh of sense perception, emotion, beliefs, and political positions marked by the lines above might be compared to the concept of *Weltanschauung*, or worldview, so central to German Romanticist thought and the Hegelian model of a dialectical unity.[4] However, it is more accurately understood as a form of Nishnaabewin: the philosophies, practices, and relationships that compose Anishinaabeg ways of life, as well as what Michi Saagiig Nishnaabeg scholar Leanne Betasamosake Simpson describes as a type of knowledge "created through the combination of heart knowledge or emotion, and thought or intellect."[5] Annharte's work as a theorist, we will see, involves the production of new Anishinaabeg concepts in a poetic practice that underscores the exemplarity of an Indigenous abolitionist feminism.

Annharte is a member of the Little Saskatchewan First Nation of Manitoba, part of the group of Ojibwe peoples that in turn forms part of a larger group of Anishinaabe Nations, including the Michi Saagiig; the ancestral territories of these peoples stretch across large parts of the Canadian prairie provinces and around the Great Lakes region of Ontario and the northeastern United States, and they share an ancestral language, Ojibwe (or Anishinaabemowin)—a language comprised of a variety of local dialects and writing systems. As Simpson explains in her 2017 book *As We Have Always Done: Indigenous Freedom Through Radical Resistance*, Nishnaabewin is a form of intelligence that encompasses "all of the associated practices, knowledge and ethics that make us Nishnaabeg and construct the Nishnaabeg world."[6] Nishnaabewin involves *Biiskabiyang*: "the process of returning to ourselves, a reengagement with the things we have left behind, a reemergence, an unfolding from the inside out—is a concept, an individual and collective process of decolonization and resurgence." Simultaneously individual and collective, a re-engagement with a past not shaped (as Marx had it) by dead capital that weighs like a nightmare, Biiskabiyang means, rather, "the embodied processes as freedom."[7]

For Simpson, Nishnaabewin emphasizes the dynamic and practical aspects of relationships between theory and practice. Commenting on her earlier book, *Dancing on Our Turtle's Back*, she notes that there:

> I explained how the transformative power of knowledge is unleashed through movement, kinetics or action, our embedded practices and processes of life; that is, one has to be fully present and engaged in Nishnaabeg ways of living in order to generate knowledge, in order to generate theory.[8]

Indeed, action is central to the concept of social relation here, where the conscious and intentional building of one's shared physical environment and relationships also makes self-determination possible. Writing about her own Michi Saagiig relations, Simpson links everyday activities of life- and world-building to Nishnaabeg creation stories:

> In this sense, in the past, Nishnaabeg woke up each morning and built Nishnaabeg life every day, using our knowledge and practices because this is what we are encouraged to do in our creation stories; these are our original instructions. This procedure or practice of living, theory and praxis intertwined, is generated through relations with Michi Saagiig Nishnaabeg land, and that is constructed and defined by our intimate spiritual, emotional, and physical relationship with it. The procedure is our grounded normativity. Living is a creative act, with self-determined making or producing at its core.[9]

While they are based in philosophically distinct traditions and describe different social arrangements, there is an affinity to be noted between Simpson's Nishnaabeg concept of living as a creative and practical act, and Marx's description of labor in capitalism as "the living, form-giving fire ... the transitoriness of things, their temporality, as their formation by living time."[10] Both share the fundamental recognition not only that our social world is made by the collective and repeated activities of humans over time—whether that process takes place by intentional decision-making or the uncoordinated yet collective expenditures of muscle and brain in the service of capital—but also that from these activities and their modes of organization spring thoughts, beliefs, feelings, and subjectivities.

Simpson underscores this very point when she observes that "colonized life is so intensely about consumption that the idea of making is reserved for artists at best and hobbies at worst. Making is not seen as the material basis for experiencing and influencing the world."[11] In this vein, she characterizes Nishnaabewin as a type of grounded normativity, a theoretical term she develops with the Dene scholar Glen Coulthard to describe the place-based knowledges and practices that ground Indigenous political systems, economies, and understandings of nationhood, emphasizing the sense in which they are "process-centered modes of living that generate profoundly different conceptualizations of nationhood and governmentality—ones that aren't based on enclosure, authoritarian power, and hierarchy."[12] Linking grounded normativity to the concept of "kwe," the Ojibwe word approximating "woman"—which as Simpson explains, "recognizes a spectrum of gender expressions"—Simpson characterizes her own life as a kwe in terms of method: as a way of generating knowledge about oneself and one's relations through daily place-based practices "of hunting, fishing, harvesting rice and medicines, ceremony, language learning, singing, dancing, making maple syrup, parenting, and storytelling," as well as through the "internal work" of "generating meaning about my life through the way I think and live." She compellingly concludes this part of her account by connecting kwe, method, and theory:

> This is not just experiential knowledge or embodied knowledge. It is not just individual knowledge rooted in my own perspectives and experiences with the abusive power of colonialism, because it is theoretically anchored to and generated through Nishnaabeg intelligence and because it takes place entirely within grounded normativity—perhaps a strangulated grounded normativity but grounded normativity nevertheless. In an entirely Nishnaabeg intellectual context, I wouldn't have to explain this at all. This would be understood because it is how our knowledge system has always worked.
>
> This is kwe as method generating kwe as theorist.
>
> This is kwe as method generating kwe as theorist, *as we have always done*.[13]

As is evident here, Simpson's ambivalent relationship to academic scholarship informs her efforts both to retain a sense of the importance of theory as a tool for critique and to distinguish kwe as theorist from settler perceptions of what theory is and who theoreticians might be. Theory in this case is rooted in a cosmology based in Aki, or "akinoomaage," the Nishnaabeg concept of drawing guidance from interactions with one's environment, and a practice conceived in terms of pointing towards and taking direction from our surroundings.[14]

Kwe-as-Theorist

Simpson's description of kwe as a method that generates concepts, subjectivities, and relationships offers a framework for reading Annharte's poetry that, in its emphasis on social relations, resonates in important ways with the Marxian sense of activity discussed in the previous chapter as a form-determining dialectic binding the abstract and the concrete. It is in this sense, too, that Annharte's work can meaningfully be read as a poetics of abolition insofar as it aligns with Ruth Wilson Gilmore's well-known argument that abolition means building a future world from what is already here, since "what the world will become already exists in fragments and pieces, experiments and possibilities . . . abolition is building the future from the present, in all of the ways we can."[15]

Indeed, the generative aspects of Nishnaabeg intelligence and its concrete daily practice are central to Annharte's poetics. In poems ranging in subject matter from cybernetic coyote grandmothers and "commie conversations" in Vancouver, to satiric commentary on policy amendments to the Indian Act, to the evocation of American Indian and Indigenous armed resistance in the late nineteenth century, we are reminded of "the affirmative Indigenous worlds that continue to exist right alongside the colonial worlds,"[16] as well as the unassimilable dimensions of these lifeworlds. In an early essay from 1994, Annharte suggests one example of this affirmative presence when she frames Indigenous storytelling in terms of a "medicine line," which she initially defines as a "boundary line between groups" or a "division of territories." Yet she also uses the concept to link oral and written forms of storytelling: "the 'medicine line' might not simply be a linear extension of a story 'told' to a story 'written.' The direction of the 'line' might also spiral up or down. I see this 'medicine line' as what connects me as a writer to the most intangible elements of a culture I struggle to understand."[17] Noting the unexplainable dimensions of her own culture, experienced in part through "sensual memory" and also understood in this essay through the image of a spider web, Annharte connects oral tradition to place and identity by framing the "Grandmother voice" as a medicine line:

> What do the stories convey to me? Right away I hear Grandmother's voice, even if the storyteller is a man. I hear the story with the ears of a grandchild. The Grandmother voice is a "medicine line" which stretches across the generations. Each woman must have this legacy of oral tradition. For me, my grandmother was a kind ant accepting influence in my life. She spoke to me in the Anishinabe language.... I think of the stories as healing because they help us connect to some part of the earth. They remind us of who we are and we are given identity.[18]

Most descriptions of the medicine line understand it as an Indigenous term for the border between Canada and the United States, a boundary line that held particular significance for the mobile peoples of the Plains Métis, for whom the northern Plains "borderlands," as Michel Hogue has pointed out, were Indigenous homelands as well as a space of migration. Some Plains Métis people referred to this new international border as the medicine line because in the late nineteenth century it offered safety from US soldiers who respected its boundary. But as Hogue argues, contradictions surfaced as the consolidation of the new settler-colonial border proved conspicuously incompatible both with the migratory practices of the Plains Métis—practices central to their economic and political organization—as well as with their existing sovereignties and territories.[19] In characterizing cross-generational, matrilineal storytelling as a medicine line, then, Annharte inverts this Indigenous spatial concept by temporalizing (indeed, spiralizing) it, further incorporating the telling of Anishinaabe history, and the constitutive violence of settler-Indigenous relations, into Anishinaabe terms. As the readings in this chapter underline, this method of conceptual reworking is a favored strategy for a decidedly urban poet concerned to critique prescriptive fictions of Indigenous authenticity and the ironic duplicity of liberal forms of recognition as they prop up the ongoing dispossession of First Nations communities in Canada. The post-contact idea of the medicine line thus suggests affirmative *and* negative forces at work, in keeping with Annharte's subsequent reflection that "maintaining an Indian identity is a struggle."[20]

Annharte's deployment of the medicine line as a concept incorporating spatial and temporal, matrilineal and spiritual dimensions offers a practical example of Simpson's notion of kwe-as-theorist, where, significantly, "kwe" and "theory" are rendered not as static, guaranteed categories of identity and knowledge, but as the result of daily practices. In this regard, and in a trope that recurs across her work, Annharte identifies with the coyote, a mythological character who often represents the role of trickster in North American Indigenous cultures, but more specifically for Annharte represents the complexities of identification itself—a longstanding interest that has inspired Mercedes Eng's apt characterization of Annharte as a "coyotrix granarchist."[21] In a series of poems titled "granny boot camp," the poem "Gynegran," makes this explicit: "Coyote is flexible and inconsistent. Adaptable contradiction." This contradiction, we are led to understand, unfolds both at the level of identity and of literal survival:

> Coyote starts something then changes mind right away.
> Tricksters had to scheme a life. Way out of trouble. Think
> quick to stay alive. Get out of the way conformity will crush.[22]

Scheming, adapting, evading: in Annharte's poems, strategies of physical and psychic survival are intrinsically connected and often evoked by way of racialized and feminized identity categories. From "Squaw" to "rez identity" to "Injunaity," some of these categories are derided by allusive wordplay or irony.[23] Others are notably drawn from street life and handled more gently—"Mama Sasquatch" and "ndn bag lady" provide figures of solidarity for Annharte's speaker[24]—while still others are overtly prized: in the "granny boot camp" series, the image of an Indigenous grandmother is positively kaleidoscopic, making her appearance as "Spider Grandmother," "MEDICINE WOMAN NOT," "Coyote chaos," "Cyber gran," but also in Cree, nsyilxcən, and Ojibwe as "Plain old kokum, gaga, tupa, nokomis."[25] In an especially humorous line, Annharte calls this figure a "Priestess, Poetess, Prophetess, / Visionary and Seer" before inserting the brand name of a multivitamin: "We must pump up that Geritol image."[26]

Racializing "Indigeneity"

Annharte's "granny boot camp" poems give us a sense of the elasticity with which her work produces new, Indigenized concepts. Yet her poetry is also remarkable for the way it moves between method and concept, activity and thought, to suggest a dialectical idea of the abstract-concrete character of "race" somewhat at odds with the specifically textual sense of the concept in recent poetry studies. In his writing on the transformative capacity of Black experimental writing, for example, Anthony Reed argues that the post-lyric work of Claudia Rankine and Douglas Kearney is alert to "the abstractness of the black subject."[27] Following Robin Kelley, Reed defines race as a contentless abstraction whose "value always seems to precede its appearance."[28] Open-ended, indeterminate, endlessly mediatized and mediated, "race" can thus be transformed in Black experimental writing in such a way that it becomes imbued with a productive capacity, as *poesis* in the ancient Greek sense and a mode of self-making. Yet where Reed's concept of "the textual nature of Blackness as a social encoding of difference" is informed by a deconstructive rejection of the logic of identity and the liberal politics of recognition,[29] Annharte's poems, as we will see below, reject such logics in a way that more directly attends to the fetters of the objective reality from which they arise, not only suggesting a content at work but specifying that content as capital.

Christopher Chen's definition of race, in his powerful essay "The Limit Point of Capitalist Equality: Notes Toward an Abolitionist Antiracism," helpfully underscores the distinction I am drawing here. Even while, in his words, it is "through race [that] black chattel slavery in the United States constituted 'free' labor as white, and whiteness as unenslaveability and unalienable property," Chen argues that race is better understood not a property or attribute of identities or groups, but as an array of ascriptive procedures that structure social life. It should therefore be grasped as a structural coercion rather than a cultural particularity or deviation from socio-political norms:[30]

> If race is thus [unhelpfully] understood in terms of difference rather than domination, then anti-racist practice will require the affirmation of stigmatised identities rather than their abolition as indices of structural subordination. Formulating an abolitionist anti-racism would require imagining the end of "race" as a hierarchical assignment, rather than a

denial of the political salience of cultural identities. "Race" here names a relation of subordination.[31]

Chen's distinction between difference and domination, affirmation and abolition, rests on an insistence that we connect race to the objective force of capitalist compulsions. His definition of race as a relation of subordination and a hierarchical assignment thus entails an assertion that cultural and textual understandings of "difference"—a term he invokes in both its poststructuralist and liberal casts—are inadequate to a political horizon that might imagine (and strategize toward) "the end of 'race' as a hierarchical assignment."[32]

Chen's argument is one of several trenchant critiques of the liberal politics of recognition that gained traction in the years immediately following the 2007–2008 financial crisis.[33] Among the most prominent of these is Coulthard's landmark 2014 study *Red Skin, White Masks: Rejecting the Colonial Politics of Recognition*, which advances the claim—now widely recognized among Indigenous studies scholars, and ironically by some university institutions themselves[34]—that "colonial relations of power are no longer reproduced primarily through overtly coercive means, but rather through the asymmetrical exchange of mediated forms of state recognition and accommodation."[35] His critique offers a pointed rejection of the influential arguments of Charles Taylor, whose well-known 1992 essay "The Politics of Recognition" advances a conciliatory interpretation of the Hegelian master-slave dialectic and its promise of "reciprocal recognition among equals." Using Quebecois and Indigenous people in Canada as key examples of "threatened minorities,"[36] Taylor suggests that the oppression of specific groups can be ameliorated by nation-states that recognize group-specific claims or allow for semi-autonomous self-government, while asserting a core set of fundamental rights such as citizenship. Coulthard challenges this remedial vision, however, on the basis that it depends on the mutual recognition of free, self-determining individuals or bodies—a recognition paradigm that, as Frantz Fanon's critique of Hegel's model demonstrates, is irrelevant within colonial contexts since "for Hegel there is reciprocity; here the master laughs at the consciousness of the slave. What he wants from the slave is not recognition but work."[37]

The Indigenous cultural identities embedded in the claims to sovereignty that both Coulthard and Simpson place at the heart of Indigenous resurgence are constitutively different from the hierarchical racial categories that Chen theorizes as "race," however. They exceed racial ascriptions nonetheless imposed on Indigenous subjects, since Indigeneity primarily names not a structural position within a set of social relations defined by colonial capitalism and genocidal violence, but an identification with a history of Indigenous cultures and traditions that predate European contact, and a line of continuity between pre-contact Indigenous life and contemporary Indigenous struggles against systematic dispossession and erasure.

At the same time, Coulthard's critique of recognition helps us to see how, as per Chen's argument, race is also reproduced as liberal versions of "Indigeneity" through a variety of processes that typecast Indigenous subjects into identities either legitimized by settler culture as exceptionally natural, authentic, creative, or spiritual, or else delegitimized as mixed-blood, welfare-dependent, anti-capitalist, or simply poor. In every case, moreover, Indigeneity is mediated by legal regimes of personhood and property, as Iyko Day points out:

> In a colonial context, the violence of [the value] abstraction carries over into the racialized modes of relation embedded in the emergence of modern legal personhood. Defined as an appropriative, self-possessed individual, the legal subject of capitalist relations conceals itself through the illusion of abstract equivalence that works to devalue personhood through property. It is a racial construction that stands in reactionary opposition to Indigenous modes of relation.[38]

If the violence of capitalist abstraction shapes the racial construction of the self-possessed individual, examples of the reactionary character of this process abound: take (for one brief example) the image of the Indigenous eco-warrior whose symbiotic and spiritual relation to the land is romantically prized until the moment she stages a sit-in to prevent pipeline development through First Nations territories.[39]

Examining representations of Indigeneity as racializing identity categories—character masks that are always insufficient to the reality of the subjects they project and that instead might be grasped in their historical moments of appearance, disappearance, and transformation—is therefore a project that Coulthard and Annharte share. In distinct ways, their work helps us to perceive these racializing appearances as mediating objects themselves and, if not to unmask them, then to at least understand some of the more specific ways in which they are internally bonded to the objective movements of capital—in other words, to grasp how social relations "assume the form of a relationship between things that objectivize themselves in the person," as we saw in Chapter 1.[40] Indeed, this is the register in which Chen connects racism, theorized as a relation of subordination and form of domination, to an abolitionist politics that necessitates "imagining the end of 'race' as a hierarchical assignment." Notably, he defines race in contrast to other forms of cultural groupings, identifications, and antagonisms:

> Overlapping with—yet conceptually distinct from—class, culture, caste, gender, nation, and ethnicity, "race" is not only a system of ideas but an array of ascriptive racialising procedures which structure multiple levels of social life. . . . To distinguish racial ascription from voluntary acts of cultural identification—and from a range of responses to racial rule from flight to armed revolt—requires a shift in focus from "race" to racism.[41]

The "multiple levels of social life" noted here include the imposition of "fictive identities" as well as "wage differentials, wealth stratification, and occupational and spatial segregation,"[42] suggesting how an abolitionist antiracism is undergirded by a dialectical sense of the material and conceptual production of race.

But what form would the abolition of race take in Indigenous contexts? Annharte's work helps us to grasp the paradoxical ease and difficulty of answering that question, particularly in the context of the recent demands of the Land Back movement for the restitution of Indigenous lands and resources, but also in light of an entangled history in which Indigenous people have long lived alongside and in antagonism with settlers, both in the entity called Canada and in its legally designated outsides, the "temporally fixed place of the reserve."[43] Annharte's abolitionist poetics, we will see, involves critiquing "fictive" Indigenous identities as much as it means exhorting her audience to quite literally help build barricades that will block "roads / railways dams."[44] Rooted in Anishinaabe grounded normativity, the anti-capitalist radicalism undergirding her poems is thus distinct from but usefully comparable to other abolitionisms, and especially comparable, I will argue, to calls for the abolition of abstract identity categories that form part of an array of communization tendencies to have emerged in recent deindustrializing decades.

Before moving to read Annharte's poetry in more detail, however, let us examine some of the political and conceptual shapes abolition has taken in this era of capitalist decline both for feminist poets and for communization theorists. Then we may turn to Harry Harootunian's conjunctural method of "deprovincializing Marx," which aids our reading of this Anishinaabe poet when it accounts for the copresence of distinct temporalities both set in play by and excluded from capital's formal modalities; from this point, we can be guided toward a more precise historical reading of an Indigenous abolitionist poetics—a poetics that, unlike other communist abolitionisms, would seek to preserve as much as it would cancel.

The Paradox of Abolition

"Abolition" is a provocative and seductive idea, as politically controversial as it can be conceptually hazy. Most immediately, the term suggests the nineteenth-century abolitionist movement to which the end of the legally sanctioned Atlantic slave trade is often attributed. This association gives the idea a positive valence of possibility, as if the abolition of what might be opposed is generally within reach. Local, national, and international campaigns to abolish nuclear weapons, the death penalty, abortion, child labor, human trafficking, pornography, and prisons all operate on the premise of a realizable outcome, despite fundamental incongruities in their political motivations and strategies. While twenty-first-century movements such as Occupy, Black Lives Matter, and Idle No More might represent more expansive forms of political engagement, they nonetheless tend to include specific demands for the abolition of concrete institutions like the Federal Reserve Bank, the police, or Canadian parliamentary law.

Yet while issue-based forms of abolition can be tracked across the political spectrum, Left-oriented movements have expressed a telling tension over the last two decades: at the same time as they have sought to affirm the positions of women; queer and trans people; Black, Brown, Asian, and Indigenous people; and the working-class or "the 99 percent," they have also articulated understandings of raced, gendered, sexuated, and classed identities as categories to be dissolved or reinvented beyond recognition. As Juliana Gleeson writes, "everyone from gay communists to millenarian Marxists to anarcho-nihilist transfeminists have proposed gender's abolition." While she observes that it "has become repeatedly obscured as a strategy by the tangled and uneven development of revolutionary thought," Gleeson nevertheless notes the persistence of gender abolition as a political demand, albeit one whose interpretation has quickly changed in recent years: from communization theory's eschatological but (in Gleeson's critique) heterosexist call, in the early 2010s, for the abolition of gender as a constitutive part of a capitalist totality, to Laboria Cuboniks's entreaty, just a few years later, to "[l]et a hundred sexes bloom!," to anti-identitarian demands by anonymous gender nihilists that since any gender deviance will be punished, "gender must go." Gleeson additionally underscores the emergence of new abolitionist solidarities, noting how "anti-racist and trans activists have converged around the cause of prison abolition."[45]

The question of what becomes of identity categories when they are understood to be both the product of an unjust society and an indispensable framework for resistance has been set in stark relief by a protracted period of economic stagnation and contraction in the Global North over the last four decades. Importantly, this economic transformation in OECD countries—which has been variously characterized as a shift from Fordism to post-Fordism, industry to finance, or Keynesianism to neoliberalism—is one in which the capitalist production process appears to need the worker and her labor less and less.[46] In this way, deindustrialization erodes the material basis for trade unionism and other twentieth-century political projects predicated on a positive conception of worker identity, a fact worth bearing in mind when we observe the renewed interest in the politics of gender abolition, the abolition of race, of work, and even the capitalist value-form.[47]

Indeed, at a moment when conversations about identity politics are at the forefront of culture war discourse, feminist poets and theorists in particular have returned to a contradiction cogently described by Denise Riley in the 1980s: in seeking to transform the category "women" from its status as an oppressed social identity, feminists have had to reinscribe this category and its baggage, for, in Riley's words, "both a concentration on and a refusal of the identity of 'women' are essential to feminism."[48] Writing about social reproduction struggles, Marina Vishmidt casts this problem as the "paradox of self-abolition":

The subject of abolition emerges through the struggle that abolition entails, yet must also arrive at a point where the militant identity emerging through struggle has to eliminate its basis in the society the movement wants to change or overcome: being a woman, in this instance. . . . [T]his is not a situation which can be dealt with by fiat, but has to be one of the modes and horizons of struggle itself, in which it will continue to unfold as a painful contradiction. Who is the subject that initiates and who comes out of the other side of self-abolition?[49]

Riley herself poses a similar question in "A Note on Sex and 'The Reclaiming of Language,'" a poem from her 1977 collection, *Marxism for Infants*:

> The work is
> e.g. to write "she" and for that to be a statement
> of fact only and not a strong image
> of everything which is not-you, which sees you[50]

Who is this not-yet self-abolishing subject, constituted by powers beyond their cognition, and thus unable to prefigure their own transformation? As Samuel Solomon notes, this poem has been read "as a relatively straightforward polemical allegory for the misrecognitions of categorical identifications and interpellations."[51] Riley's title acerbically pokes fun at linguistic feminism—or at least the idea that language might be a site for political transformation—and as Solomon observes, she is clearly skeptical of feminist injunctions to "reclaim the language" since, "in all of her work, language *has us* as much as we can ever dream of having it."[52]

To be sure, Riley's speaker's frustration with that "strong image / of everything which is not-you, which sees you" suggests a sense of language as a sort of referential compact with late capital, a mediating technology in a system compelled to cast difference into identity. Next to this critique, we can note an engagement with more concrete abolitionist acts of sabotage, riot, destruction, and refusal in Black US poetry emerging from the 1960s onwards, a tendency linked explicitly to the waves of militant struggle that emerged in that decade in response to police brutality, high unemployment, and poor living standards. Gwendolyn Brooks's *Riot*—published in Detroit in 1969, following the uprisings of the "long hot summer" of 1967—and Amiri Baraka's *Black*

Magic: Sabotage, Target Study, Black Art, published the same year, mark signal examples of a poetics of abolition that takes up violent struggle as a political rationale and *cri de coeur*.[53]

One salient way to periodize the poetic interest in abolition in advanced capitalist economies over the last half-century would be to read it in correspondence with a post-1968 Francophone analysis of how political strategies correlate to shifts in the relationship between capital and labor in an era of economic downturn. The debates in communization theory between Theorie Communiste and Troploin, for example, tend to pivot on the question of when and under what conditions the abolition of capitalist society becomes possible to imagine. For Theorie Communiste, the "communization thesis," which is to say the immediate destruction of all capitalist social forms without any transitional phase, is itself eminently historicizable: it only becomes thinkable once the worker-centered affirmation of the proletariat begins to look untenable. At this point—a moment Robert Brenner and Joshua Clover have persuasively tied to the late 1960s and early 1970s, and especially 1973[54]—a new cycle of struggle emerges in the wake of worker struggles, and this time carries abolition in itself as its immanent horizon because it can no longer feasibly seek to secure a better position for laborers.[55] According to this periodizing model, cycles of social struggle are tied to cycles of capital accumulation: in what Marx calls the tendency of the rate of profit to fall, the relationship between capital and labor enters crisis as a result of a contradiction internal to capital's own logic, whereby technological advances increase productivity by reducing the ratio of costly waged labor in the production process, yet in doing so expel the only real source of value: human labor.[56] Significantly for communization theorists, as intra-capitalist competition evens out and a new business cycle begins, new laborers are hired on less favorable terms. This useful framework helps us to understand a less remarked-upon feature of poetry since the 1970s: a tension that emerges when sociological identity categories no longer serve as points of identification and affirmation, but as external constraints and limits to be abolished: a mode of thinking in poetry that can be tracked in relation to "the changing mode of *reproduction* of capitalist social relations as a whole according to the dialectical development of the relation between classes."[57]

Yet the meaning of a politics and poetics of abolition is fundamentally recast if we set this striation of capitalist history—one in which historical time unfolds through periodic shifts in the capital-labor relation—in further dialectical relation with capitalism's interconnected attempts to subsume non-capitalist social formations through institutions of settler colonialism. As Harry Harootunian has consequentially argued, Western Marxism has generally neglected this route. Instead, the Frankfurt School and Italian autonomist Marxists advanced the idea that the domination of "the commodity relation" represented capitalism's highest form, its "final externalization and naturalization."[58] As Harootunian explains, "this became the dominion of the abstract, of value over the concrete, and the appearance of the individual, who creates its own nature and is without history."[59] Capitalism's triumph has thus been figured in terms of the "regime of real subsumption" as it mediated late capitalist society—its ways of thinking, modes of production, and cultural expressions—to the point of "completion," in an enveloping of social relations the world over. Yet for Harootunian, the turn to a mode of cultural critique based on the supposed "autonomous" nature of the commodity form serves to parochialize Marx's arguments, resulting in an adherence to "a rigid conception of a Marxian historical trajectory constrained to upholding a particular progressive narrative all societies must pass through, on the template of a geographically (and culturally) specific location exemplified by England,"[60] and an "evolutionary pathway based on a universal model requiring replication everywhere."[61]

In this way, Western Marxism also ushered in a distancing from economic analysis in favor of cultural inquiry, "especially in the domain of aesthetic production, art and literature," a shift that Harootunian argues risks sacrificing history itself as the subject of inquiry. Harootunian's central point, however, is that subsumption via the commodity relation has never been the only configuration through which social groups have been yoked to processes of capital accumulation, and that these yokings—appropriative, extractive, expropriative—require their own analysis and historicizing frameworks. Thus, what he calls "deprovincializing Marx" involves "not simply an expanded geographic inclusion but a broadening of temporal possibilities unchained from a hegemonic unilinearism."[62] Harootunian reconfigures Marx's concept of formal subsumption—Marx's term for capital's action of drawing into itself and appropriating preexisting non-capitalist labor processes[63]—to argue for the copresence of distinct temporal structures in capitalism:

The operation of formal subsumption set up the temporal structure of every present, through its mission to appropriate what it found useful in prior practices and procedures. If capitalism seeks to establish the force of the value form and achieve a sameness in the commodity relation, *it paradoxically also produces the very difference it is trying to eliminate* with its propensity to challenge every present with a new content in part derived from the past and the shadowing trace of primitive accumulation.[64]

Capitalism undermines its logical drive towards sameness (abstract equality) because it is *itself* a product of history, "derived from the past." Harootunian's approach thus emphasizes how the formal subsumption of labor is precisely that: a formal modality that develops in dialectical relation with its own (past) content, and alongside other distinct and ongoing processes of primitive accumulation as they separate proletarians from their means of reproduction.

It is worth underlining that Harootunian's critique does not exactly apply to (nor is it aimed at) the value-critical framework that communization debates take as their basis for a theory of how the reproduction of the capital-labor relation enters crisis. These analyses do not take the commodity relation nor "the regime of real subsumption" as their starting point; rather, they share Harootunian's emphasis on capital's formal movements to argue that secular pressures internal to capitalism govern transitions in the world economy. And yet these recent studies of capitalist crisis and its social manifestation are analytically limited by their focus on the Global North. Given how, as David Lloyd and Patrick Wolfe note, capital's crisis of profitability has led to "a renewed movement of enclosure" and a time of "a second commons,"[65] Harootunian's intervention urges us to consider how a model of crisis focused on the changing relationship between capital and labor in advanced capitalist countries connects to different configurations of capitalist development and sociality.

It can be helpful, therefore, to set Harootunian's insistence on the distinct temporal structure of "every present" next to analyses of cycles of struggle toggled to the capital-labor relation, for it allows us to reconfigure (not to mention de-exceptionalize) the rise of abolitionist desires in deindustrializing settler societies as they intersect with—or run up against—forms of Indigenous abolitionism tied to different striations of time. But this is just part of the broader advantage his method enables, a fact that becomes clearer when Harootunian explains that while Marx's categories of formal and real subsumption were in fact what allowed him to conceive of capitalism as a historical totality—"to literally imagine it," and thereby subject it to analysis—this does not negate the role of contingency within capitalism's development:

> This is not to suggest that forms of subsumption, and especially the vastly overlooked idea of hybrid forms of subsumption Marx mentioned in *Capital*'s chapter on absolute and relative surplus value, are simply substitutes for the overstated category of transition, nor is it to gesture toward some form of historicist stagism in disguise. *It is, however, a way to reinvest the historical text with the figure of contingency and the unanticipated appearance of conjunctural or aleatory moments.* Marx referred to such specific processes in several texts (apparently first in notebooks and in *Grundrisse*) and emphasized the coexistence of different economic practices in certain moments and the continuing persistence of historical temporal forms, rather than merely "remnants," from earlier modes in new historical environments.[66]

Emphasizing how the "unanticipated appearance of conjunctural or aleatory moments," is bound to the unevenness of forms of accumulation and "the coexistence of different economic practices," Harootunian describes how capitalism appropriates older modes of production in Asia and Africa through hybrid forms of subsumption, so that "practices from the non-economic realm" are "pressed into the service of capitalist production" while remaining non-capitalist in themselves.[67] Indeed, he repeatedly underscores that Marx saw formal subsumption as an ongoing process that, in addition to forms of primitive accumulation, also takes place alongside capitalism in its "developed form."

Harootunian's interpretation of *Capital* and the *Grundrisse*—and his rejection of Western Marxism's real subsumption thesis in favor of a critique more akin to a value theory of social forms—suggests a methodological and historical framework for reading for forms of struggle that cannot be slotted so neatly into "cycles" linked to corresponding cycles of accumulation. Indeed, this seems an essential component for a feminist reading method that might hope to dialectically account for distinct temporal orders and striations of history, and one thereby capable of imagining how abstraction comes about in the expansive sense discussed in the Introduction as a coerced movement of social forms. If "the continuing persistence of historical [pre-capitalist] temporal forms"[68] that Marx himself emphasized includes Indigenous social modalities on the land of Turtle Island as they exist in entangled relation with settler societies such as Canada, this version of Marx offers a better way of grasping capital's conjunctural relation to Indigenous people as it seeks to eliminate them via state violence, or harness them via "profoundly asymmetrical and nonreciprocal forms of recognition."[69] What is more, it also tells us something about capital's non-relation to the unassimilable dimensions of Indigenous social worlds, or more relevantly, about *their* non-relation to capital.

How might we return such a method to a reading of Annharte's work—the object that necessitated it in the first place? To recall a key theme from the previous chapter, this is also a hermeneutical question about how poems, too, emerge from a history of aleatory, contingent, conjunctural moments that we might say is syncopated to the ambivalent and dialectical processes through which individuals (dis)identify. If models of social antagonisms based on cycles of struggle and accumulation are insufficient for grasping identity categories as mediating concepts beyond one specific economic configuration particular to the Global North, then reading the work of a Little Saskatchewan Anishinaabeg poet not only requires thinking about its relation to value and accumulation on the basis of a more capacious analysis of capitalism's unevenness—one that considers other temporal forms as more than merely "remnants"—but also reading for what poetry such as Annharte's can tell us about these different historical striations. As the readings below suggest, this approach can adjust or even invert our understandings of the content of Indigenous antagonisms—a political question Simpson rhetorically addresses when she asks, "what if the driving force in Indigenous politics is self-recognition rather than a continual race around the hamster wheel of settler colonial recognition?"[70] But it is also a register of nonidentity that surfaces in Annharte's disarming use of "the enemy's language,"[71] a vernacular politics of *both/and*, that we can connect to Harootunian's notion of the unanticipated appearance of conjunctural or aleatory moments (moments to which Annharte alludes, in another recurring motif of her work, as "weasel pops"[72]).

Apostrophes and Donuts

Self-recognition implies an affirmative force that, as I have been suggesting, also marks a politics of (self)abolition—one that must be distinguished in Indigenous contexts from a feminist struggle that, as per the feminist adage that the only way out is through, understands "woman" as an unavoidable but abolishable political ground. Indeed, a Marxist-feminist critique of abstract identity categories is dialectically recast by an abolitionist poetics grounded in Nishnaabewin. And it must be, if we are to depart from a situation in which liberal arts study of Indigenous cultures is often limited to an academic exercise, as one of Annharte's poems points out:

> no white guilt table of contents
> hidden white privilege footnotes
> how much commentary does it take
> to build a career on our backs?[73]

What Annharte dryly calls "commentary" as opposed to critique or analysis underscores the self-serving dynamics of settler-colonial cultural economies. The couplets excerpted here are typical of Annharte's style of using short lines and a mixture of free verse and staccato rhythms, in this case to amplify the speaker's rebuttal to the glassy condescension of benevolent settler opinion. They appear in a poem sardonically titled, "help me I'm a poor Indian who doesn't have enough books," mocking an implied idea that knowledge comes packaged in commodity book form. Yet while Annharte's title also alludes to the ways in which capital-L literature and academic literary criticism are implicitly coded as white, it may also betray a genuine anxiety regarding the intransigency of a situation where the author herself, a theorist in her own right with a degree in English, is acutely aware of the state-inflicted debt problems and poverty experienced by many First Nations communities in Canada, where "CanAmerican Lit is so apartheid," and in addition where, as Annharte sees it, "colonized writers do not find out their own history so when literary critics step in, sort, catalogue, interpret and assess writing, they are more than happy to accept a non-Indigenous evaluation."[74]

Mockery in Annharte's work is thus by no means limited to the function of a rejoinder to settler misconceptions. Rather, it is a rhetorical critical strategy designed to reposition the speaker on her own terms. "Toulouse Art

Trick," for example, confronts us with questions about what we expect from poetry when the slapstick humor of its apostrophe marks a complex relation between goofiness, femininity, and race, in the process compelling a studied misalignment with "serious" literary endeavors:

> Let us duel. You and me right here not outside. Voyez-vous ça exercise bra? Tits jammed. Still a weapon. Belly gapes from dressing gown, Toulouse. Sash is draped over the chair back. Might tie you up if you want. Aieee, safety pin closure. Fat sticks out. All my fat is me and may intimidate you. If left out of life, fat is company. Forgive me this excess, mon chéri.
>
> Enough me. Back to you, Toulouse. Would you sketch crotched out panty hose? Not a trick question. Ouvre is Louvre.[75]

In the tightness of an exercise bra, a safety pin, and panty hose, as well as the implied proximity of speaker and addressee, the suspense of this poem is built on the pressure of its elastic tension, which serves here to dramatize the barely contained threat of a gendered and racialized excess, hyperbolically figured as an overspill of fat and rhetorically encoded as an apostrophic monologue of self-conscious, feminized chatter.

Henri de Toulouse-Lautrec—the French post-Impressionist painter who was not only famous for his images of dancers at the Moulin Rouge but also for his short stature (he suffered from an unknown genetic disorder and stood four feet eight inches tall)—functions initially as a cipher here for European bourgeois culture *tout court*, the poem's inanimate addressee and the missing half of the "duel" played out by short sentences of the poem as they swing back and forth. The formal contradiction staged by the fact that there is actually only one side in this duel, however, discloses an emotional contradiction in which the speaker is at once powerful and powerless: while she playfully teases and belittles "'Toulouse" with the threat of stabbing by a safety pin about to pop, and mocks him by punning on his name to conjure the deliberately inane image of a belly gaping from a dressing gown, Annharte's hyperbole also suggests a self-conscious awareness of its own auto-referentiality, staging an internal drama via the mute absence of a well-known artist who stands in here for middlebrow Eurocentrism. "Forgive me this excess, mon chéri" is thus an ironic plea, in part because the speaker is aware that the self-appointed arbiters of appropriate culture are emphatically not listening.

There is another doubleness to this apostrophe, however, and as Reg Johanson has noted, what Annharte describes as her "guerrilla backchat" is not addressed (primarily at least) to a white settler audience. In a discussion of Annharte's self-descriptions as a "word warrior," a "bitch," and a "circuit speaker for Horrible Anonymous," Johanson observes that:

> The weird jouissance the colonizer experiences at reading denunciations of himself and in the experience of guilt that they produce is circumvented by ridicule and humour. Listening "from the perspective of a First Nations person," for Annharte, means hearing for the knowledge and experience shared by other First Nations people. It is they who "get" the joke. The decolonizing word warrior, then, is a figure of the critic who is turning away from dialogue with, or the education of, the oppressor to address her own people.[76]

Indeed, even though the grammatical object of the line, "All my fat is me and may intimidate you" is Monsieur Toulouse, the poem does not exactly address him even as it moves to ask: "did you, Toulouse, only paint mistresses? . . . Would you devote your best brush strokes to snagged fish nets abandoned by fat ladies?"[77] While Toulouse-Lautrec, a disabled man of short stature who suffered much scorn himself, is perhaps not the most uncomplicated target, it is worth remembering his role as a suitably general cipher for Eurocentric bourgeois art. Annharte's fun-making draws attention to the fat-phobic implications of his idealizing representations of svelte dancers, sex workers, and domestic workers—easily accessible subjects who made good material for post-Impressionist art—and yet the point is not that a fat Indigenous woman would be purposely excluded from these stereotypically French erotic projections, but rather that she would never appear in this Europeanized visual field in the first place.

The gaudiness of a pun like "Toulouse Art Trick," matched here by cheesy snippets of tourist French and the expressive shrillness of "Aieee," contributes to the poem's bawdiness, too, as the speaker suggests, "Might tie you up if you want" before reaching new heights of artifice to knowingly insist on pursuing this one-way dialogue: "Enough me. Back to you, Toulouse." Indeed,

Annharte's deliberately garish puns seem to accumulate as a meta-pun—a self-reflexive parody of the racist stereotype of the overemotive racialized subject, a trope Sianne Ngai calls "animatedness" to refer to "the exaggeratedly emotional, hyperexpressive, and even 'overscrutable' image of most racially or ethnically marked subjects."[78] For Ngai, "animation seems closely related to apostrophe—lyric poetry's signature and, according to Jonathan Culler, most "embarrassing" rhetorical convention, in which absent, dead, or inanimate entities are made present, vital, and human-like in being addressed by a first-person speaker."[79] Most pertinent about the apostrophe of this poem, however, is that the addressee is neither present, vital, nor human-like: on the contrary, he is only made *more* dead in contrast to the expressive speaker. The poem's nuanced attention to audience is signaled by this contrast—energetically communicative, intractably absent—insofar as it serves to dramatize the paradoxical hypervisibility and invisibility of this improperly embodied speaker.

Yet all of this leads to a contradiction that turns out to be the winning ticket, as expressed by Annharte's final sentence: "My concealed weapon will be my fat."[80] As the speaker hopes that her bodily excess will allow her to escape the sexual objectification to which Toulouse-Lautrec's subjects are submitted, we may also infer that her rhetorical excess is a strategy for turning away from the avant-garde (read: white) poetry reader. This is a tactical joke, a form of Nishnaabewin in which an Indigenous reader might especially recognize and share. It is both parodic and sincere, and as such circumvents settler-imposed stereotypes, which as Ngai implies, take the fact that animatedness is "of the body" as confirmation of a self-evident truth, a sign of the racialized subject's supposed authenticity or naturalness.[81]

To put it another way: unlike Toulouse-Lautrec, whose paintings fashionably made use of lowly feminized subjects to create high art, we might say that the abolitionist drive of Annharte's poetry takes form in her staunch refusal to reproduce the codifications that sustain hierarchical assignments for Indigenous and feminized subjects and produce the representative regimes through which they are recognized. Indeed, in their intersecting connotations and antagonistic power bearings, Annharte's stagings here mark a strategically layered relation to multiple audiences. Her poetry has been awkwardly associated with the avant-garde poetics of the Vancouver-based Kootenay School of Writing,[82] and its experimentalism is likely influenced by a summer spent working at Red Deer College in 1988 with the sound poet bpNichol and time spent at Naropa Summer Writing Program on Pan American and Eco-Poetics in 1992.[83] But it is more clearly rooted in her extensive involvement with Indigenous activist organizations and writing groups. As Pauline Butling and Susan Rudy note, in the preface to a 2005 interview:

> [Annharte's] community activist work began in the 1960s, starting with a summer job at the Native Friendship Centre in Winnipeg in 1963. She started going to the National Indian Youth Council gatherings in the U.S. and became a founding member of the Canadian Indian Youth Council. In Vancouver in the 1960s she joined the Native Alliance for Red Power. She has also worked on various projects designed to improve the life of urban Indians and has been active in several writing groups, including the Aboriginal Writers' Group in Regina in the 1980s and the Carnegie Centre Writing Group in Vancouver in the 1990s.[84]

In the context of her involvement with the Red Power movement and Indigenous urban organizing, we might consider Annharte's themes of "basic grannydom" (to use her own moniker) as part of a vernacular class politics required to be a granny of a certain kind: one where commentary on the baldness of a "90-year-old vagina" is no big deal—"grass did not grow on her race track that much"[85]—and where basic grannydom also means that everyday misogynist street talk is afforded little charge: "'You old fat bitch.' She was not fazed out by that talk."[86] Indeed, the queer and working-class multivalences of everyday speech are made pleasurably obvious in her poetry: while Annharte explains, "I do think of myself as a 'word warrior'"—a widely used term for Indigenous writers in Canada[87]—she soon follows this by noting, "Then again. I jokingly refer to myself as a "word slut.""[88] In the series "granny boot camp," titles such as "Her Erection" and "CY-BRO-GRAN-MOC" announce poems in which anecdotal retellings of street life are allusively connected to other poems in the book that explicitly draw their experimentalist strategies from the everyday experimentalisms of survival: in "bin diver art," for instance, the semiotic disruptions of a late twentieth-century avant-garde parataxis are reconfigured into a set of emphatically embodied but no less formal disruptions engendered by the neurological dynamics of dumpster diving: "devoid family pill works neck jerks forward backward spine / tingles arch back brain chemicals splash froth trough only a / synapse ago."[89]

Not all of the poems in *Indigena Awry* lean on humor. "Lady Earth Diver," for example—a poem in which the speaker describes the disappearance of her mother and the consequent loss of her Indigenous language—stands out in the subdued contrast of its understatement. Yet Annharte's committed avoidance of poetic gravitas and the idea of sincerity associated with lyric voice are also part of her identification as an Anishinaabe urban poet, and one (as she puts it) "of Ojibwe persuasion":[90] the "Invisible Indian / going to high school in the city"[91] who later sardonically observes, "Hollywood Indians line up. Whoop it up and please de-scalp / this time,"[92] and who regards public discourse with dry comic suspicion, noting, "It's hard to be a political correct squaw / my secret: don't ever open mouth."[93] Given how Annharte elsewhere notes that Ojibwe speakers "always seem to be laughing heartily when speaking the language," that "it's impossible to be 'too serious' and the language itself is picturesque,"[94] it would be fair to surmise that her poems, even when written entirely in English, are inflected by the humor, rhythms, and figurative codes of Ojibwe language and culture.

In the same tenor, Annharte's Indigenous speaker is vividly interpellated as an urbanite global citizen in the prose poem, "multicultural timbit," where a search for a "Timmies" (a Tim Horton's coffee franchise) in Toronto airport unfolds as a comedy of errors. The speaker, who wants a "Timbit," wryly notes: "if I spoke in hand signals, the message that I want a Tim Horton donut might be mistaken for a terrorist threat."[95] This speaker is by turns a participant in globalized consumerism and excluded from it: she compares herself not to a ring donut, in fact, but to a Timbit, the sugar-glazed doughball cut like a negative from the center of the donut. She tells us she is "on the way to Quebec and must bust through the language barrier," which in this case means replacing one colonial language with another, a fact that brings different meaning to her playful derision of French mannerisms: "he gives me a tip on how to speak French by adopting a fake accent and drooping a lip à la Chrétien. Shrug often too."[96] Other moments signal more immediately disconcerting occurrences: "The flight attendant on the plane did not give out a *Globe and Mail* to me. Did she figure out I was 'anglais' and 'autochuck'? To her, I might be part Métisse but do not speak Michif."[97] The speaker's outsiderness is not only signaled here by her exclusion from the Francophone culture represented by a French edition of the *Globe and Mail*, the newspaper of liberal Canada (and ironically because Annharte is perceived to be "anglais"), but also by her inability to speak Michif, an official language of the Métis First Nations in Canada and a cross between Cree and French.

Indigeneity and Identification

The fundamental importance of ancestral land and territories to the self-determination of Indigenous people means that local specificities are central to Indigenous political resurgence. At the same time, and in contrast to stigmatizing representations of Indigenous people as "monocultural, unrealistic, doomed, chauvinistic, or 'tribal,' "[98] the subject of "multicultural timbit" really *is* global and has been made so by force—perhaps into the mutable figure of "Indigena Awry" to which the collection's title gestures. Thus, the layered registers of global and local, intimate and public, and especially Annharte's mimesis and parody of the language of neoliberal multiculturalism invite us to read these social forms for their conjunctural historical character, especially when she sets them in relation to pivotal moments of colonial history.

The Indian Act of 1876 is invoked several times in *Indigena Awry*, for instance, once as "the Indian Act shoved down our throats,"[99] and elsewhere by connotation, in "half breeds," or in the borders of the "rez" (Indian reservation).[100] Designed under the auspices of assimilation, the Indian Act's colonial policy has systematically dispossessed Canada's Indigenous population, most notoriously by way of an 1894 amendment that mandated the establishment of the residential school system, but more broadly through a set of laws that continue to invent and re-invent Indigeneity as "race" via the border technologies of Indian reservations, marriage laws, and generational cut-offs.[101] As Darryl Leroux notes, drawing on legal theorist Pamela Palmater's work:

> [T]he Indian Act has long sought to alter the Crown's legal relationship with sovereign Indigenous nations to one between Canada and individual "Indians." By racializing what are political entities through technologies such as blood quantum and the generational cut-off now used in the Indian Act, the Canadian government ensures its current and future access to Indigenous lands.[102]

Racialization thus enables land access. And, as Audra Simpson explains, it does so in large part by dispossessing Indigenous women of their rights to land and community membership:

[Canada] brought Anglo-Victorian law into the community and used "race" to define Indigeneity, then instilled heteronormative marriage with the power to define legal personhood and thus to *remove* Mohawk women from their territories, their homes, and their families upon marriage to non-Native men.... The Indian Act, a specific body of law that recognizes Indians in a wardship status to Canada—not a nation to nation arrangement by any stretch—created the categories of personhood and rights that severed Indian women from their communities when they married white men. It did the reverse to Indian men; white women *gained* Indian status upon their marriage into an Indian community.[103]

As Simpson notes in reference to the Mohawk Nation of Kahnawà:ke, the European model of patrilineal descent imposed by the Indian Act supplanted the traditional means for defining kinship and determining community belonging through the mother's clan.[104] While the out-marriage provision was repealed in 1985 by an amendment known as Bill C-31, leading thousands of Indigenous women to apply to have their Indian status reinstated, Coulthard highlights how some First Nations bands themselves dismissed women's concerns—from gender equality rights to housing access—as "untraditional, and by extension, as deleterious to Indigenous liberation."[105]

Addressing such contradictions, the Binizaá feminist critic Isabel Altamirano-Jiménez has pointed out that while Indigenous people's specific understandings of a more generalized concept of Indigeneity existed "prior to its global articulations,"[106] the term "Indigenous" has been (re)produced in an era dominated by neoliberal state policies, the World Bank, the International Monetary Fund, and NGOs in a much narrower sense as a form of nationhood: one Indigenous people have strategically adopted to assert land rights and articulate Indigenous identities transnationally (as in the case of specific groups in Latin America and Southeast Asia who otherwise rely for survival on subsistence economies[107]) yet one that functions simultaneously as a racializing category that invisibilizes the heterogeneous and place-specific meanings of "Indigeneity" for those who actually identify through Indigenous cultural groupings. Thus if a settler-imposed version of Indigeneity as a racial concept offers some compromised protection from forms of state violence, like resource extraction and land expropriation for those at the margins of third world economies, its abstract character as a social form is also a powerful technology of settler statecraft, too. As Brenna Bhandar also underscores, Native legal status "retains a degree of flexibility and mobility as something that is passed on and transmitted, a sign that has economic, cultural, and social value, but at the same time is regulated and controlled by the state."[108]

Annharte's poetry is thereby attuned to a long history of direct and indirect domination that produces "Indigeneity" as a manageable identity category for the legal and political needs of a settler state, but also—as we have seen—to how Indigeneity appears as "race" in even more malleable ways as it transmogrifies through a series of contradictory social forms and subjectifications. Indeed, another genre of settler-colonial versions of "Indigeneity" emerges from the category's reproduction by white settlers looking for alternatives to mainstream society. As Scott Lauria Morgensen explains, for example, queer white writers in the United States in the 1980s attempted to encourage lesbians and gay men away from "narratives of perversion" and toward a vision of queer liberation inspired by Native Two-Spirit expressions of gender and sexuality. Commenting on Judy Grahn's 1984 book *Another Mother Tongue: Gay Words, Gay Worlds*, Morgensen observes how Grahn "describes white U.S. gay men and lesbians as needing Native cultural authenticity to learn to speak in their own 'mother tongue.' Yet, as her title indicates, that tongue remains 'another' when modern non-Natives adopt Indigenous identifications in their pursuit of liberation." Noting the glaring problem with Grahn's settler-colonial vision of "a universal gay pattern strongly linked to berdache," Morgensen explains how "positing an Indigenous embrace for queer exiles from a white settler society lets [Grahn] imagine switching allegiances to play 'Indians' against her own people." This is a false allegiance, Morgensen argues, that leads queer settlers to "impersonate" Indigeneity in weak critiques of settler society that ultimately amount to reconciliations with it.[109]

More to the point: as Coulthard has influentially and persuasively argued, settler forms of Indigeneity entice Indigenous individuals to identify with asymmetrical forms of recognition channeled through cultural codes and psychic appeals. Building on Frantz Fanon's critique of Hegel's recognition paradigm, *Red Skin, White Masks* demonstrates how the politics of recognition in settler-colonial countries of the Global North relies on official policies and unofficial cultural practices of "acknowledging" and affirming acceptable versions of Indigenous identity, in a historic transformation of settler-colonial relations that uses indirect, covert means to set the terms for struggles over Indigenous sovereignty and non-capitalist modes of production by transforming the ground on which opposition is likely or even possible.[110] Thus, in Coulthard's own Dene community, antagonisms increasingly take the form of "narrowly conceived cultural claims" that do little to change material conditions.[111] As the Coast Salish-based Warrior Publications point out, ongoing negotiations between the Canadian government and band councils means that Aboriginal "self-governance" and economic self-sufficiency depends on selling or leasing land, resource exploitation, and taxation. "In this way," as they put it, "self-government will really be the self-administration of our own oppression."[112]

In order to account for these relatively new colonial accumulation strategies, Coulthard proposes shifting the terms of analysis from *capitalist relation* to *colonial relation*, so that "the inherent injustice of colonial rule is posited *on its own terms and in its own right.*"[113] This methodological shift offers a way to avoid a series of assumptions common in Left theory that ignore histories of Indigenous thought and practice—a mistake made especially stark by redistributive arguments for "the return of the commons," which fail to recognize that:

> [I]n liberal states such as Canada, the "commons" not only belong to somebody—*the First Peoples of this land*—they also deeply inform and sustain Indigenous modes of thought and behaviour that harbour profound insights into the maintenance of relationships within and between human beings and the natural world built on principles of reciprocity, nonexploitation and respectful coexistence.[114]

Coulthard's proposal that the colonial relation be understood "not as a primary locus or 'base' from which these other forms of oppression flow, but rather as an 'inherited background field' within which market, racist, patriarchal and state relations *converge* to facilitate a certain power effect" instead comes to rest on an intersectional analysis in which capital is figured "*in relation to or in concert with* axes of exploitation and domination configured along racial, gender, and state lines."[115] Arguing that it is the acquisition of land rather than proletarianization that constitutes the dominant background structure shaping settler colonialism in Canada, he notes that "there is much more at play in the contemporary reproduction of settler-colonial social relations than capitalist economics," since a "host of interrelated yet semi-autonomous facets of discursive and nondiscursive power" must be accounted for:

> Although it is beyond question that the predatory nature of capitalism continues to play a vital role in facilitating the ongoing dispossession of Indigenous peoples in Canada, it is necessary to recognize that it only does so in relation to or in concert with axes of exploitation and domination configured along racial, gender, and state lines.[116]

Coulthard's approach, framed against the economic determinism of a "scientific" Soviet Marxism, thus suggests an Althusserian model of structural causality in which the economic is considered as one of a set of categories (alongside culture, ideology, the juridical, and the political, in Althusser's formulation) constituting a "synchronic system of social relations as a whole":[117]

> Given the resilience of these equally devastating modalities of power, I argue that any strategy geared toward authentic decolonization must directly confront more than mere economic relations; it has to account for the multifarious ways in which capitalism, patriarchy, white supremacy, and the totalizing character of state power interact with one another to form the constellation of power relations that sustain colonial patterns of behavior, structures, and relationships.[118]

Like Althusser, Coulthard insists on the semi-autonomy of different levels of the social. And yet: we might consider how economic relations are nothing but the "constellation of power relations" Coulthard describes above. If, as this book argues, capital is an impersonal force that works on and through subjects, institutions, and state formations, in the process opportunistically torquing pre-capitalist forms of difference in order to manage its own contradictions, then dispossession (the appropriation of land and resources) and exploitation (the appropriation of surplus value from labor under cover of the wage) are inextricably bound at the level of capital's concept—which is to say, bound to its function of abstraction and dissimulating movement.

Coulthard's multi-systems approach, which also echoes the unitary theories of 1980s Marxist feminism, thereby separates the political and the economic in ways that risk underestimating capital's dialectical, uneven, but always totalizing relation to social forms: the mediating objects and processes it uses to its advantage, whether that means making them value-productive or not. To recall the discussions of previous chapters: what is "power" if not capital's propensity to produce "new configurations in which the inner connection get more and more lost," as the "components of value ossif[y] into independent forms"?[119] As Harootunian's argument suggests, however, we might draw on a different reading of Marx to assert the unique orientation of multiple colonial relations and temporalities, and to re-read his concepts of formal subsumption and primitive accumulation to understand moments of renewed enclosure and accumulation by dispossession in relation to a global crisis in profitability,[120] indeed, to "find a Marx concerned to conceptualize the *differentia specifica* of the tyranny of the capitalist wage relation."[121]

Recognizing the basic bond between capital's totalizing movement and its (increasingly lost) inner connections makes the overriding import of Coulthard's critique all the more crucial, since his attention to the coercive structure of recognition optics, and to what he calls "the risks of interpellation" for Indigenous people, is tied to his support for more uncompromising—abolitionist and transformative—forms of political struggle.[122] Commenting on the Manichean relations Fanon identifies in *Black Skin, White Masks*, Coulthard explains how:

> In the context of internalized colonialism, the material conditions of poverty and violence that condition the colonial situation appear muted to the colonized because they are understood to be the product of one's own cultural deficiencies. In such a context, the formation of a colonial "enemy"—that is, a source external to ourselves that we come to associate with "our misfortunes"—signifies a collapse of this internalized colonial structure.[123]

The question of how to locate the "enemy" promptly joins critique to political strategy. Moreover, we might aver that Coulthard's argument that the liberal politics of recognition constitutes a continuation of colonial systemic violence by less overt means finds its poetic accomplice in *Indigena Awry*, where the "silent compulsions" of capitalist accumulation are shown to be inseparable from—in fact, *make their appearance as*—the production of Indigeneity as raced, gendered, and classed.

Indeed, as Annharte's poetry suggests, Indigenous people are often subjectivized by capital through what Bhandar calls "a nexus, a juridical knot, between identity and relations of ownership."[124] The antagonisms of her work are accordingly directed toward both colonial legal forms (the Indian Act, or the state imposition of colonial languages) and settler structures of feeling (the ostensible benevolence of academic commentary, or the racial paranoia of anti-terrorist rhetoric), in an attempt to interrogate and undermine the affective attachments, manipulative solicitations, and recognition-based demands that serve to reproduce colonial structures of domination. We could therefore say that the enemy posited by *Indigena Awry* is not a thing, but the relational dynamics of an entire system. Simpson posits the inverse in the practice of grounded normativity, which *also* "isn't a thing; it is generated structure born and maintained from deep engagement with Indigenous processes that are inherently physical, emotional, intellectual and spiritual."[125] In this way, Annharte's critique suggests a dialectical sense of the abstract-concrete connections between subject and system, and a profound understanding of how, in Coulthard's terms, "negative emotions . . . mark an important turning point in the individual and collective coming-to-consciousness of the colonized."[126]

For though the serial poems of *Indigena Awry* sometimes read like a series of ruminative anecdotes, we get a taste in "multicultural timbit" of the gently self-deprecating manner in which they couch a totalizing desire to kaleidoscopically reference both "heres" and "elsewheres" at once. This strategy enables Annharte to figure what Harootunian also helps us to perceive as the conjunctural relations of distinct historical temporalities in all their aleatory contingencies. "Indigenous Verse Ability," for another example, suggests in its title the contradictory imposition foisted on Indigenous subjects to be versatile in their "performance" of Indigeneity. The poem begins:

> Right off, ingenious character needs to apply
> any part-time genius rez identity on or off
>
> Right on, dress accordingly use convenient
> Scalp wig or beaver hat trap appendage bag
>
> Always, fuk wid Indin expert tease please
> even if disabled walk with crutch is not even

> Never, forget internal voice represents eternal
> Injunaity croak sing songs of constant repetition[127]

Following the first couplet's invocation of the legalities of "rez identity," and the attempts of both the Canadian state and First Nations band council governments to litigate nationhood and "reserve" status, these lines poke fun at the racist romance of Indigenous "genius" as well as its abstraction as a part-time job; at the notion that "identity" could be signaled by dressing accordingly; and further, at the idea that doing so entails wearing an obvious signifier like a beaver hat. Annharte's strategy of conflating by connotation the affective, feminized, performative aspects of flexible labor with the affective, feminized, performative demands of a politics of recognition suggests the inseparability of these forms of domination, enacting a conjunctive (rather than disjunctive) strategy something like what Jeff Derksen calls a "rearticulation of aesthetic [here we might add, settler] expectation."[128] In this way, the poem also casts doubt on any possible separation, at the level of capital's concept at least, between gender and settler-colonial reproductions of "Indigeneity" as axes of oppression that could be analyzed in isolation from each other and not, as I have been arguing, as the social modalities of a global system of hierarchies of difference and uneven relations of value.

This is what Leanne Simpson might call *kwe-as-theorist* at work. Annharte's dramatic irony encodes a list of instructions—do this, do that (but don't really do it)—followed by another instruction to "fuk wid Indin expert." At the same time, the poem suggests that an "eternal / Injunaity" persists inside, in the speaker's "internal voice," in a satiric misspelling that itself alludes to what might be understood as the dialectical character of Indigeneity in settler-colonial contexts, or in Simpson's terms, "a strangulated grounded normativity but [a] grounded normativity nevertheless." Fucking with anthropologists, government officials, and—it must be said—literary critics like the present author may be "a critical language game in the conditions of settlement,"[129] but it is also a potent political strategy that can help to guard and sustain Indigenous modes of living, which as Simpson highlights are also modes of production:

> Engaging in deep and reciprocal Indigeneity is a transformative act because it fundamentally changes modes of production of our lives. It changes the

relationships that house our bodies and our thinking. It changes how we conceptualize nationhood. Indigenous intelligence systems set up, maintain, and regenerate the neuropathways for Indigenous living both inside our bodies and the web of connections that structure our nationhood outside our bodies.[130]

Nevertheless, in "croak sing songs of constant repetition," the last line of the section excerpted here, we may again detect a double meaning insofar as its illocutionary function not only evokes the self-determining practice of Nishnaabeg song and storytelling but also carries a weary tone of bored fatigue. The poem's sense of the ongoingness of settler-colonial dispossession thus leads to the suggestion that even the most meaningful practices of Nishnaabeg resurgence can end up feeling rote. But ancestral purity and political fixity were never Annharte's goal:

> I do enjoy the mention of cultural purity but I quickly get bored because it does not seem to have anything to do with the hodge-podge reality that makes up my world. I want to find those "medicine lines" that heal the emptiness and loneliness that I sometimes feel because of how true the stereotypes of Natives have become. The caricatures are believed. I have "pure Indians" in my family but I have "pure bullshitters," too. I like to be equally proud of them. . . . Actually, I think I am part "bullshitter" or at least I know how to exaggerate.[131]

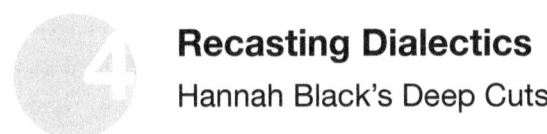

Recasting Dialectics
Hannah Black's Deep Cuts

IN HER 2013 ESSAY "Reading Dialectically," Carolyn Lesjak defends Marxist literary criticism against the disciplinary conservatism of a "return to literature" in academic literary studies since the early 2000s:

> The impulse to be affirmative, to talk about what texts do rather than what they don't do, occludes the negation upon which such affirmation is based— . . . the ontological assumptions structuring what appears "in the text"—but unlike a dialectical reading, offers no way of actually registering or thinking the occlusion that structures the surfaces being privileged.[1]

Surveying a range of new "isms" and conservative currents that have gained increasing prominence in literary criticism—New Formalism, New Narrativism, and cognitive science studies, among others—Lesjak connects this affirmative impulse to a generalized injunction to reclaim the pleasure of reading and to appreciate literary texts at face value, a critical disposition that even extends to the neo-Darwinist Stephen Pinker's attempt to route worthwhile literary reading through a biologizing concept of literature's appeal to human nature.

Lesjak contends that, after the heady theory days of the 1960s through the 1990s, the deepening crisis in the humanities—increasingly defunded and (already in 2013) subject to right-wing ideological attack—sends literary scholarship into comfortable retreat as "middle-level research," a position occupied without irony or chagrin by the non-heroic critic whose aim is not to master the text but to appreciate it: "the overarching message seems to be: scale back, pare down, small aims met are better than grand ones unrealized, reclaim our disciplinary territory and hold on to it."[2] Her point, however, is not to dismiss the relevance of a text's surface or the intractable materialism of the archive, but to think about how "notions of surface and depth can be seen in productive tension or unease with each other,"³ and in this regard her methodology—which draws pointedly on Fredric Jameson's arguments about the representation of historical time in his 2009 book *Valences of the Dialectic*—provides a salient way to read a very wide range of contemporary cultural production.

The work I will read with it later in this chapter is Hannah Black's 2022 novella *Tuesday or September or The End*, a work part-fiction, part-prose poetry that can also be productively read in dialogue with Black's recent sculpture and video works. Black is perhaps best known for her open letter to the curators of the 2017 Whitney Biennial, in which she powerfully protested the exhibition of the white artist Dana Schutz's 2016 painting, *Open Casket*, which depicts the famed photograph of the body of Emmett Till, a fourteen-year-old who was brutalized and murdered after being accused of flirting with a white woman at a Mississippi grocery store in 1955.⁴ But as we will see, Black's longstanding interests in outlawed and otherwise denigrated forms of political activity, particularly as they draw on an internationalist history of Black radicalism and contest institutionalized forms of representation, define exhibitions such as *Ruin/Rien* (2020)—a collection of sculptural and video works arranged around the central motif of a copy of C. L. R. James's *The Black Jacobins* (a text we will return to in a moment)—as much as they undergird the political imaginary of *Tuesday or September or The End*. In particular, her 2022 shows—*Politics* and *Broken Windows*—foreground the dialectics of affirmation and negation as they dramatize antagonisms between, on the one hand, the democratic and institutional arena of public policy and electoral representation, and on the other, the politics of riots and looting, which Black notes is "figured as a kind of frivolous or excessive or histrionic or purely acquisitive act, as if it were a high femme activity."⁵

I want to suggest that in Black's hands, toggling between surface and depth is a lyric strategy for advancing a theory of history that is also a theory for revolution and requires from its reader new, more capacious, and deeply invested methods of dialectical reading. While Lesjak notes Jameson's emphasis on narrative, specifically, as the literary form that possesses a "unique capacity to hold multiple temporalities together" and is therefore able "to make time and history appear,"⁶ my aim here is to offer an example of a work of speculative fiction that depends as much on lyric tropes as it does on narrative strategies to accomplish that feat. As Lesjak observes after Jameson, such literary undertakings mark a theoretical endeavor to grasp a momentary sense of the dynamism of time and space, one that cannot be resolved into philosophical concepts and "only becomes visible at moments of temporal coexistence, of simultaneity, of the contemporaneity without coalescence of several distinct subjectivities at once."⁷

But why narrative and not poetry for Jameson? In *The Modernist Papers*, a collection of loosely connected essays on modernist literature published between 1979 and 2005, Jameson's readings of modern poetry—from William Carlos Williams's *Paterson* to Gertrude Stein's *Lectures in America*—are framed by a claim that "any successful dereification of these now institutionalized texts" must read them as failures, since "only failure makes possible human experience as such, where success binds and alienates us more securely and inextricably into an external world of things," under conditions that "make modern art impossible in the first place."⁸ But Jameson describes only two ways in which poetry might meaningfully attempt (and fail) to oppose capitalist ideology when he compares postmodern Language poetry, "a kind of analytic decomposition of alienated commercial language from the inside," to earlier modernist works of the twentieth century, which made "the speculative leap into a Utopian and radically other type of language."⁹ In Jameson's telling, an older modernist project, which sought to restore the fragmented subject's unity on a symbolic level by way of the sublimity of aesthetic abstraction, becomes the ground—both canceled and preserved—for an anti-representational, anti-humanist understanding of language as the unrecoverable source of capitalist "degradation" in postmodern texts. Language writing thus gets its comeuppance in Jameson's reading of Bob Perelman's poem "China," in his famous 1984 essay, "Postmodernism: Or, The Cultural Logic of Late Capitalism," which features Perelman's poem as the model of a writing practice that is symptomatic of the reification of language, and not (as it imagines) executing its critique. Essays by George Hartley and Rob Halpern have since challenged this characterization,¹⁰ but such work continues to be regarded, as *Valences of the Dialectic* would attest, as relativist and dehistoricizing, and framed in terms of "the complacency of the postmoderns, wallowing in their various time-intersections without any concern for any ontological universal of Time that might possibly arise from them."[11]

A failed Utopia or total degradation: as if these options for the practice of an oppositional poetry weren't limited enough, modernist strategies of abstraction have, Jameson argues, ultimately served to repress the contradictions and concretions of the social—especially in the case of Wallace Stevens's "seemingly ahistorical" abstract landscapes. Stevens's canonization in the academy as "the supreme manifestation of New Critical poetic and aesthetic values" finds its basis in his insistently departicularized lyric:

> The repression of the social origins of this neutralized landscape, henceforth given as a kind of abstract "vocabulary," a set of neutral counters for the exercise of poetic speech (not unlike those formal, geometrical vocabulary units of the great architectural modernists such as Le Corbusier), is determined by the subject-object framework of Stevens's poetic practice which we will characterize as rigorously epistemological in all the worst senses of this word. In Stevens we never have anything but an abstract subject contemplating an object world which is thereby construed as being equally abstract.[12]

"Lyric" is barely mentioned in *The Modernist Papers*, but here in Stevens's "set of neutral counters for the exercise of poetic speech" it enters through modernism's back door. Stevens's work was met with high approval from New Critics such as Cleanth Brooks and John Crowe Ransom, in whose journals he published.[13] And even if, as Virginia Jackson and Yopie Prins write, New Criticism was but one critical interval of "a longer history of abstraction in which various verse genres . . . were collapsed into a large, lyricized idea of poetry as such,"[14] it is easy to see how, in his critique of Stevens as New Criticism's poster child, Jameson further reifies the collapse between lyric and verse, implicitly opposing poetry *tout court* to the kinds of narrative literary works in which the movement of History may be grasped. Elsewhere in *The Modernist Papers,* lyric is either framed in terms of its being rightfully rejected, as in Ezra Pound's *The Cantos*—which cannot be read according to "any conventional conception of lyric poetry or even of poetry itself in general"[15]—or lyric is irrelevant because, as with Jameson's reading of Williams's mid-century epic poem *Paterson*, the dialectical reader will find not a lyric but a narrative poem, and one where Williams's occupation as a local physician underwrites his speaker's allegorical, totalizing gaze. Like Dr. Destouches going about his work as a *médicin des pauvres* in Louis-Ferdinand Céline's classic novel *Voyage au bout de la nuit*, the figure of Mr. Paterson encounters people from all social classes and can "similarly offer a vehicle for the cognitive mapping of American society."[16]

Stevens's paradoxically modernist lyric style is conservative principally, however, because its authority rests on the way it feigns a form of collective speech. For Jameson, this abstract vocabulary takes up the "familiar modernist practice of a unique personal or private style" and misleadingly presents the "private voice" as "somehow impersonal again, as though this style were in reality something like an older rhetoric, with its collective, prepersonal capacities, its preexisting of the individual speaker who only needs to move in it as in an element."[17] In supplying his abstract vocabulary with a mythologized, dehistoricized appearance of sociality, in other words, Stevens disavows the material constitution of the poem. Other writers fail better: *Paterson*, for example, "knows in its deepest structural impulses ... that it must not succeed, that its conditions of realization depend on a fundamental success in failing, at the same time that it must not embody any kind of will to failure either."[18] Yet Stevens's work is a strong example of a characteristic Jameson persuasively applies to modernist literature more broadly, which is its constitutive failure to achieve the ontological unity it seeks, at least in part as a result of "the great fact of personal style"—and, it is tempting to read, lyric style. Especially significant here is Jameson's description of how the modernist text ends up caught in a sort of false mediation that further obscures its historical constitution: a Stevens poem may reach for something "immediate and impersonal," but it is inevitably converted into "a mere example of some imaginary essence (signed Faulkner, Stevens or whatever)." In modern writing, the drive for invention may have resulted in a new "system of signs," but what followed was "the moment in which that very system triumphantly mastered its content, became a frozen mannerism."[19]

Albeit more a series of interspersed critiques than a systematic account, we thus find in Jameson's reflections that anti-capitalist poetry knowingly or unknowingly fails either because it is contaminated already (as in Language poetry), or because—like the poems of Wallace Stevens, a businessman after all—it is modernist and thus deluding itself that "genuine aesthetic construction" is still possible (and here it fails doubly, Jameson explains, because such a project requires no small amount of self-deception and hubris).[20] Otherwise, we might surmise from implication, there is no point in asking poetry to do historical work because it is *lyric*, a genre of political retreat invented by twentieth-century critics and premised on the fiction of an ahistorical interior voice. Yet at the heart of these relegations lies an acknowledgment of the social composition of literary and artistic genres themselves. This leads one to ask again why so much Marxist literary criticism, following Jameson, continues to proffer the novel as its paradigm—a form that, as Joshua Clover points out, was "capital's *second nature* given literary form" in a value-producing, industrial capitalism: one that Clover argues can now only repeatedly and perhaps fruitlessly be observed, in a period of terminal economic decline, in its failure to reconcile capitalist subject with capitalist world as it once did.[21]

For what good does it do to repeatedly observe art's failure? Clover makes a fair point. Yet however limited we may find Jameson's attention to contemporary poetry, his critique of modernist writing is instructive in two aspects in particular, I want to argue, where modernist poets may well have failed but where contemporary post-lyric strategies could, in qualified but important ways, succeed. Not least of interest here, first, is Jameson's invocation of "an older rhetoric, with its collective, prepersonal capacities"—from which Stevens's poems purport to speak. This fantasy collectivity, at any rate no longer possible after the onset of industrial capitalism, contrasts with Jameson's underscoring of what G. S. Sahota notes in a review of *The Modernist Papers* as "all that is abstracted, distorted, or ignored" by modernism, by which Sahota means the non-white traditions and inventions constitutively excluded from Western literary canons and ways of reading.[22] Second, and relatedly, we might attend to what modernist poetry could not manage to achieve as a result of its limits—namely those "moments of temporal coexistence, of simultaneity, of the contemporaneity without coalescence of several distinct subjectivities at once"[23]—not only to ask what kinds of poetic writing might achieve this "contemporaneity-without-coalescence" without resorting to postmodernist dissolutions of History, but also to figure out how such writing relates to historical modes of lyric and narrative, and indeed to that non-capitalist (and apparently non-racialized) "older rhetoric" and its collective capacities.[24]

To outline the possibility of a dialectical account of these temporal coexistences, Jameson draws on Paul Ricoeur's distinction between two philosophies of time foregrounded by linguistic critics: first, the psychological theory that grammatical tenses "merely express more fundamental human experiences of temporality," and second, the structuralist claim that "language and its forms" are in fact what *produce* the effect of lived temporal experience.[25] While Ricoeur's solution of a humanist "third way," an existential notion of time in which "reading the deployment of linguistic tenses itself expands and modifies our experience," is just as unsatisfying, he argues, it is nevertheless in Ricoeur's attempt to account for the intersection and incommensurability of these distinct concepts of time that Jameson finds "a new methodological key"—one in which the differences between philosophies of time conceived in terms of movement, number, or space enable us:

> to triangulate the "reality" of time and temporality beyond any specific finite representation or figuration. *Or perhaps it would be more accurate to say that figuration is itself this intersection between several incommensurable representations.* . . . At any rate, we here for the first time glimpse a figural possibility capable of being transferred to narrative as such: what gives us an insight into the temporalities of (fictional) narrative is not the virtue of one of these accounts over the other, it is their very multiplicity as such, their intersection.[26]

For Jameson as for Ricoeur, narrative strategies of emplotment, character, narrative voice, and point of view allow us to grasp a sense—as opposed to a formed concept—of Time and temporality, a time unified and driven, in Jameson's account, not by phenomenological or existential human experience, as Ricoeur has it, but by capital's impersonal compulsions (something closer, in this way, to the Aristotelian notion of an objective time of the universe).

These are the moments where History appears, and for Jameson they make possible a narrative figuration of time that avoids reduction to any single temporality or representation. But, and this is my point, the figural possibility of the "reality" of time need not take narrative as its vehicle, whether or not we agree with Jameson and Ricoeur that narrative is fundamental to our human experience of time as a sequence of events and thus to our interpretation of all other textual genres.[27] In the discussion to come, we will see how the supple, sensitive, distinctly Jamesonian reading method outlined in "Reading Dialectically" can, among other things, reveal a strategic disloyalty to categories of literary genres and their associated tropes, specifically where works like *Tuesday or September or The End* engage in such tactics to theorize the relation between totality and difference, or between (feminized, racialized) subject and (feminizing, racializing) system.

To be sure, the novella mobilizes many of the narrative techniques that Jameson finds useful: character type, the traumatic return of the repressed, scenes of Socratic dialogue. In the traditional arc of the bildungsroman, *Tuesday or September or The End* even accompanies its protagonist through an emotional journey of beginning, middle, and end, and in this way risks comparison with the oft-solipsistic self-discoveries of contemporary autofiction more than it does the paratactic disorientations of postmodern New Narrative writing, which might also count as a stylistic precursor. But as we will see, this narrative arc is infused with lyric tropes and forms: from a mute alien object that serves, like a Grecian urn, as a receptacle of lyric apostrophe and vehicle for self-discovery, to a series of melodic refrains employed, much in the lyric tradition, as remedy to the "disorder and meaninglessness of experience."[28] Perhaps most importantly, though, Black's lyricism—and as we will see, her willed Prometheanism and recuperated fanaticism—connects with a totalizing, distinctly American tradition of lyric rooted both in African American sorrow songs and in Black radicalism. Before we move to read it, therefore, I want to propose another "methodological key" that comes to seem imperative.

Recasting Dialectics

Jameson would hardly be the first to argue that the concrete infrastructural processes of colonialism and imperialism are formally encoded and obscured in modernist abstraction.[29] But the dialectical method he develops across his work, beginning with the 1981 publication of *The Political Unconscious: Narrative as a Socially Symbolic Act*, offers a way of reading this connection that (if we admit that anti-empiricist truth claims about capitalist societies can in fact be made[30]) comes to make all other approaches seem inadequate, principally because the dialectic is unique in its adaptive capacity for its own reconstitution. Once adjusted by Marx, this Hegelian method of thinking the whole combines a speculative and deductive logic with an openness to its own negation, to allowing material history to renovate its own architecture. And the negativity of dialectic is key to admitting contingency and difference as part of any historical account: for Hegel, not only is the negation of a thing as determinate as what it negates, but the bifurcating action of the negation produces something different, meaning that the negation of the negation "results in an affirmation, but a different affirmation from that originally negated," in Michael Inwood's words.[31] A dialectical totality is consequently "a result, an articulation rather than an assumption," as Marina Vishmidt and Zoe Sutherland explain, and a model that "both allows for contingency and lends a determinate framework to what would otherwise be a simple 'conjunction' or 'intersection' of more or less decontextualized particulars."[32] In its Marxist, Jamesonian version, we thus find a spatial dialectic—temporalized *and* systematic—of abstract and concrete negations, and one that, I will additionally argue, is also open to being "recast," in Fred Moten's sense of the term.

"Not In Between," the opening essay in Moten's three-volume study, *consent not to be a single being* (2017), is all about dialectics, in fact. In his reading of C. L. R. James's account of the Haitian revolution in *The Black Jacobins*, the Caribbean provides an exemplary historical coordinate for what Moten calls the "not-in-between,"[33] a concept he locates more specifically in the difference between Toussaint L'Ouverture's educated fidelity to the statist project of the French revolution, on the one hand, and his "untutored" Lieutenant, Dessalines, who "unlike Toussaint, [took] his men into his confidence" in battle, on the other.[34] Invoking the not-in-between to refuse the binary of (white) "enlightenment" and (black) "darkness," however, Moten characterizes Black radicalism in terms of its emergence from an incommensurable yet "irruptive" striation of historical time.[35]

Trickily for Marxists, he approaches this task by attending to the textual and sonic elements of James's prose, noting Jacques Derrida's critique of the privileging of speech over writing in *Of Grammatology* in order to read James's account of the Haitian revolution for its "resistant aural performances, as the function of a materialist aesthetics and an aestheticized political economy of *appositional collision*." In "the not-in-between that both marks and is James's phrasing," Moten finds "a serrated lyricism": a linguistic innovation that amounts to "a theoretical achievement which is nothing less than a complex recasting of the dialectic" (what he elsewhere calls a "cut dialectic").[36] In a suggestive early passage, for example, Moten implies that the utopian kernel of the commodity—what we find in its contradictory double character as use and exchange value—is both distinctively Black and distinctively lyric, because the slave-commodity does in fact "scream" its "open secret." Therefore:

> This means an attention to the lyric, to the lyric's auto-explosion, to the auto-explosion the lyric gives to narrative. This means paying attention to the thing (to what screams its fetish character and the whole of its secret against the [deafness of the] proper) that notes the presence of that desire, that takes into account the lyric's infusion with narrative, that sees the historicity and political desire of the lyric precisely as the refusal that animates and is one possibility of the fetish character, the possibility of free association and total representation that emerges from a transference that is only possible in the form of the open secret, by thinking the rhythm of world and thing.[37]

There are a number of ways to interpret the concept of lyric Moten presents here, including by reference to the Heideggerian notion of the "thing" through which he has previously theorized "the case of blackness."[38] In another key passage that cuts against Marxist methods, he teasingly conflates economics and magic in order to set up an opposition between lyric and narrative, where "meaning is cut and augmented by the very independent syntaxes and outer noises—politico-economic spells and spellings—that James would record."[39] These independent syntaxes and outer noises suggest less an internalized outside—in the sense of the "universally devalued" yet value-mediated forms of reproductive labor that Vishmidt and Sutherland have theorized as a negative totality[40]—and more an incommensurability: James records, in Moten's reading, "a collusive interplay in the work that is not in between but outside of the broad-edged narrative/historical trajectory of a familiar dialectical lineage."[41]

But Moten's characteristic turn to textuality, I would argue, does not easily reduce to a dissolution of material history into ahistorical theoretical figures, as Anthony Reed among others has contended.[42] Rather, speech-based particulars such as anacrusis, arrhythmia, dialect, and accent serve instead to mark the difference—the "not-in-between"—between the real movement of history and its representations, perhaps even to track those mediations, or in Moten's words, to disclose "the interanimation of theory and history."⁴³ Sound and speech are imperative to this project, where:

> [L]iterary voice and political theory and practice are disrupted by ... a sound that bends the regulatory musicological frame of notes, the hermeneutic insistence of the meaning of words, the national imperatives of European idioms, the dialect that reconstitutes dialectic as reason, historical motive, liberatory polyrhythm. There is, in [*The Black Jacobins*], a lyric disruption of a certain Europeanized notion of public/national history and historical trajectory as well as an exterior/African disruption of the interiority of European lyric. The property sang, the commodities shrieked.⁴⁴

The lyric disruption of the not-in-between, Moten suggests, could enable us to overcome the limits of the dialectic's European provenance by accounting for a much more "entangled" relation between thought-systems and their historical trajectories. Indeed, Moten notes his dissension from Cedric Robinson's claim that the revolutionary consciousness of Black radicalism developed not in relation to a European Left's struggle with its bourgeoisie, but independently of it, both in separation from the historical trajectories of Marx and Hegel and as a "separate revolutionary culture, another origination of resistance":

> This break or arrhythmia: is it a complete detachment from that temporal/historical trajectory or is it a displacement, a retemporization disruptive of the very idea of absolute break and, by extension, an augmentative curvature of old harmonic notions of convergence or hybridity, a dissonant bending of the dialectic and its notes? Again, I think James's content, when seen in the context of a closer look at the mechanics of his phrasing, moves in another implication—not of the irrelevance of the [European] bourgeoisie and by extension, in the breaking from or out of the evolutionist chain and closed dialectic of historical materialism, but in a dialectical bending of that dialectic that stems from a radical consciousness that cuts and anticipates, but is at the same time cut and anticipated by, Marxism.⁴⁵

Moten's relation to Marxism becomes clearer in a passage like this, where the valences both of deferral and difference in the concept of *différance* are conceived in terms of "retemporization," allowing for a theory of time based not on a groundless chain of significations or complete ontological break, but for a frame in which the sonic and textual elements of lyric offer a way to "recast" dialectics—a move, it bears noting, that is deeply dialectical in itself. In James's phrasing, Moten thus finds a theoretical maneuver in which figuration is synonymous with spatio-temporal movement, one in which "figuration is itself this intersection between several incommensurable representations," to put it in Jameson's terms[46]—terms that, I am suggesting, do not merely describe the not-in-between but share its basic conceptual contours.

Moten further clarifies this sense of how Black diaspora recasts dialectics when he distinguishes the not-in-between from the poststructuralist notion of hybridity it might more readily be understood to impute. Indeed, James's phrasing is important for Moten precisely because it does *not* align with what he characterizes as the apolitical "hesitation" of postcolonial theory. In this sense he compares James's critique of Toussaint's hesitation to "a certain postcolonial aura that is structured around such hesitation," framed here as "a kind of hybridizing encounter of the in between, an oscillative lingering eternally prefatory to action, whose value depends upon the ongoing and necessarily groundless—and therefore doubly paradoxical—assertion that 'freedom's basis [is] in the indeterminate.'"[47]

Hence, if the postcolonial aura is "eternally prefatory to action," Moten's not-in-between is, on the contrary, *actionable*: "The not-in-between of this opposition would be some kind of syncopated but nonhesitational phrasing. . . . It would be not in between enlightenment and darkness, narrative and lyric, all of that."[48] This lyric recasting of the dialectic—an intersecting yet incommensurable "cut" in the dialectic—is nevertheless "cut and anticipated" by Marxism. And while Robinson insists on the Black radical tradition as a culture formed in separation from the European proletariat, Moten regards it dialectically, reading James's phrasing for its "syncopation," finding:

> Leaps! Leaps! Leaps! A mystery of *aufheben*. This is why Hegel is so important for James, why the nature of the dialectic is so crucial. Because it is all bound up in the relation of the bourgeoisie to the proletariat, in how to get from one to the other, in how one fulfils the etiolated universalism of the other. This is the future in the present, the invasion from the inside, socialism in the factory.[49]

The Hegelian language of leaps highlights the speculative dimensions of the analysis I have been drawing on across this book: an attempt to account for the "real" of value relations and their inverted social forms, and one that offers us a way to think the production of difference as part of a systematic and contradictory social whole. In this sense, too, Moten's language resonates with Lesjak's invocation, drawing on Slavoj Žižek's early work, of the "leap of faith" required to account for the constitutive force of value's mediations, unthinkable within the empirical limits of the social sciences, as well as her description of Jameson's theory of the violent intersections of multiple temporalities as engendering "something like a cut into the social."[50]

Transposing these problems of discrete temporal experiences and their interferences into literary terms of narrative and lyric is a distinctly theoretical endeavor too, as Moten underlines when he notes how James attempts to raise the rhythm of his phrasing "to the level of theoretical principle and historical motive."[51] In this vein, Moten highlights (with italics) James's allusion to Wordsworth's famous dictum, where James writes:

> [T]he violent conflicts of our age enable our practised vision to see into the very bones of previous revolutions more easily than heretofore. *Yet for that very reason it is impossible to recollect historical emotions in that tranquility which a great English writer, too narrowly, associated with poetry alone.*[52]

The recollection of historical emotions must be conceived otherwise, in Moten's reading, since "here, poetry is understood not only to have no monopoly on such tranquility but is also perhaps given as that which is in excess of tranquility itself." Again, we might note Moten's care to characterize this excess not in terms of infinity or plenitude but as "a lyric and dialectical drive that brings the noise of such emotion."[53]

The not-in-between thus theorizes the dialectical interference and contiguity between tranquility (Wordsworth) and colonial "turbulence" (James). Dialectical, because the language of "excess" in this passage is nevertheless framed within the terms of a violent (and not merely theoretical) negative dialectic, as "the refusal of an oscillation that seems, ultimately, to be part and parcel of the dialectic, the failure of its own internal resources to achieve the *Aufhebung* toward which it is directed," a failure that "manifests itself in the colonial encounter."⁵⁴ Reading the colonial encounter as the concrete manifestation of a capitalist contradiction offers a potent answer indeed to Jameson's question in *Valences of the Dialectic*, where he asks, "what is a spatial contradiction, in other words? What can be the spatial equivalent of the negative or of negation?"⁵⁵

Lyric Perversion

Moten's notion of James's untutored, Black, arrhythmic phrasing theorizes lyric as a dialectical disruption and "retemporization," an aesthetic mode based in movement, but also one that shares conceptual overlap with Jameson's sense of a type of figuration located at the intersection of incommensurable temporalities. What does that retemporization look like in poetry? One answer to this might be found by observing how the Black diasporic spatial configuration that informs this lyric's totalizing drive is already present in the African American folk songs in which American lyric is rooted. In her analysis of W. E. B. Du Bois's depiction of nineteenth-century sorrow songs, for example, Andrea Brady notes that in Du Bois's rendering, the sorrow song "seems to come from nowhere ... and everywhere":

> It is an intrinsically American art form, deeply embedded in the conditions of its production; and a transcendent music that escapes those constraints and ascends to "the right hand of God." It is a distillation or sublimation, a pure form; but it is also drastically female, in its message "seldom voiced by man," its swelling and growing, and subjection to rape and defilement. It is diachronic, derived from the "Ancient of Days" but a "new song," "born anew out of an age long past," weaving "old and new" together.⁵⁶

In contrast to Du Bois's view of the diachronic distillation of African American song—which is "embedded in" its conditions of production yet paradoxically also "escapes" them thanks to its feminized ability to weave "old and new" together—Brady shows how the New Critical idea of lyric developed by Southern Agrarian Critics, with Cleanth Brooks and John Crowe Ransom at the center, was built on the simultaneous fetishization and exclusion of traditions such as the sorrow song. In this way, Brady's critique demonstrates what it is, precisely, that the fetishization of Wallace Stevens's "abstract vocabulary" most directly abstracts. Ripe with racial fantasies of Southern paternalism ultimately rooted in the plantation, the folk song and the collectivity of the "throng" provided a foundational myth for New Critics, who found the historically specific actuality of African American traditions inconvenient to their theory of the impersonal, departicularized qualities of a universalizing lyric poetry. Thus, in New Criticism emerging from the South, "African Americans are 'a folk' whose cultural activities provide experimental data to furnish theorists contemplating 'poetic origins' of a more European type"[57]:

> The song of the race that is really the thought of an individual spoken aloud comes very close to collapsing one naïve vision of folklore into the liberal lyric as defined by [John Stuart] Mill (lyric as the etiolated voice of the confined individual), or the spontaneous overflow of powerful feeling recollected in tranquillity (perhaps the supposed tranquillity of Emancipation, the period in which white collectors assumed these songs of suffering would pass away).[58]

Clearly, neither the liberal lyric nor Wordsworth's concept of poetry are what Moten identifies in the lyric disruption of James's phrasing. But nor are these versions of lyric completely separate from that disruption—an "irruption" and noise that records colonial abstractions of the sorrow song's lyric and in doing so returns those abstractions to their disavowed historical referent. The concept of "not-in-between" thus helps us to grasp the figuration of the intersection of several incommensurable representations: that which might "make time and history appear," but also that dialectical movement whereby, in Moten's words, "one fulfils the etiolated universalism of the other"[59]—or to put it in value-critical terms, a movement whereby social forms beget social forms.[60]

From here we can pose a few questions: What happens when the collectivity of the throng appears in a new guise, in the form of rioters and revolutionaries, as in Black's novella? How best to read lyric tropes when they are taken up in post-internet writing to perform the kind of dynamic, figurative dialectical thinking Jameson reserves for narrative? If lyric is not an object of thought—as the New Critics treated it—but a historically loaded literary category as well as "a mode of perception and an instrument for thinking,"[61] can it be saved from the dustbin of Marxist literary criticism, replete with its contradictorily racialized, feminized, and mushy associations?

One challenge here has to do with the level of analytical abstraction required for us to connect the constitutive racial exclusions of modern lyric to a history of capitalist accumulation. While Stevens's work, for example, prestigiously appears in the journals of New Criticism, the racial character of its content is not detectable here at an empirical or textual level—to put it simply, it is not that Stevens's poems are nostalgic for the plantation. Rather, these histories are encoded and mediated at the level of social form, where they appear obscured in an abstracted vocabulary of the so-called universal, one to which critics append a Europeanized brand of lyric. Critique thus involves moving between distinct (interfering, incommensurable) orders of history and their encoded representations, an activity of "transcoding," as Sianne Ngai underscores in her framing of Jameson's larger project.[62]

In addition to highlighting the spatial and radically inclusive nature of reading dialectically, its sensitivities to difference and its resulting critical potency, Lesjak's argument can therefore help us to see how *Tuesday or September or The End* is typical of a wider range of recent literary experiments that seem to invoke dialectical reading, intuitively suggesting a shared project of bringing the false separation of surface and depth into crisis.[63] In *Tuesday or September or The End*, we find not a liberal lyric, which in Brady's description marks a synthesis of the particular elevated to the condition of the universal, but a dialectical lyric capable of dialectical leaps.[64] Older methods of dialectical interpretation such as reading for symptoms or unveiling hidden structures no longer suffice for reading works such as this, not simply because the diagnosis will be predictable—in other words, susceptible to "reified protocols of reading" and attached to "old lessons already learned," rote gestures that, as Lesjak notes, ultimately mark a failure to be properly dialectical—but more importantly because these works gesture themselves to the inadequacy of such critical unmaskings. They do so implicitly yet powerfully when they attest to the paradoxically fragmentary and unified nature of lived experience and the impossibility of knowing (at least in any provable way) how that experience is constituted, and in the political impasse they register when they observe that, *yes, this is fucked up*—an impasse, I am arguing, with negative and utopian implications.[65]

Moreover, as we will see, the need for a more intense and ambitious dialectical reading arises because *Tuesday or September or The End* conveys a sense that the surface *is* the truth of the matter. This is not the same thing as pointing out the "obviousness of domination," as Lesjak describes one strategy of surface reading.[66] Rather, it is a way of acknowledging that the "real" of capital is nothing but the social forms through which it takes shape and that these forms of appearance require interpretation.[67] As Lesjak has it:

> What is needed is a better way of reading surfaces as perverse rather than as obvious, as never identical to themselves in their "thereness," and always found within and constitutive of complex spatial relations, both seen and not seen, deep and lateral, material and figural—all of which requires a more rather than less expansive reading practice: more interpretation, more dialectical complexity, a more rather than less invested critical position, because relations, after all, cannot be seen in any solely literal sense.[68]

In other words, there is only one world, the world of appearance, but "what is appearance an appearance of, and what appears in appearance?"[69] The need for an "invested" critical position, rather than a supposedly neutral or balanced one, emerges from a problem central to our age of new fascisms, which from state-sanctioned genocides to conservative sex panics, often depend on a disingenuous insistence that things are indeed identical to their appearance. *It is what it is!*

Acknowledging the perversity of surface forms can also help us to see how lyricism in *Tuesday or September or The End* is distinct from what Anna Kornbluh describes as the "declensionist blur" and "auto-authorizing, lyrical, fragmented first-personalism" of recent autotheory—one element of an "immediacy style" of topical, transparent art that reifies capitalist logics even as it purports to challenge them.[70] Indeed, we find something different here, since *Tuesday or September or The End* infuses narrative with lyric *precisely* in the service of mediation, to think unity-in-difference but also—to take Jameson's definition of figuration as what happens at the intersection of incommensurable representations of time—to figure freedom in what I will outline below as the work's negative dialectical movement. In this utopian spirit, Hannah Zeavin usefully observes that the novella is "about how we might know who we are when our normal referents are muted, deleted, upended."[71]

For the same reason, Lesjak's critique also offers a politicized ground from which we may respond to the problem of lyric reading, which as Jackson and

Prins underline, means that "reading lyric, where *lyric* is the object of interpretation, necessarily involves lyric reading, where *lyric* is part of the interpretive process to be called into question."[72] Lyric reading must account for lyric's recent evolution, from G. W. F. Hegel's "perfect idea" of lyric as "the pure representation of subjectivity" and historical progress towards enlightenment, to a much more general idea of lyric as the genre of personal expression, which now seems self-evident "only because twentieth-century literary criticism made it up."[73] The question of the lyric and lyric reading is one that, more than narrative or dramatic forms (to invoke Goethe's three "natural" forms of poetry), is about the relationship between individual subject and an unknowable totality, and more specifically—insofar as this is always a problem for lyric—about the limitations of one's epistemological horizons.[74] As such, could lyric, in its histories and reinventions, not be a fruitful genre for thinking about identity formation and revolution (in short, doing Marxist critique)? Or, to put the question of reading appearances differently, if moments of a systematic whole take on feminized and racialized forms that appear to be disconnected from that whole, can lyric help us to understand their constitution without smoothing over the infinitely variable textures of their difference, their patchy legibility, their subsumption into more cognizable forms of oppression and identity?

As we have seen, Moten's not-in-between suggests a historically situated way to imagine difference through a method of "retemporization," in the "cut" of the dialectic effected by lyric negativity, and it would make sense to read his intervention, in addition, as a response to Marxism's record of inattentiveness to feeling, sense perception, and experience, those phenomenological levels at which difference is often registered. Such inattentiveness is something Lesjak notes, too, when she highlights another counterintuitive connection between Jameson's spatial dialectic and poststructuralist thought—this time to compare Jameson's focus on how the interferences of multiple historical temporalities unsettle "the 'lightning flash of simultaneity of self and world' privileged by temporal models of identity" with Eve Sedgwick's Buddhist conception of transindividuality, which also centers spatial relations in its emphasis on touch as opposed to sight in order to conceive of identity as "*in proximity*," thereby theorizing a sensory plane of knowledge that Sedgwick calls "realizing" as opposed to merely "knowing." For both theorists, Lesjak observes, reading becomes a practice of "seeing what we know" rather than "knowing what we see," and on this point she insists, "no accumulation of documents, however large, can do this kind of [lateral] interpretive work: the problem isn't a dearth of knowledge but the gap between knowing and realizing or acting."[75] Indeed, Sedgwick's notion of an "aching gap in the real" further informs Lesjak's emphasis on the leap of faith required to grasp capitalism as a moving, systematic totality of social relations.[76] And as we shall see, for Lesjak as for Black, dialectical interpretation consequently means "extending the very frame of time" beyond the history of capitalism,[77] expanding outwards to geological and even cosmological time, and doing this by way of identifying—and in Black's case, lyrically dramatizing—some dialectical reversals to which we shall return.

Refusing to Know

If surfaces are always more than themselves, *Tuesday or September or The End* depends on this insight for its opening gambit. Divided into chapters toggled to the first six months of 2020, and thus set during the beginning of the COVID-19 pandemic, Black's novella follows two central characters, Bird and Dog, investigating their psychic interiors in conjunction with a set of implied analytical frameworks and debates drawn from contemporary Marxist discourse regarding global economic contraction and the limits of electoral politics in the United States. We begin with Bird, the book's protagonist, as she reflects on her job in a high-end New York City salon. This type of work, an interior monologue suggests, gives Bird an advantage as a totality theorist: in a pointedly detached manner she considers how "something must have gone wrong" in her clients' lives for them to choose this particular salon, where rolling CNN news blares from the TVs and a cut and color costs around five hundred dollars. Yet, "Technically nothing had gone wrong in their lives; they had a lot of money. All that had gone wrong in their lives had also gone wrong in the life of the world."[78]

Bird senses she is uniquely attuned to what has gone wrong in the world, since "her eye had been trained through generations of heavy chromatic meaning para-originating in the Caribbean, where her parents were born, via London, where she was born, to New York City, where she now lived." In a fundamental way then, Black diaspora structures Bird's ability "to perceive movements in the general mood."[79] Framed as a type of cross-generational, "chromatic" racial training, this attunement to the affective vicissitudes of everyday late capitalist life allows Bird to perceive what in one way seems like a cinematic "atmosphere of saturated, narrative repetition" approximating "simulation or psychosis," but in the end, as she notes with irony, is "probably something much more drab, like the slow death of a form of society."[80]

Political-economic slow death indeed forms the backdrop to the ensuing fragmented narrative, as Black makes reference to the 1971 Nixon shock, when "President Narwhal," as Nixon is cast, "cut the regulative link between the dollar and gold and set capital free into its imaginary."[81] The era of secular stagnation, to use Alvin Hansen's term for persistently slow economic growth and low business investment, leads inevitably to political malaise: "Human life at that point was like a fucked-up car. Some people who understood how it worked could drive it a certain distance, but it would eventually have to be taken to the scrapyard and recycled into something more bearable."

In this tenor, too, we are introduced to Bird's boyfriend Dog, whose democratic political attachments are set in contrast to Bird's misanthropy: "As a social democrat, he sought to embrace popular feeling."[82] It is hard to miss Black's playful snarkiness here: a distancing both from the perceived or real injunction to identify with abstract social categories—witness her satirical take on the supposed authority lent by the familiar refrain of identification, "*as a* [fill in the blank]"—and, we might intuit in connection, from the affective and political contours of socialism itself, signaled by Dog's dogged commitment to the "Moley Salamanders" election campaign and his earnest hopes for reformist measures. As we subsequently learn, Bird only half-supports this canvassing work, which she suspects is misguided. Yet at this early point in the novella, social democrat Dog seems to constitute an element of the backdrop: more a characterological outline (to borrow a term from Jane Hu) than a subject with history and drives.[83] The constitutive violence of this society is further signaled in its absurdities: Democratic Party nominees "defend themselves against having to provide universal healthcare" by making it sound "stupid and complicated," and Dog works days in a call center, where he spends "so much of the life he believed he could waste making people cry on the phone."[84]

We might observe that with its outsized farce and barely veiled aliases for political figures—President Llama and President Pig also feature—*Tuesday or*

September or The End rhetorically mirrors an Augustan satire. Yet the book is better read not as a Leftist version of the conservative, enlightened rationality of a Jonathan Swift or Alexander Pope commenting imperiously on "the intrepidity of these diminutive mortals,"[85] but rather as a case for exiting traditional political binaries altogether, finding "a way out of no way," as Dianne Swann-Wright puts it.[86] Indeed, as the contours of this strange, proximate world develop, Black increasingly refrains from casting her characters and their motivations as selfish, nihilist, or simply stupid, as the reader may initially be inclined to expect, and instead sets a scene that she will later use to dramatize an evental break—one that takes form in both cognitive and inescapably visceral, experiential ways for Bird as well as for Dog.

Because as it happens, there is one presaging and comedic sign of an alternative, politically radical trajectory: the presence of aliens. From Bird's perspective at the beginning of the story, this detail is presented as just that: another factoid in a weird and weirdly acceptable world of "freaky" weather, blaring TVs, five hundred dollar haircuts, and Dog, who is lost in the "glowing window of his phone," where he submissively allows "catastrophe to scroll through him."[87] Sure, people are "enraptured by the alien object," but Bird feels no curiosity:

> Bird was stubborn and did not want to give herself an interesting encounter with the alien material. She would prefer to continue to be wrong, which did not require her to turn to face her wrongness. So, while the world was raving about and obsessed with the alien object, in Bird and Dog's apartment it was equal parts alien and mundane. It was a rod of unknown material with a pattern on its surface. And the truth was, nothing else was yet known.[88]

The gap between the surface of the alien object and the "truth" implies an analogy between the "rod of unknown material" and Bird, who would "prefer to continue to be wrong" and remain unknown to herself. Recalling Lesjak's point about the spatial interference of multiple temporalities as they unsettle the apparent simultaneity of self and world, we might ask what an "interesting encounter" between the two would look like. What kind of self-recognition,

Black seems to ask, would be required for Bird to "face her wrongness" and become interested in the alien's plane of history, its radical nonidentity?

A lyric reading adjusts our understanding of this literary device. While the alien object obviously riffs on extraterrestrial invasion narrative tropes, its alterity does more interesting work when we consider its function as a figure of lyric metaphor. The alien object is silent, graceful, unknown in its constitution: "It really did look like oak, like the professor had said, but seemed to have been produced by technological methods."[89] For much of the novella, it remains "mute, awaiting interpretation."[90] And like Keats's Grecian urn or Francis Ponge's jug, the mute alien object offers a capacious metaphor: for Keats, as Barbara Johnson notes, the urn's muteness is a feminized poetic ideal, the perfect object of lyric apostrophe, superior in its silence. There is a crucial advantage to choosing an urn over, say, a Grecian frieze:

> Urns can be metaphors for the relation between form and content, but also between body and soul, expression and intention. Like the most general description of a human being, they have an inside and an outside. Whether we speak of eating or of thinking, we see the human being as a thing with interiority, an outside with something happening inside. Thus, urns are not so much anthropomorphic as humans are urnomorphic.[91]

Yet an urn is a human invention; humans are "urnomorphic" only insofar as urns are an externalization of human labor and imagination in the first place. The alien material stretches the parameters of this well-worn lyric trope not only outwards—from the realm of human history to a cosmological striation of spatialized time—but radically inwards too, towards the repressed interiority of individualized trauma.

Hence, we are introduced to a socially shared yet socially isolating idea of trauma early in the novella, in a scene in which Bird "reminded Dog that they were living in a suicidal society in which a majority of people were surveilled, indebted, drugged and traumatized—that life itself had been dishonored."[92] In the same scene, we learn of Bird's own trauma, notably when Dog weaponizes it in an argument to remark on its uselessness for generating mass social movements. Yet Bird agrees: "Emotional wounds had no structuring capacity: though sometimes she picked up her pain thinking it could provide a strut or brick, it melted immediately in the warmth of her grasp into dark, liquid rot."[93] Trauma is useless to Bird because it is ungraspable and deathly: not world-making but decomposing. Thus, while readers are invited to speculate about its origins and constitution, along with Dog and Bird's clients, who wonder if the alien is "sleeping" or related to ancient civilizations,[94] only Bird refuses this speculation, and in doing so refuses not only the wish to know the unknown object but to recognize—or as Sedgwick might say, "realize"—herself in relation to it. Bird's capacity for reading, her attunement to the "general mood," and her adeptness at reading her clients is therefore limited, Black implies, by her resistance to any knowledge of the alien's constitution that might also require self-knowledge, or the making accessible of repressed trauma.

Knowing and realizing, identity and alterity: lyric considerations help to foreground the role of dialectics in *Tuesday or September or The End*, emphasizing the speculative dimensions dialectics give to both theory and reading. Indeed, speculation is also central to the book's more dialogical scenes, where Black highlights its role in political practice, too. In a chapter titled "February: The Death of Social Democracy," Bird and Dog engage in a loosely Socratic dialogue opposing electoral and state-based socialist politics to the abolitionist pursuit of insurrectionist revolution. It is Bird and not Dog who holds out for speculative thought in this case, however, linking it to the capacity to imagine other social arrangements. Notably, this orientation requires "belief" and "faith in the infinite possibility":

> Bird said that [Dog] always underestimated belief,
> because of his narrow view of politics. She said
> that social revolution required faith in the infinite
> possibility that simmers underneath the movement
> of chance.
>
> Then it required a god, said Dog, and therefore mass
> murder, given the current conditions.
>
> A god, said Bird, is just a concept that teaches
> a daily life. It's like how the possibility of social
> transformation is kept alive by everyday practices
> such as crime and love of friends, practices that

> seem minute in comparison to the scale of the problem—race, capitalism, etc—but that reveal that the problem is unfolding in all its spectacular beauty/terror at the animal scale of a day.
>
> She stated that an abolitionist who didn't believe in abolition in their lifetime was a reformist. The question was too urgent to be left to the glacial mechanisms of policy and politics. The anarchists knew better than the socialists what to do: smash, burn, redistribute immediately.[95]

Bird's refusal to take interest in the alien and therefore in herself begins to look different from this vantage point. Unlike Dog, Bird is able to move between scales to not only imagine a capitalist totality "unfolding in all its spectacular beauty/terror at the animal scale of a day," but more importantly, to conceive the "possibility of [total] social transformation."

What prevents her from moving toward the freedom she desires? On one level, Black suggests, the answer is indeed Bird's personal trauma: we learn that her "emotional wounds," as Dog calls them, stem from her childhood, and are emblematized for Bird by "a technically incestuous affair" with her stepbrother, a transgression unknown to Dog and one that Bird understands as the private scandal that organizes her psyche and signifies "her innate wrongness."[96] Yet Bird's trauma also arises as a "kaleidoscopic flickering" that wakes her in the night, "a disturbance in the body joining forces with a disturbance in the world."[97] Implicitly acknowledging the obviousness of the connection by scarcely needing to point it out, Black thereby figures Bird's individual, specific trauma in the context of a larger one shaped by Atlantic chattel slavery:

> Carried forward by the abolition of authority and the authority of abolition, America had been born with the sun in the sign of hurt, and everyone knew what happened next. What they didn't know about was Bird's childhood.[98]

"What happened next" of course alludes to a long history of white supremacist terror, slave rebellions, abolitionist and civil rights struggles impelled by the institution that "birthed" America. Yet Black suggests that while Bird's capacity for revolutionary action emerges in part from this history of collective "hurt," it is simultaneously hampered by a connected, individual hurt—an impeding sense of innate wrongness that is further compounded by the masculinized pragmatism of democratic socialism personified by Dog.

Indeed, Dog's pragmatism takes on a markedly secular form that Black opposes to the cosmological framework that offers meaning for Bird. In "February," both Bird and Dog contract the COVID-19 virus, yet in the feverish "weird shared dream" into which they descend, Black describes how "they were together and apart from each other. They were sunk in their own bodies. A seam of strangeness opened up between them."[99] For Bird, the "shared virus took the place of sex," suggesting the "secret identity of sex and death."[100] Yet more importantly, Bird's experience of the coronavirus brings with it a hermeneutic based on the language of astrology, chance, stars, and planets, as "her fever-thoughts teemed with planetary significance," and she senses the beginning of "a new Plutonic cycle." Black's prose is bluntly allegorical in this section, as she invokes the 1776 signing of the Declaration of Independence alongside a reference to the inauguration of global capitalism, here figured as "the new rhythm of a process incarnating death/sex as an abstract world system." This striation of capitalist time, we learn, is both powered by and replaces "meaning": "They capitalized the kaleidoscope and revolutionized the institution. The power of meaning had been leached out of the world like oil. Commoditized, liquidized meaning powered fractures in the texture of relation."[101]

Recalling Marx's distinction between personal and impersonal domination, whereby "personal relations of domination and servitude" are replaced, in modern capitalism, by "the power of money, which is impersonal,"[102] we might feasibly imagine that "meaning" here gestures metaphorically to a world in which social relations are immediately apprehensible. It is fittingly likened to oil, evoking capital's oil-dependent history, from the whaling ships of *Moby Dick* to the present dominance of OPEC. And it is worth underscoring how, as it simultaneously registers difference and similarity, this simile not only evokes capitalism's oil-dependent history, but leans on the metaphorical powers of oil as a substance that quite literally embodies the force of a social relation, suggesting "the historical specificity of oil as it becomes a medium, rather than a mere object, of exchange," as Jeff Diamanti insightfully describes its role in the futures thinking of petroleum corporations.[103] Meaning is thus not only what "powers" capitalist development; it is also what gets abstracted—"leached out," in Black's words—by capital's irrational (in this case, meaningless) drive towards self-expansion. "Meaning," in this sense, is lyrically figured as both a practical activity and a feeling-thought, the non-capitalist mediation of the social that might yet return.

For Bird, then, whose "fever-thoughts [teem] with planetary significance," cosmological forces offer not an escapist anti-politics but an insurrectionary energy guided by an image of a world unbounded by abstract capitalist time and, importantly, one in which meaning is restored: "now a new Plutonic cycle was about to be born. Cosmic hour of reckoning! Shivering, Bird groped her way along the hallway to the bathroom. Her thoughts were not her own."[104] Dog, on the other hand, is admonishing: he advocates planning, reason, measured actions, the "boring" and reformist work of improvement: "Riots did not run cities. In the end, in between admittedly welcome moments of rupture, it was all about the hard, boring work of improving local conditions, he said. Not glamorous."[105] Amusingly perhaps, Dog's condescending pragmatism begs comparison with Lesjak's picture of "middle-level researchers": *scale back, pare down, small aims met are better than grand ones unrealized.*

The novella's narrative arc suggests that Bird and Dog may not be locked in this antimony, however. The pragmatist-idealist binary staged between them replays what Jordy Rosenberg outlines as the perceived conflict of secularism, whereby modern forms of empirical or rational secularism of the late seventeenth and early eighteenth centuries narrate themselves as the antidote to the fanaticism and fervor of religious abstractions.[106] This cleavage, Rosenberg writes, "splits time into a 'now' of objectivity, and a 'then' of credulous passions. Such a periodization . . . enhances the allure of an 'after' that ushers in rationality, dispels superstition, and renounces fiery universalism for cool, secular relativism."[107] Yet, in a critique that resonates with Moten's notion of an entangled model of dialectics, Rosenberg also highlights how the easy split between religious enthusiasm and enlightenment rationalism obscures the dialectical nature of their co-dependent development, where, though divergent in content, the *formal* integration of religious and civil abstractions shapes not only the ideology of the state but also its aestheticization. As a result:[108]

[T]he question, rather, has to do with the dialectical incorporation of religious forms into the logic of capitalist modernity itself. This incorporation, as we know from Marx's critique of Bruno Bauer in "On the Jewish Question," voices an eerie analogical echo between religious abstractions and the abstraction of the citizen-subject.[109]

A religious icon or a rights-bearing citizen: both ideas are propelled by enthusiasm. And even if it results at times in what Ngai might call "bad mediations"[110]—meaning concepts that are themselves reified—enthusiasm is revealed here as a mediating tool for thinking totality, either as a social mass of abstract citizens that can be managed and planned through governments and institutions, or else as an unknowable constellation governed by unknowable forces.

Black's own sense of the formal proximity between Bird's and Dog's politically divergent enthusiasms is suggested when the two are later reunited among a wellspring of riots and communizing encampments at the end of the novella, thereby seeming to complicate the conflictual dance of their early dialogue. Albeit distinctly unfinished, this formal resolution to the plot is anticipated, too, by Bird's own suspicion of idealist abstractions: where President Pig has "murdered the dying language of politics and resurrected it as abstract poetry," for example, Bird unfavorably compares such dubious poetry—as Jameson might—to the presence of aliens who conversely provide "a kind of cosmic self-consciousness, like being narrated."[111] Later in *Tuesday or September or The End*, moreover, the mediating capacities of abstractions seem to represent an untrustworthy source of reassurance in the face of border closures: "President Pig had closed the borders and she would not be permitted to return home. The catastrophe was personal/impersonal, like the Leo/Aquarius polarity in astrology. Her mind reached for this comforting abstraction amid concrete tumult."[112]

While abstractions in thought could serve as instruments of analysis or forms of delusion, and are therefore neither "good" nor "bad" in themselves, their mediating function is where political contestation takes place. Indeed, we could read the novella's denouement as the utopian and collective abolition of the integrative pact of religious and civil abstractions, as riots take over, precincts burn, police defect, and a "nine-month public debate about what the form of the city commune would be" ensues: "During the month of June, all prisoners were officially released, medical debt was cancelled, rent was abolished and millions of dollars of public money was given to mutual aid groups around the city."[113]

In Black's very last twist, Bird and Dog run into each other, by chance or fate, "as the people declared the New York Commune from the ruins of City Hall."[114] Yet it is not so much Bird's abolitionist position that wins out against Dog's socialism but, to take Rosenberg's figure for a politics of hope, her critical enthusiasm that does. Underlining the fact that religious spirit—and we might substitute utopian, cosmological, even theoretical spirit here—arises from specific material contexts and practical activities, Rosenberg observes how "such a perspective does not rule out the possibility of resistant, liberationist theologies for which religion's offer of hope, communal comfort, and utopian thought has provided a real social basis for collective action and the unyielding resistance to exploitation and immiseration."[115]

Identity/Cosmology

The eventual break of the novella thus takes lyric rather than narratological form: following an awkward reunion with her stepbrother Alpaca, who has encouraged her to return from New York to her childhood city of London, Bird finds herself trapped, "alone under national lockdown," in a featureless Airbnb apartment. Mirroring capital's own logical drive to abstract whatever it can, the apartment looks like it is "designed according to a principle of total equality to make exactly no one feel at home."[116] Following three days in bed in a haze of grief and Xanax, Bird emerges into an altered state:

> In the void she was surprised to find walls and a
> floor, even furniture, chairs and a table picked out by
> someone else
> In the void she saw her grandmother curled over her
> sewing in failing light void light, when Bird went to
> switch on the lamp above the grandmother's blank
> gaze stopped her in her tracks what's that okay no
> strong light in the void
> She saw Alpaca at sixteen turning to her with his hair

grown out a little too long, blurred lines and edges
In the void she saw all her good and bad decisions, she
revisited her decisions, but could she call them that,
blown through her life by wild intensity of feeling?[117]

In the repeat of a lyric refrain, Black returns Bird to her childhood and teenage years. Though the images of Bird's grandmother and of Alpaca juxtapose scenes of both comfort and pain, they are cushioned somewhat with blurred edges, "no strong light." But lyric, in this case, also does the work of showing how poetry is "in excess of tranquility," how it "brings the noise," as Moten argues.[118] Thus, Bird's own "wild intensity of feeling" is not recollected in tranquility, as Wordsworth's enduring definition of poetry has it, but with profound unease as she considers how it has structured her entire life, leading her to question the autonomy of her past decisions. Another refrain describes how Bird tries "saying her own name out loud now and then to remind herself her being had tangible contours from without if not from within,"[119] simultaneously evoking the African American history of the politics of naming and the psychic fragmentations of an interior trauma. Still other lyrics take on a paratactical mode to figure relationality, as in, "Mothers birds skies distances visions mothers," or:

... a blasted fragment of liver, a torn shred of spleen, a
boneless wing on which childhood had left signs of
greed or hunger, teethmarks
Want and need cannot after all be cleanly
distinguished so that even someone as dedicated to
feeling as Bird could walk too far in the direction of an
outside authority that she knew on some level it was
her destiny to abolish in herself[120]

Again, interior and exterior stand in lyric relation, not only to allude thematically to the cop in your head, or the dichotomy between capitalist greed and hunger in the gut, but to mark a decidedly formal occurrence in which the human temporality of narrative is split open into a time of "destiny" and "vision," of intersecting temporalities of trauma, a "void" time of aching gaps and the failure of *Aufhebung* that "manifests itself in the colonial encounter."[121] Black is careful to frame this lyric event both spatially and temporally: Bird is suffused with "planetary exhaustion . . . not jet lag, not even human," as "the crown of time tighten[s]."[122]

In this practiced vision, to recall James's phrase about seeing into the bones of previous revolutions, reading dialectically means moving, *Political Unconscious*-style, between horizons and semantic levels, from the level of the encodings of literary genres to the level of world history. I would like to offer a final example here of Black's own achievement in this regard, by highlighting a scene in which Bird accompanies Alpaca on a pandemic mission to deliver food to elderly Black residents in the neighborhood. As Bird acerbically observes, "[Alpaca] had started a volunteer-run food delivery service for black elders in the community. . . . He used the word *community* a lot now."[123] She nevertheless dons a billowing hazmat suit and accompanies her stepbrother to a damp block of flats to visit Horse, an elderly man living with dementia. Left alone for an hour with Horse, who we learn "was in prison for a long time" and has few visitors, Bird notices the posters on the walls: one depicting Black Jesus, in which "the historically implausible availability of blue dye had not been corrected alongside Christ's melanism," and another, Malcolm X, "in what she knew now was his final, craziest year."[124] This configuration provides the setting for a dialogue between Bird and Horse that moves across historical temporalities and notably contrasts the tonal patterns of natural conversation with its disjunctive content. It is worth excerpting a few sections of the dialogue, first to note how ambitiously Bird begins it:

> She looked at Horse, on the bed. She wanted him to look like her father, but Horse was thinner and darker and dying.
>
> "We have to come from somewhere," she said. "Even if it's outer space."
>
> "Call this food?" asked Horse.
>
> They listened to Alpaca leave.[125]

Though she has been informed by Alpaca of Horse's dementia, Bird seems to intuitively enter this polytemporal pact, in which it is not the content but the form of dialogue and shapes of language that constitute communication:

> "I used to think you get older and the past falls away. But it comes closer. I think about it all the time. It's a kind of emblem or a shield. It used to stand in between me and Dog. Like I was hoarding secret proof that he couldn't love me. I think that's how it was."
>
> "I think animals do know. It's us who don't know. The question is how to get the government out of the head." His accent was reassuringly Jamaican despite the odd content of his speech.[126]

Bird and Horse speak to each other as if talking in song lyrics: their simple, measured sentences are of roughly equal length; Horse's accent reassures Bird, providing a familiar form to a strange content. Lyric thus heavily inflects their dialogue, as if preparing the ground for an interlude of sorts, a moment in which Bird confides that she had sex with her stepbrother: "I feel embarrassed—ashamed of having been born, is that possible? But why is shame my only feeling for my life?" she asks. In reply, Horse begins speaking from another temporality, this time cosmological:

> Horse's eyes rolled deeply back in his skull and then appeared to be swallowed by his forehead, to return as three new eyes, round and black. The dark skin of Horse's body glowed a dull red. The multiple lids of his three eyes fluttered. His skin slowly took on a new texture and color, something like polished oak.[127]

Bird "immediately accepts" Horse's inhabitation by the aliens, who explain that they are "activated by signs of basic culture, such as the incest taboo."[128] But who is Bird addressing, exactly, when she confides her feelings of shame? If Horse, her addressee, is tuned into another striation of historical time, and subsequently crosses from a personal history to a cosmological one—and from one subjectivity to another—we might interpret this moment as one in which Bird speaks both to herself and to a larger totality. Indeed, it is a distinctly figural moment, one in which multiple temporalities are given representation in the flow of conversation and structures of lyric address, and in which Bird finds a way to locate herself within larger (known and unknown) systems. This dialectical method, as Lesjak notes, implies "a kind of knowing that no longer relies on self-reflexivity as the means toward the apprehension of history":

> [A] spatial dialectic refigures the coming to consciousness associated with self-consciousness as a "mode of quasi-spatial enlargement: to the old non-reflexive I or ordinary consciousness there is added something else, which allows us to grasp that former non reflexive self as itself an object within a larger field." Seeing what we know entails seeing not only larger sociotemporal relations spatially, but our very identity, as well.[129]

Indeed, to recall an argument from Chapter 1, there is no coming to (ordinary) consciousness by way of an "uncovering" of ideology, since ideology can now be understood as "a radically historical modality of capital itself."[130] Instead we must refigure ourselves through a mode of "quasi-spatial enlargement."

Combining lyric and narrative, lyric and dialogue, thereby becomes a strategy in *Tuesday or September or The End* not only for moving between capitalist and (imagined) non-capitalist spaces and times, but also juxtaposing them to retain a sense of their incommensurability. In the process, Black marks difference all the way down, from planetary movements to the inside of a prison cell, from the birth of America to a dissociated scroll on an iPhone. As "a disturbance in the body joining forces with a disturbance in the world," in her words, lyric introduces anarchist notes as it bends, cuts, or recasts the dialectic, and in doing so registers the enduring contingency at the heart of capital's logic, which as Marx argues, proceeds on the basis of the spontaneous and unplanned collective activity of commodity owners.[131] Reading for new forms of lyric is not so much a case of meaning-making being passed to the reader in postmodern style, then, and more a situation in which lyric strategies encourage poet and reader to meet as dialecticians: a situation that depends not only on the unique capacity of dialectical method to renovate itself, as Moten suggests, but also on the capacity of art to shape thought in its movement as opposed to its representations.

Reading dialectically encourages us to understand such moments of recognition—of self, of others, of a literary trope or a revolution—as always incomplete, as a positive form of appearance that must also be read for its negative character, as well as within an incomprehensible, textured, and moving system that is not only situated in historical (capitalist) time but the deep time of geological and planetary formations. In this way, the transindividuality that reveals identity to be a state of dispossession, as Lesjak argues *pace* Sedgwick, is socially bound to larger systems that are themselves subject to noncapitalist, geological, and even cosmological forces. This recognition requires a politics undergirded not by class consciousness but by an ability to read the world in its constitutive relations and in the nonidentity of its appearances, in a flash of the negative or a deep cut in the social.

Notes

Introduction

1. Karl Marx, *Grundrisse: Foundations of the Critique of Political Economy*, ed. and trans. Martin Nicolaus (London: Penguin, 1973), 164. In addition to its more direct reference to Marx's well-known phrase, my hope is that for some readers, this book's title will also allude to the way feminized backs have served as potent metaphors for late twentieth-century feminist activist writing, as in *This Bridge Called My Back: Writings by Radical Women of Color*, a signal text of women of color feminism edited by Cherríe Moraga and Gloria Anzaldúa; the long-running feminist periodical *off our backs* and the later publication *On Our Backs*, a lesbian erotica magazine whose title was intended to satirize the anti-pornography "prudish" politics of *off our backs*. See *This Bridge Called My Back: Writings by Radical Women of Color* (Watertown: Persephone Press, 1981); *off our backs* (1970–2008); *On Our Backs* (1984–2006).

2. As Marx puts it, "the various proportions in which different kinds of labour are reduced to simple labour as their unit of measurement are established by a social process that goes on behind the backs of the producers; these proportions therefore appear to the producers to have been handed down by tradition." See Karl Marx, *Capital: A Critique of Political Economy*, vol. 1, trans. Ben Fowkes (London: Penguin, 1991 [1976]), 135.

3. I am thinking here of the way an abstract poetics associated with the modernist innovations of poets like Gertrude Stein and Louis Zukofsky was often opposed to lyrical expression in late twentieth-century avant-garde poetics. What inspired the experimental genres that became known, for better or worse, as Language poetry—a movement contentiously institutionalized in US universities in the 1980s and 1990s—emerged in part from Russian formalism and Objectivist poetry, and (theoretically at least) from Jacques Derrida's critique of linguistic structuralism, but also in contrast to the expressivist poetics of the New York School. Such writing was at times characterized as a way of treating language as "material," but feminist challenges to the male-dominated poetics of Language poetry nevertheless underscored the persistence of the opposition between a subject-less abstraction and lyrical expression in their work to dismantle it at the junctures "where Lyric meets Language." For examples of key

texts, see Ron Silliman, "The New Sentence," in *The New Sentence* (New York: Roof Books, 1977); Steve McCaffery, "The Politics of the Referent," *Open Letter* 3, no. 10 (1977); for feminist work that challenges and complexifies these avant-garde modes, see Lyn Hejinian, "The Rejection of Closure," in *The Language of Inquiry* (Berkeley: University of California Press, 2000), 40–58; and *American Women Poets in the Twenty-First Century: Where Lyric Meets Language*, ed. Juliana Spahr and Claudia Rankine (Middletown: Wesleyan University Press, 2002). See also Virginia Jackson's list of studies of American lyric she persuasively calls "fictions of racial continuity" in *Before Modernism: Inventing American Lyric* (Princeton: Princeton University Press, 2023), 2n3.

4. In her influential essay "Rules of Abstraction," Leigh Claire La Berge points out that financial print culture tended to describe finance as "complex" at the same time as academic studies described it as "abstract." La Berge notes in addition that the same print culture also moved to describing finance as "simple"—a dichotomy that warrants investigation into "how and when finance is both experienced and critiqued as pivoting between representable/unrepresentable, simple/complex, and concrete/abstract." See Leigh Claire La Berge, "Rules of Abstraction: Methods and Discourses of Finance," *Radical History Review* 118 (2014): 94–95.

5. For a helpful guide to these concepts as they are developed both in *The Phenomenology of Spirit* (1807) and in *Science of Logic* (1812), see Andy Blunden, *Hegel for Social Movements* (Chicago: Haymarket Books, 2020). For a recent argument for the pertinence of Hegel's categories for thinking about reproduction, see Rebecca Carson, *Immanent Externalities: The Reproduction of Life in Capital* (Chicago: Haymarket Books, 2023).

6. Theodor Adorno, *Minima Moralia: Reflections from Damaged Life* (London: Verso, 2005), 15.

7. Sianne Ngai, *Theory of the Gimmick: Aesthetic Judgment and Capitalist Form* (Cambridge, MA: Harvard University Press, 2020), 191; italics in original removed. Ngai's helpful language of binding recalls Adorno's concept of the "binding force" of works of art. See Theodor Adorno, *Aesthetic Theory*, trans. Robert Hullot-Kentor (London: Continuum, 1997), 334.

8. See Isaak Illich Rubin, *Essays on Marx's Theory of Value*, trans. M. Samardzija and F. Perlman (Montréal and New York: Black Rose Books, 1973), 37. With this in mind, we might entertain another Marxist valence to the poet Robert Creeley's oft-cited formulation that "form is never more than an extension of content." Robert Creeley, Letter to Charles Olson, 5 June 1950, in *The Selected Letters of Robert Creeley*, ed. Rod Smith et al. (Berkeley: University of California Press, 2014).

9. Diane Elson, "The Value Theory of Labour," in *Value: The Representation of Labour in Capitalism* (London: Verso, 2015 [1979]), 171.

10. Bhanu Kapil, *Ban en Banlieue* (New York: Nightboat Books, 2015), 6; and Kay Gabriel, "Shut Your Mouth," in *A Queen in Bucks County* (New York: Nightboat Books, 2022), 4.

11. Marx, *Grundrisse*, 104.

12. For a helpful commentary on this aspect of Marx's critique, including his use of the verb "reflects" to express the simultaneously objective and inverted (or distorted) appearance of value, see Michael Heinrich, *How to Read Marx's Capital: Commentary and Explanation on the Beginning Chapters* (New York: Monthly Review Press, 2021), 148–149.

13. Best frequently employs this clarifying phrase, "function of abstraction," both in her earlier book, *Marx and the Dynamic of the Capital Formation: An Aesthetics of Political Economy,* and in her 2024 book, *The Automatic Fetish: The Law of Value in Marx's Capital.* Her explanation of her choice to put it this way, rather than use Alfred Sohn-Rethel's term "real abstraction" (now more well-known to Marxist critics), is notable for the way it briefly acknowledges the discrepancy between her concept of capital as a social modality based on the movement of a perceptual physics, and Sohn-Rethel's concept of the "social synthesis" based on the action of exchange. Best's interesting footnote reads as follows:

> Sohn-Rethel's category of "real abstraction" addresses similar concerns as the movement I tend to call "the function of abstraction" in *Marx and the Dynamic of the Capital Formation.* Unfortunately, Sohn-Rethel's formulation was not on my radar in 2003 when I carried out that study of *Capital I,* and the benefits of learning from Sohn-Rethel were lost to me for that project. I stick with my own reading and formulation of Marx nonetheless because, for better or worse, I know what I intend to capture and say with it, and my formulation and Sohn-Rethel's are not fully flush.

Beverley Best, *The Automatic Fetish: The Law of Value in Marx's Capital* (New York: Verso, 2024), 9n10; see also *Marx and the Dynamic of the Capital Formation: An Aesthetics of Political Economy* (New York: Palgrave Macmillan, 2010).

14. Best, *Automatic Fetish,* 10–11.

15. Best, *Automatic Fetish,* 2.

16. Best, *Automatic Fetish,* 10.

17. Best, *Automatic Fetish,* 11.

18. Fredric Jameson, *The Political Unconscious: Narrative as a Socially Symbolic Act* (Ithaca: Cornell University Press, 1981), 40.

19. Marx, *Capital,* vol. 1, 256.

20. Marx, *Capital,* vol. 1, 257.

21. Marx, *Capital,* vol. 1, 772.

22. While some might justifiably point to Georg Lukács's work here, I exclude it only because his concept of reification is in important ways distinct from the concept of value mobilized in this study, and not because his work is not relevant to the kind of critique I set out here. For a clarifying exploration of this distinction in the context of Gillian Rose's critique of Lukács's thought as "a type of methodological Marxism, where the totality is imposed rather than derived from contradictory experience," see

Michael Lazarus, "The Legacy of Reification: Gillian Rose and the Value-form Theory Challenge to Georg Lukács," *Thesis Eleven* 151, no. 1 (2020): 80–96.

23. For two important exceptions in studies of race, value, and North American literature and culture, see Seb Franklin, *The Digitally Disposed: Racial Capitalism and the Informatics of Value* (Minneapolis: University of Minnesota Press, 2021); and Iyko Day, *Alien Capital: Asian Racialization and the Logic of Settler Colonial Capitalism* (Durham: Duke University Press, 2016). For a helpful synthesis and presentation of critical social theory in the Frankfurt School tradition, see Werner Bonefeld and Chris O'Kane, eds., *Adorno and Marx: Negative Dialectics and the Critique of Political Economy* (London: Bloomsbury, 2022).

24. See David Trotter, "Stainless Steel Banana Slicer," *London Review of Books*, 18 March 2021, https://www.lrb.co.uk/the-paper/v43/n06/david-trotter/stainless-steel-banana-slicer. Notably, Ngai is described here as a critic of ideology and aesthetics with a "post-Marxist perspective," in some strange language-work that eschews the fact that the Western Marxism of Theodor Adorno and Fredric Jameson is essential to Ngai's earlier arguments in *Ugly Feelings* (2005) and *Our Aesthetic Categories: Zany, Cute, Interesting* (2012), but more tellingly, ignores Ngai's explicit rejection, in *Theory of the Gimmick*, of post-Marxist concepts of real subsumption and general intellect in favor of a value-critical argument that the gimmick "has, or *is*, a value theory of labor" (Ngai, *Theory of the Gimmick*, 34–37). Trotter accordingly brackets the two chapters containing expositions of Marx's arguments and commentary on the abstraction of the form of value ("these chapters seem to belong to a different book altogether") because they supposedly detract from "the gimmick's special interest as an idea" and "risk losing sight of its inherent toxicity." Not only does this paternalistic admonition mistakenly assume that ideas can be analyzed in separation from economic abstractions, but it misses Ngai's core point about the gimmick, which is that the gimmick identifies, in an analogous way to Marx, the "erroneous appraisal of value in general—and through this, an entire system of relations based on the mismeasurement of wealth" (Ngai, *Theory of the Gimmick*, 51).

25. Sianne Ngai, *Ugly Feelings* (Cambridge, MA: Harvard University Press, 2005), 130.

26. See Margaret Ronda, *Remainders: American Poetry at Nature's End* (Stanford: Stanford University Press, 2018); Jasper Bernes, *The Work of Art in the Age of Deindustrialization* (Stanford: Stanford University Press, 2017); Christopher Nealon, *The Matter of Capital: Poetry and Crisis in the American Century* (Cambridge, MA: Harvard University Press, 2011), and *Infinity of Marxists: Essays on Poetry and Capital* (Leiden: Brill, 2023); by Sianne Ngai: "Visceral Abstractions," *GLQ* 21, no. 1 (2015): 33–63, and "Bad Timing (A Sequel): Paranoia, Feminism, and Poetry," *differences* 12, no. 2 (2001): 1–46; by Joshua Clover: "Autumn of the System: Poetry and Financial Capital," *Journal of Narrative Theory* 41, no. 1 (2011): 34–52; "Retcon: Value and Temporality in Poetics," *Representations* 126, no. 1 (2014): 9–30; and Benjamin Crais, Veronica Davis, and Carson Welch, "A Conversation with Sianne Ngai and Joshua Clover," *Polygraph: An International Journal of Culture and Politics* 29 (2024): 13–38.

27. Luke Roberts, *Living in History: Poetry in Britain, 1945–1979* (Edinburgh: Edinburgh University Press, 2024); Christopher Chen, *Literature and Race in the Democracy of Goods: Reading Contemporary Black and Asian North American Poetry* (London: Bloomsbury Academic, 2022); Walt Hunter, *Forms of a World: Contemporary Poetry and the Making of Globalization* (New York: Fordham University Press, 2019); Samuel Solomon, *Lyric Pedagogy and Marxist-Feminism: Social Reproduction and the Institutions of Poetry* (London: Bloomsbury Academic, 2019); and Andrea Brady, *Poetry and Bondage: A History and Theory of Lyric Constraint* (Cambridge: Cambridge University Press, 2021). For a brilliant account of the figural and rhetorical character of subsistence ways of living and histories of dispossession from the British Romantic period to the 1980s, see also Lenora Hanson, *The Romantic Rhetoric of Accumulation* (Stanford: Stanford University Press, 2022).

28. Dawn Lundy Martin, *Life in a Box Is a Pretty Life* (New York: Nightboat Books, 2015), 5.

29. Marina Vishmidt, "Bodies in Space: On the Ends of Vulnerability," *Radical Philosophy* 2, no. 8 (2020): 34.

30. Christopher Nealon, "Abstraction, Intuition, Poetry," *ELH* 88, no. 2 (Summer 2021): 387–420.

31. The term "open text" originally comes from Umberto Eco's 1959 essay, "The Poetics of the Open Work." See Umberto Eco, *The Role of the Reader: Explorations in the Semiotics of Texts* (Bloomington: Indiana University Press, 1984), 47–66.

32. Carolyn Lesjak, "Reading Dialectically," *Criticism* 55, no. 2 (Spring 2013): 252.

33. Recent studies that discuss feminization and racialization as co-constitutive processes include Brenna Bhandar, *The Colonial Lives of Property: Law, Land, and Racial Regimes of Ownership* (Durham: Duke University Press, 2018); Gargi Bhattacharyya, *The Futures of Racial Capitalism* (Cambridge: Polity Press, 2024); Sita Balani, *Deadly and Slick: Sexual Modernity and the Making of Race* (New York: Verso, 2023); Jules Gill-Peterson, *A Short History of Trans Misogyny* (New York: Verso, 2024).

34. Hennessy also draws instructively here on David Valentine's argument linking the term "feminization" to "gender nonconformists": poor, Black, and Latinx people living in New York City in the 1990s, many of them sex workers, whom Valentine opposes to "the "respectable class identifications of (especially white and professional) gay men and lesbians." Rosemary Hennessy, *Fires on the Border: The Passionate Politics of Labor Organizing on the Mexican Frontera* (Minneapolis: University of Minnesota Press, 2013), 130. For other value-critical interventions in queer and trans Marxism, see Jordy Rosenberg and Amy Villarejo, eds., "Queer Studies and the Crises of Capitalism" (special issue), *GLQ* 18, no. 1 (2012); Kevin Floyd "Automatic Subjects: Gendered Labor and Abstract Life," *Historical Materialism* 24, no. 2 (2016): 61–86; Naomi Cohen, "The Eradication of Talmudic Abstractions: Antisemitism, Transmisogyny, and the National Socialist Project," *Verso Blog*, December 19, 2018; Jo Aurelio Giardini, "Trans Life and the Critique of Political Economy," *TSQ: Transgender Stud-

ies Quarterly 10, no. 1 (2023): 48–53; and Amy De'Ath, "Gender and Social Reproduction," in *SAGE Handbook of Frankfurt School Critical Theory*, ed. Beverley Best, Werner Bonefeld, and Chris O'Kane (Thousand Oaks: SAGE, 2018), 1534–1550.

35. Hennessy, *Fires on the Border*, 131.

36. Beverley Best, "Wages for Housework Redux: Social Reproduction and the Utopian Dialectic of the Value-Form," *Theory & Event* 24, no. 4 (2021): 905–906. Best explains this point in the course of a lesson on how value makes its social appearance in its inverted form as price, where "the competitive disadvantage of female-gendered labor-power pushes its price below its otherwise comparatively higher value and below the price of male-gendered labor-power." This "price-depressed" labor-power is what posits gender itself when it identifies workers as male or female.

37. Jay Prosser, *Second Skins: The Body Narratives of Transsexuality* (New York: Columbia University Press, 1998), quoted in Hennessy, *Fires on the Border*, 126.

38. Hennessy, *Fires on the Border*, 131, 134. This point perhaps recalls Hennessy's earlier critique (in her 2000 book, *Profit and Pleasure*) of Judith Butler's discursive concept of gender as one that skips over the task of actually historicizing the historical contexts it invokes. See Rosemary Hennessy, *Profit and Pleasure: Sexual Identities in Late Capitalism* (New York: Routledge, 2000), 115–121.

39. Donna Haraway, "A Cyborg Manifesto: Science, Technology, and Socialist-Feminism in the Late Twentieth Century," in *Manifestly Haraway* (Minneapolis: University of Minnesota Press, 2016), 38.

40. Cameron Awkward-Rich, "On Trans Use of the Many Sojourner Truths," in *Feminism Against Cisness*, ed. Emma Heaney (Durham: Duke University Press, 2024), 47–48. As Awkward-Rich notes, Rubles was declared insane and committed to Stockton Asylum, where they died of tuberculosis eight years later. See also Nat Raha, "The Limits of Trans Liberalism," *Verso Blog*, September 21, 2015, https://www.versobooks.com/en-gb/blogs/news/2245-the-limits-of-trans-liberalism-by-nat-raha.

41. Stuart Hall, "The Centrality of Culture: Notes on the Cultural Revolutions of Our Times," in *Selected Writings on Marxism*, ed. Gregor McLennan (Durham: Duke University Press, 2023 [1997]), 332. This is not to argue that "the scenarios of representation," as Hall calls them in his 1988 essay "New Ethnicities," are merely expressive of capital's logics, but to set out another way of conceiving their relationship to capital altogether. See also Stuart Hall, "New Ethnicities," in *Selected Writings on Race and Difference*, ed. Paul Gilroy and Ruth Wilson Gilmore (Durham: Duke University Press, 2023 [1988]), 248.

42. Marie Annharte Baker, *Indigena Awry* (Vancouver: New Star Books, 2012), 49, 52.

43. Silvia Federici, "Wages Against Housework" (Bristol: Power of Women Collective and Falling Wall Press, 1975), 1. Despite the methodological promise of early Marxist-feminist texts for a Marxist feminism that is not merely trans inclusive but recognizes the central importance of trans studies and politics, the trans body, and the lived realities of trans people for any Marxist critique of gender worth its name, it

bears noting that Federici's more recent work, *Beyond the Periphery of the Skin*, is openly transphobic in its insistence on the category "woman" as the political preserve of cisgendered childbearing women and in its reactionary attack on "body remakes." See Silvia Federici, *Beyond the Periphery of the Skin: Rethinking, Remaking, and Reclaiming the Body in Contemporary Capitalism* (New York: PM Press, 2020); for a knowledgeable review, see Cory Austin Knudson, "Beyond the Periphery of the Skin— Silvia Federici," *Full Stop*, 28 May 2020, https://www.full-stop.net/2020/05/28/reviews/cory-austin-knudson/beyond-the-periphery-of-the-skin-silvia-federici/.

44. Federici, "Wages Against Housework," 2.

45. In Samuel Moore and Edward Aveling's translation of the third German edition of *Capital*, and in Ben Fowkes's well-known translation in the 1981 Penguin edition, this term is translated as "inner connection." Other commentators have chosen to translate "*inneres Band*" as "inner bond," however, and this is the term that appears in A. V. Miller's translation of Hegel's *Science of Logic*. In his 1874 *Logik*, the German idealist Rudolf Hermann Lotze writes of the "inner bond that unites the attributes of a thing to a whole," and it is in this spirit that I use the term here. See Karl Marx, "Afterword to the Second German Edition [of *Capital*]," in *The Marx-Engels Reader*, ed. Robert Tucker (New York: W. W. Norton, 1978), 301; Karl Marx, *Capital: A Critique of Political Economy*, vol. 3, trans. David Fernbach London: Penguin, 1991); Georg Wilhelm Friedrich Hegel, *Hegel's Science of Logic*, trans. A. V. Miller (London: Penguin, 1991); Rudolf Hermann Lotze, *Logik, Erstes Buch, Vom Denken* (Hamburg: Meiner, 1989 [1874]), 38.

46. Maya Gonzalez, "The Gendered Circuit: Reading *The Arcane of Reproduction*," *Viewpoint Magazine*, 28 September 2013, https://viewpointmag.com/2013/09/28/the-gendered-circuit-reading-the-arcane-of-reproduction/. Gonzalez is simultaneously riffing on Leopoldina Fortunati's apt title for her 1981 text, *The Arcane of Reproduction*. See Leopoldina Fortunati, *The Arcane of Reproduction: Housework, Prostitution, Labor and Capital* (New York: Autonomedia, 1989).

47. Marx, *Capital*, vol. 3, 970.

48. See, for example, Imre Szeman, "Who's Afraid of National Allegory? Jameson, Literary Criticism, Globalization," *South Atlantic Quarterly* 100, no. 3 (2001): 803–827; Ellen Meiksins Wood, "Capitalism and Human Emancipation." *New Left Review* 167 (1998): 3–20; Rosemary Hennessy, *Profit and Pleasure: Sexual Identities in Late Capitalism* (New York: Routledge, 2000); and, more recently, Joshua Clover, "Value | Theory | Crisis," *PMLA* 127, no. 1 (2012): 107–114; and Christopher Nealon, "Introduction: The Matter of Capital, or Catastrophe and Textuality," in *The Matter of Capital: Poetry and Crisis in the American Century* (Cambridge, MA: Harvard University Press, 2011), 1–35.

49. Michèle Barrett, *Women's Oppression Today: The Marxist/Feminist Encounter* (London: Verso, 1988), x.

50. For a useful chronology that situates Western Marxism among other interpretations of Marx's work, see Ingo Elbe, "Between Marx, Marxism, and Marxisms: Ways

of Reading Marx's Theory," *Viewpoint Magazine*, 21 October 2013, https://viewpointmag.com/2013/10/21/between-marx-marxism-and-marxisms-ways-of-reading-marxs-theory/.

51. Barrett, *Women's Oppression Today*, 30–31.

52. It is worth observing how Coward's argument that "there is no general and essential economic existence of the relations of production—there is only the particularity in which they are secured" might be put to a more sympathetic reading if we notice the way this language reaches for a concept more like social form, framed as the "particularity" in which economic relations are "secured." See Rosalind Coward and John Ellis, *Language and Materialism: Developments in Semiology and the Theory of the Subject* (London: Routledge, 1977), 69, quoted in Barrett, *Women's Oppression Today*, 34.

53. Barrett, *Women's Oppression Today*, 37, 35.

54. Barrett, *Women's Oppression Today*, xv, 29. Barrett is writing in conversation with Heidi I. Hartmann's well-known essay, "The Unhappy Marriage of Marxism and Feminism: Towards a More Progressive Union," *Capital & Class* 3, no. 2 (1979): 1–33, among many other Marxist-feminist interventions into what became known as the "systems debates." For a careful overview, see Cinzia Arruzza, "Remarks on Gender," *Viewpoint Magazine*, 2 September 2014, https://viewpointmag.com/2014/09/02/remarks-on-gender/.

55. Michèle Barrett, *The Politics of Truth: From Marx to Foucault* (Cambridge: Polity Press, 1991), 24–25.

56. See Stuart Hall, "Race, Articulation, and Societies Structured in Dominance," in *Selected Writings on Race and Difference*, ed. Paul Gilroy and Ruth Wilson Gilmore (Durham: Duke University Press, 2021 [1980]), 195–245; and Kevin Floyd, *The Reification of Desire: Toward a Queer Marxism* (Minneapolis: University of Minnesota Press, 2009).

57. Beverley Best, "Distilling a Value Theory of Ideology from Volume Three of *Capital*," *Historical Materialism* 23, no. 3 (2015): 3.

58. See Mario Tronti, *Workers and Capital* (London: Verso, 2019 [1966]).

59. Federici, "Wages Against Housework," 5.

60. Federici, "Wages Against Housework," 1; italics in original. Unless noted otherwise, emphasis is in the original.

61. Mariarosa Dalla Costa and Selma James, *The Power of Women and the Subversion of the Community* (Bristol: Falling Wall Press, 1972), 49.

62. For two more examples, see Fortunati, *The Arcane of Reproduction*; and Lise Vogel, *Marxism and the Oppression of Women: Toward a Unitary Theory* (New Brunswick: Rutgers University Press, 1983). For recent developments of these premises in feminist accounts informed by value theory, see Endnotes, "The Logic of Gender: On the Separation of Spheres and the Process of Abjection," *Endnotes* 3 (2010): 56–90; Roswitha Scholz, "Patriarchy and Commodity Society: Gender Without the Body," *Marxism and the Critique of Value*, ed. Mathias Nilges, Josh Robinson, Neil Larsen, and Nicholas

Brown (Chicago: MCM', 2009), 123–142; and Amy De'Ath, "Gender and Social Reproduction," *SAGE Handbook of Frankfurt School Critical Theory,* ed. Beverley Best, Werner Bonefeld, and Chris O'Kane (Thousand Oaks: SAGE, 2018), 1534–1550.

63. Werner Bonefeld, *Critical Theory and the Critique of Political Economy: On Subversion and Negative Reason* (London: Bloomsbury, 2014), 41–42.

64. Alfred Sohn-Rethel, *Intellectual and Manual Labour: A Critique of Epistemology,* ed. and trans. M. Sohn-Rethel (London: Macmillan, 1978), 44, 33–34.

65. Brenna Bhandar and Alberto Toscano, "Race, Real Estate, and Real Abstraction," *Radical Philosophy* 194 (2015): 9.

66. Sohn-Rethel, *Intellectual and Manual Labour,* 4.

67. Bonefeld, *Critical Theory,* 82–86.

68. Silvia Federici, *Caliban and the Witch: Women, the Body, and Primitive Accumulation* (New York: Autonomedia, 2004), 63–64.

69. In a succinct essay on this point, Juliana Spahr and Joshua Clover note capital's imperative to "make differential," explaining that "differentials are a necessary basis for the imperative to *make productive,* since productivity within capital requires differential valuations." See Juliana Spahr and Joshua Clover, "Gender Abolition and Ecotone War," *South Atlantic Quarterly* 115, no. 2 (2016): 292.

70. See Jacques Derrida, "*Différance,*" in *Margins of Philosophy,* trans. Alan Bass (Chicago: University of Chicago Press, 1982), 1–27; and Peggy Kamuf's introduction to the essay in *A Derrida Reader: Between the Blinds* (New York: Columbia University Press, 1991), 59–60.

71. Eve Sedgwick, *Tendencies* (Durham: Duke University Press, 1993); and Lisa Lowe, *The Intimacies of Four Continents* (Durham: Duke University Press, 2015). Other important studies we might note here abound, but some of the most salient surely come from queer theory, notably Lee Edelman's *No Future: Queer Theory and the Death Drive* (Durham: Duke University Press, 2004) and Jack Halberstam's *The Queer Art of Failure* (Durham: Duke University Press, 2011).

72. Best, "Value Theory of Ideology," 114.

73. Jonathan Culler, *Theory of the Lyric* (Cambridge, MA: Harvard University Press, 2015), 2. Culler's opening claim in *Theory of the Lyric* is that this shift "is extraordinarily limited and limiting. It leads to neglect of the most salient features of many lyrics, which are not to be found in ordinary speech acts— from rhythm and sound patterning to intertextual relations," and that the development of "a novelizing account of the lyric" ignores the possibilities of the Western lyric tradition, "from ancient conceptions of lyric as a form of epideictic discourse (the rhetoric of praise or blame, focused on what is to be valued) to modern proposals to consider lyric as 'thoughtwriting': writing thoughts for readers to articulate" (2–3).

74. Virginia Jackson, *Before Modernism: Inventing American Lyric* (Princeton: Princeton University Press, 2022), 51, 9. Jackson locates this disavowal and omission not least in her own publication, with Yopie Prins, *The Lyric Theory Reader: A Critical Anthology* (Baltimore: Johns Hopkins University Press, 2014).

75. Jackson, *Before Modernism*, 43, 16, 41.

76. Sonya Posmentier, "Lyric Reading in the Black Ethnographic Archive," *American Literary History* 30, no. 1 (2018): 2.

77. See Sianne Ngai, *Our Aesthetic Categories: Zany, Cute, Interesting* (Cambridge, MA: Harvard University Press, 2015), esp. 18–28; and *Theory of the Gimmick*.

78. Theodor Adorno, *Notes to Literature* (New York: Columbia University Press, 1992), 96–97.

79. Ngai, *Our Aesthetic Categories*, 99; Shierry Weber Nicholsen, *Exact Imagination, Late Work: On Adorno's Aesthetics* (Cambridge, MA: MIT Press, 1999), 149.

80. Marina Vishmidt, "Maintenance of What: On Reproduction in an Extra-Systemic Sense." Paper presented at the annual meeting for the Marxist Literary Group: Institute on Culture and Society, Banff, Alberta, June 13–18, 2014.

81. Diane Di Prima, *Dinners and Nightmares* (San Francisco: Last Gasp, 1998 [1961]), 44.

82. Ngai, *Our Aesthetic Categories*, 24.

83. Federici, "Wages Against Housework," 2.

84. June Jordan, "1977: Poem for Mrs. Fannie Lou Hamer," in *Directed by Desire: The Collected Poems of June Jordan* (Port Townsend: Copper Canyon Press, 2005), 276.

85. Alice Notley, "But He Says I Misunderstood," in *Grave of Light: New and Selected Poems 1970–2005* (Middletown: Wesleyan University Press, 2008), 25.

86. Federici, "Wages Against Housework," 3.

87. As many feminists before me have noted, this worker is nearly always gendered male in *Capital*. This seems even more of an oversight given Marx's own observation, in this chapter on "Machinery and Large-Scale Industry," that "in so far as machinery dispenses with muscular power, it becomes a means for employing workers of slight muscular strength . . . the labour of women and children was therefore the first result of the capitalist application of machinery!" See Marx, *Capital*, vol. 1, 547.

88. Federici, "Wages Against Housework," 3; my italics.

89. Alice Notley, "January," in *Grave of Light*, 47.

90. For a summary of this development see Lesjak, "Reading Dialectically," 239–248.

91. Nealon, "Abstraction, Intuition, Poetry," 396.

92. Karl Marx, "Chapter 48: The Trinity Formula," in *Capital*, vol. 3, 953–970.

93. Eve Kosofsky Sedgwick, "Queer and Now," in *Tendencies* (London: Routledge, 1994), 5.

94. Emma Heaney, "The Trans Allegory and International Studies: A Conversation with Emma Heaney," Queen Mary, University of London, 16 March 2021, https://www.youtube.com/watch?v=_nxQAz6iJ3U&themeRefresh=1.

95. Emma Heaney, "Introduction: Sexual Difference Without Cisness," *Feminism Against Cisness*, ed. Emma Heaney (Durham: Duke University Press, 2024), 5.

96. Heaney, "Sexual Difference," 5.

97. Thank you to Colleen Lye for this helpful formulation of my argument.

98. Surprisingly, however, this "return to Marx"—a reading of Marx as a critic of capital's dissimulating movement—also suggests modes of reading that ask us to think again about Marxism's relation (or non-relation) to deconstructive and psychoanalytic interpretive methods in the work of critics such as Barbara Johnson, Judith Butler, David Marriott, Lee Edelman, and Hortense Spillers.

99. In this sense especially, *Behind Our Backs* is aligned with Christopher Chen's important work on contemporary poets' attention to capitalist strategies of racial comparison. In *Literature and Race in the Democracy of Goods*, Chen argues that contemporary poets explore a relational "grammar" that stems from the way that "differential valuation functions as a mechanism of enforced racial comparison, which shapes and launders a history of racist practices while systematically reproducing racial groups in relation to each other over time." Christopher Chen, *Literature and Race in the Democracy of Goods*, 5, 23–29.

100. Fredric Jameson, *The Political Unconscious: Narrative as Socially Symbolic Act* (Ithaca: Cornell University Press, 1981), 81.

101. Marx, *Capital*, vol. 3, 969.

102. See Lawrence H. Summers, "Accepting the Reality of Secular Stagnation," *Finance and Development Magazine*, International Monetary Fund, March 2020, https://www.imf.org.

103. See Sean O'Brien, "Detecting the Present: Contemporary Neo-Noir and the Case of American Decline," *Polygraph: An International Journal of Culture and Politics* 29 (2024): 43.

104. Robert Brenner, *The Economics of Global Turbulence: The Advanced Capitalist Economies from Long Boom to Long Downturn, 1945–2005* (London: Verso, 2006).

105. O'Brien, "Detecting the Present," 44, 56.

106. See Jason E. Smith, *Smart Machines and Service Work: Automation in an Age of Stagnation* (London: Reaktion Books, 2020); Phil Neel, *Hinterland: America's New Landscape of Class and Conflict* (London: Reaktion Books, 2020); Screamin' Alice, "On the Periodisation of the Capitalist Class Relation," *SIC: International Journal for Communisation* 1 (2011); and Endnotes, "Misery and Debt," *Endnotes* 2 (2010): 20–51, and "A History of Separation," *Endnotes* 4 (2015): 71–85.

107. The claim that the *only* source of value is abstract labor may seem shocking to some, but it is one that Marx went to great lengths to demonstrate and that recent readings of his work discuss at length. For one compelling disagreement on this topic, see Fred Moseley, *Marx's Theory of Value in Chapter 1 of Capital: A Critique of Heinrich's Value-Form Interpretation* (London: Palgrave Macmillan, 2023).

108. Annie McClanahan, *Dead Pledges: Debt, Crisis, and Twenty-First Century Culture* (Stanford: Stanford University Press, 2016).

109. Jamie Merchant, *Endgame: Economic Nationalism and Global Decline* (London: Reaktion Books, 2024), 11.

110. Marx also acknowledges that the concrete is "the point of departure in reality and hence also the point of departure for observation [*Anschauung*] and conception."

The key passage is as follows:

> It seems to be correct to begin with the real and the concrete, with the real precondition, thus to begin, in economics, with e.g. the population, which is the foundation and the subject of the entire social act of production. However, on closer examination this proves false. The population is an abstraction if I leave out, for example, the classes of which it is composed. . . . if I were to begin with the population, this would be a chaotic conception [*Vorstellung*] of the whole, and I would then, by means of further determination, move analytically towards ever more simple concepts [*Begriff*], from the imagined concrete towards ever thinner abstractions until I had arrived at the simplest determinations. From there the journey would have to be retraced until I had finally arrived at the population again, but this time not as the chaotic conception of a whole, but as a rich totality of many determinations and relations.

See Marx, *Grundrisse*, 100–101.

111. See, for example, Rae Armantrout, "Why Don't Women Do Language-Oriented Writing?," *L=A=N=G=U=A=G=E* 1, February 1978, https://eclipsearchive.org/projects/LANGUAGEn1/pictures/025.html.

112. See Jasper Bernes, "The Feminization of Speedup," in *The Work of Art*, 120–148; and Kristin Grogan, "Let the Plants Reproduce!" *Post45*, 18 July 2021, https://post45.org/2021/07/let-the-plants-reproduce/.

113. The formal experimentation of Mayer's personal work has been ignored by those who find its lyric qualities to be a political limitation. See, for example, Barrett Watten, *Total Syntax* (Carbondale: Southern Illinois University Press), 56–57.

114. The wonderfully helpful language of capitalism's "elsewheres" is originally (I believe) Christopher Nealon's. See Nealon, "Abstraction, Intuition, Poetry."

115. Elson, "Value," 129–130.

116. Leanne Betasamosake Simpson, *As We Have Always Done: Indigenous Freedom Through Radical Resistance* (Minneapolis: University of Minnesota Press, 2017), 30.

117. See Harry Harootunian, *Marx After Marx: History and Time in the Expansion of Capitalism* (New York: Columbia University Press, 2015).

118. Annharte, "Gynegran," in *Indigena Awry,* 49–50.

119. Hannah Black, *Tuesday or September or The End* (New York: Capricious, 2022), 30.

120. Lesjak, "Reading Dialectically," 239.

121. Fred Moten, "Not In Between," in *Black and Blur* (Durham: Duke University Press, 2017), 2.

122. Black, *Tuesday or September or The End*, 10.

123. Lesjak, "Reading Dialectically," 259.

Chapter 1

1. Vivian Gornick, "Consciousness," in *Taking a Long Look: Essays on Culture, Literature and Feminism in Our Time* (London: Verso, 2022 [1978]), 195.

2. Gornick, "Consciousness," 197.

3. Gornick, "Consciousness," 199, 211.

4. Gornick, "Consciousness," 198.

5. My thinking here is informed by Julie Beth Napolin's critique of a figure she calls "the *conditional white woman* (rather than *Karen*)." This figure is invoked, in Napolin's example, by the journalist Steven Thrasher's commentary on an incident where an Asian American man was forcibly removed by police from an overbooked United Airlines flight after refusing to give up his seat. Thrasher observes that "I simply can't believe a blond white woman would have been yanked around by a cop in this way." Napolin cautions against the use of this rhetorical figure, not in defense of white women but because it invokes an imaginary impossibility that forecloses political action: "the reader or listener is called into a space of imagining a fictional act of violence committed against the white woman. But the space is also empty because non-occupiable: no one can live there. It is not a site from which one can act, care, or join a battle or collectivity." In Gornick's example, we are called to imagine the absence of injurious feminization for some subjects from the starting point of its actuality for others, and this provides the basis for solidarity. And yet Napolin's point about how that non-occupiable space is politically unhelpful is one we might do well to consider here too. See Matthew Armstrong-Price and Julie Beth Napolin, "Adjacent Histories: Reading Riley's 'Am I That Name?' Against Contemporary Debates in Feminism," *History of the Present: A Journal of Critical History* 11, no. 2 (October 2021): 219; and Steven W. Thrasher, "Thanks to United Airlines, Is Flying While Asian Something to Fear?" *Guardian*, 11 April 2017, https://www.theguardian.com/commentisfree/2017/apr/11/united-airlines-flying-while-asian-fear.

6. Beverley Best, "Distilling a Value Theory of Ideology from Volume Three of *Capital*," *Historical Materialism* 23, no. 3 (2015): 104.

7. Fredric Jameson, "Cognitive Mapping," in *Marxism and the Interpretation of Culture*, ed. Cary Nelson and Lawrence Grossberg (Urbana and Chicago: University of Illinois Press, 1990), 347–360.

8. Werner Bonefeld, *Critical Theory and the Critique of Political Economy: On Subversion and Negative Reason* (London: Bloomsbury, 2014), 56.

9. Bonefeld, *Critical Theory*, 24.

10. Gayle Salamon, *Assuming a Body: Transgender and Rhetorics of Materiality* (New York: Columbia University Press, 2010).

11. Theodor Adorno, *Aesthetic Theory*, quoted in Jonathan Flatley, *Affective Mapping: Melancholia and the Politics of Modernism* (Cambridge, MA: Harvard University Press, 2008), 82.

12. Flatley, *Affective Mapping*, 82.

13. Flatley, *Affective Mapping*, 82.

14. Sianne Ngai, *Theory of the Gimmick: Aesthetic Judgment and Capitalist Form* (Cambridge, MA: Harvard University Press, 2020), 2. Ngai later links these unparticularized appraisals to a "rigorously maintained worldlessness" in Torbjørn Rødland's photography series—a gimmick that seems to reference an impersonal principle (*Theory of the Gimmick*, 220).

15. Denise Riley, *Am I That Name: Feminism and the Category of "Women" in History* (Minneapolis: University of Minnesota Press, 1988), 5.

16. Alice Echols, *Daring to be Bad: Radical Feminism in America 1967–1975* (Minneapolis: University of Minnesota Press, 1989), 5.

17. Gornick, "Consciousness," 203.

18. Jeska Rees, "A Look Back at Anger: The Women's Liberation Movement in 1978," *Women's History Review* 19, no. 3 (2010): 340.

19. Rees, "A Look Back at Anger," 340.

20. This is Sophie Lewis's apt characterization. Indeed, the trajectory of the rigid and ontologizing concept of sex class as it was invoked by radical and revolutionary feminists, especially in 1970s Britain, points to some of the theoretical roots of contemporary trans exclusionary radical feminisms. But it is worth noting how far radical feminism strayed from Firestone's own view of sexual liberation in which women would be freed from their "biological destiny": take her utopian vision from the final chapter of *The Dialectic of Sex*:

> [I]n our new society, humanity could finally revert to its natural polymorphous sexuality—all forms of sexuality would be allowed and indulged. The fully sexuate mind, realized in the past in only a few individuals (survivors), would become universal. Artificial cultural achievement would no longer be the only avenue to sexuate self-realization: one could now realize oneself fully, simply in the process of being and acting.

Shulamith Firestone, *The Dialectic of Sex: The Case for Feminist Revolution* (London: Verso, 2015 [1970]), 187; see Sophie Lewis, *Full Surrogacy Now* (London: Verso, 2019), 120.

21. For a useful overview of these positions, see Rees, "A Look Back at Anger."

22. See Ingo Elbe's excellent overview and critique of traditional, "party-form" Marxism in "Between Marx, Marxism, Marxisms: Ways of Reading Marx's Theory," *Viewpoint Magazine*, 21 October 2013, https://viewpointmag.com/2013/10/21/between-marx-marxism-and-marxisms-ways-of-reading-marxs-theory.

23. Caroline Sheldon, "What Is Male Supremacy?" Paper presented at What Is Male Supremacy? conference, London, 1978, quoted in Rees, "A Look Back at Anger," 343.

24. At the 1978 Women's Liberation Movement Conference, revolutionary feminists submitted a debate proposal that the socialist-influenced six demands of the women's liberation movement be abolished. See Rees, "A Look Back at Anger," 347.

25. This is Althusser's useful phrase. See Louis Althusser, "Cremonini, Painter of the Abstract," in *Lenin and Philosophy and Other Essays*, trans. Ben Brewster (New York and London: Monthly Review Press, 1971), 231.

26. For a key text outlining revolutionary feminism's principles and aims, including its challenge to socialist feminism's influence in the women's liberation movement, see Sheila Jeffreys's conference paper, "The Need for Revolutionary Feminism," delivered at the 1977 National Women's Liberation Movement Conference and reprinted in the socialist-feminist journal *Scarlet Woman*, http://sheila-jeffreys.com/the-need-for-revolutionary-feminism-by-sheila-jeffreys-1977/.

27. Samuel Solomon, *Lyric Pedagogy and Marxist-Feminism: Social Reproduction and the Institutions of Poetry* (London and New York: Bloomsbury, 2019), 10.

28. Ehn Nothing, "Queens Against Society," *Street Transvestite Action Revolutionaries: Survival, Revolt, and Queer Antagonist Struggle* (Untorelli Press, 2013), 6, https://untorellipress.noblogs.org/files/2011/12/STAR.pdf.

29. Cei Bell, "The Radicalqueens Trans-formation," in *Smash the Church, Smash the State: The Early Years of Trans Liberation*, ed. Tommi Avicolli Mecca (San Francisco: City Lights Books, 2009), 121–122.

30. "The Combahee River Collective Statement," Library of Congress, https://www.loc.gov/item/lcwaN0028151/.

31. Michaele Ferguson, "Dead Dogma and the Limits of the Feminist Political Imagination: Thinking #MeToo as Consciousness-Raising," *Theory & Event* 25, no. 2 (April 2022): 275–303; and Nancy Fraser, *Fortunes of Feminism: From State-Managed Capitalism to Neoliberal Crisis* (New York: Verso, 2013).

32. Endnotes, "The Logic of Gender: On the Separation of Spheres and the Process of Abjection," *Endnotes* 3 (2010): 67.

33. Silvia Federici, "Feminism and the Politics of the Common in an Era of Primitive Accumulation," in *Revolution at Point Zero: Housework, Reproduction, and Feminist Struggle* (New York: Common Notions, 2012), 147.

34. Marina Vishmidt, "Female Entropy: Social Reproduction as Problem and Medium," in *Of Other Spaces: Where Does Gesture Become Event?*, ed. Sophia Yadong Hao (Berlin: Sternberg Press/MIT, 2019).

35. Vishmidt, "Female Entropy," 32.

36. Marina Vishmidt and Zoe Sutherland, "Social Reproduction: New Questions for the Gender, Affect, and Substance of Value," in *The New Feminist Literary Studies*, ed. Jennifer Cooke (Cambridge: Cambridge University Press, 2020), 147.

37. See FTC Manning, "Closing the Conceptual Gap: A Response to Cinzia Arruzza's 'Remarks on Gender,'" *Viewpoint Magazine*, 4 May 2015, https://viewpointmag.com/2015/05/04/closing-the-conceptual-gap-a-response-to-cinzia-arruzzas-remarks-on-gender.

38. See for example, Endnotes, "Misery and Debt: On the Logic and History of Surplus Populations and Surplus Capital," *Endnotes* 2 (2010): 20–51; Michael Denning, "Wageless Life," *New Left Review* 66 (2010); and Warwick Research Collective, *Combined and Uneven Development: Towards a New Theory of World-Literature* (Liverpool: University of Liverpool Press, 2015).

39. Beverley Best, "Wages for Housework Redux: Social Reproduction and the Dialectic of the Value-Form," *Theory & Event* 24, no. 4 (2021): 909, 898.

40. Best, "Wages for Housework Redux," 910.

41. Best, "Wages for Housework Redux," 908.

42. Best, "Wages for Housework Redux," 911.

43. For value-theoretical takes on this argument, see Endnotes, "The Logic of Gender"; Roswitha Scholz, "Patriarchy and Commodity Society: Gender Without the Body," in *Marxism and the Critique of Value*, ed. Mathias Nilges, Josh Robinson, Neil Larsen, and Nicholas Brown (Chicago: MCM', 2009), 123–142; and Amy De'Ath, "Gender and Social Reproduction," *SAGE Handbook of Frankfurt School Critical Theory*, ed. Beverley Best, Werner Bonefeld, and Chris O'Kane (Thousand Oaks: SAGE, 2018), 1534–1550.

44. Best, "Wages for Housework Redux," 911.

45. Best, "Wages for Housework Redux," 911.

46. Karl Marx, *Capital: A Critique of Political Economy*, vol. 1, trans. Ben Fowkes (London: Penguin, 1991 [1976]), 165.

47. Karl Marx, *Capital: A Critique of Political Economy*, vol. 3, trans. David Fernbach (London: Penguin, 1991), 969.

48. Bonefeld, *Critical Theory*, 23.

49. See Georg Lukács, *History and Class Consciousness: Studies in Marxist Dialectics*, trans. Rodney Livingstone (Cambridge, MA: MIT Press, 1971), 306.

50. See Marx's section on "the expanded relative form of value," in *Capital*, vol. 1, 155–156.

51. Beverley Best, "Distilling a Value Theory of Ideology from Volume Three of *Capital*," *Historical Materialism* 23, no. (2015): 113.

52. Juliana Spahr, "Love Scattered, Not Concentrated Love: Bernadette Mayer's *Sonnets*," *differences* 12, no. 2 (2001): 100.

53. Bernadette Mayer, "Note on Sonnets," in *Sonnets* (New York: Tender Buttons, 2015), 119.

54. See Sianne Ngai's chapter "Paranoia," in *Ugly Feelings* (Cambridge, MA: Harvard University Press, 2005), 298–331, and Spahr's reading of Mayer's sonnets in "Love Scattered."

55. For an argument to this effect, see Naomi Schor's influential book, *Reading in Detail: Aesthetics and the Feminine*, (London: Routledge, 1987).

56. Maggie Nelson, *Women, the New York School, and Other True Abstractions* (Iowa City: University of Iowa Press, 2007), 122.

57. Nelson, *Women*, 122.

58. For two passionate and incisive critiques of the turn to "bodies" and matter in contemporary feminist theory, see Marina Vishmidt, "Bodies in Space: On the Ends of Vulnerability," *Radical Philosophy* 2, no. 8 (2020): 33–46; and Kevin Floyd, "Automatic Subjects: Gendered Labour and Abstract Life," *Historical Materialism* 24, no. 2 (2016): 61–86. For critiques of the new materialism of Grosz and others, see Jordy Rosenberg's argument about the depoliticizing temporal horizons of these studies in "The Molecularization of Sexuality: On Some Primitivisms of the Present," *Theory and Event* 17,

no. 2 (2014): 15–30; Sara Ahmed's response to the charge of "biophobia" in feminism, "Imaginary Prohibitions: Some Preliminary Remarks on the Founding Gestures of the 'New Materialism,'" *European Journal of Women's Studies* 15, no. 1 (2008): 23–39; Alberto Toscano's defense of Marxist materialism as an analysis of social abstractions, "Materialism Without Matter: Abstraction, Essence and Social Form," *Textual Practice* 28, no. 7 (2014): 1221–1240; and Sean O'Brien's critique of Grosz's *The Nick of Time*, "What's the Matter with Matter? Reproduction in Contemporary Materialist Feminisms," *GUTS Magazine*, 11 August 2013, http://gutsmagazine.ca/issue-one/whats-the-matter-with-matter.

59. Nelson, *Women*, 127.

60. Nelson, *Women*, 120.

61. Ann Vickery, *Leaving Lines of Gender: A Feminist Genealogy of Language Writing* (Hanover and London: University Press of New England, 2000), 15.

62. In her study of US American modernist poetry by white men, DuPlessis frames this as an "omnivorous" and "imperial" attitude. See Rachel Blau DuPlessis, *Purple Passages: Pound, Eliot, Zukofsky, Olson, Creeley and the Ends of Patriarchal Poetry* (Iowa City: University of Iowa Press, 2012), esp. 6–26.

63. Gillian White, *Lyric Shame: The "Lyric" Subject of Contemporary American Poetry* (Cambridge, MA: Harvard University Press, 2014), 175–176.

64. White, *Lyric Shame*, 189.

65. White, *Lyric Shame*, 161.

66. *Unnatural Acts*, Issue 2, The Poetry Project, 11 November 1972. See also Libbie Rifkin, "'My Little World Goes on St. Marks Place': Anne Waldman, Bernadette Mayer and the Gender of an Avant-Garde Institution," *Jacket* 7, April 1999, http://jacketmagazine.com/07/rifkin07.html.

67. Particularly for Rae Armantrout and Charles Bernstein. See Rae Armantrout, "Why Don't Women Do Language-Oriented Writing?," *L=A=N=G=U=A=G=E* 1, February 1978, https://eclipsearchive.org/projects/LANGUAGEn1/pictures/025.html; and Charles Bernstein, "Stray Straws and Straw Men" (1976, 1977), in *Content's Dream: Essays, 1975–1984* (Evanston: Northwestern University Press, 2001).

68. Bernadette Mayer, "Experiments," *L=A=N=G=U=A=G=E* 3 (June 1978): 4.

69. Cindy Sissokho, "Grace Before Jones: Black Image-Making and the Gaze," *Ocula Magazine*, 16 December 2020, https://ocula.com/magazine/features/grace-before-jones-camera-disco-studio/.

70. See Vishmidt, "Bodies in Space." For related arguments about resistance to concepts of social abstractions, see Jordy Rosenberg, *Critical Enthusiasm: Capital Accumulation and the Transformation of Religious Passion* (Oxford: Oxford University Press, 2011); and Alberto Toscano, "Last Philosophy: The Metaphysics of Capital from Sohn-Rethel to Žižek," *Historical Materialism* 27, no. 2 (2019): 289–306.

71. Jasper Bernes, *The Work of Art in the Age of Deindustrialization* (Stanford: Stanford University Press, 2017), 142.

72. Moving from the moment to the totality, Bernes's central claim, drawing on

Luc Boltanski and Eve Chiapello's theory of capital's internalization of "artistic critique," is that the ideas of experimental artists and poets in the postwar era provided important coordinates for new modes of labor organization that emerged in the postindustrial Global North.

73. Tiqqun, *The Cybernetic Hypothesis* (Los Angeles: Semiotext(e), 2020); and Gavin Walker, *The Sublime Perversion of Capital* (Durham: Duke University Press, 2016). Indeed, such renderings of capital swerve uncomfortably close to what Christopher Nealon calls the "antihumanist tone," found everywhere from Afropessimist arguments to the tech offices of Silicon Valley, which insists on the insignificance and rapaciousness of humans "in tones both wonderstruck and baleful." See Christopher Nealon, "The Antihumanist Tone," in *Affect and Literature*, ed. Alex Houen (Cambridge: Cambridge University Press, 2020), 267–283.

74. Jasper Bernes, "The Test of Communism," 7 March 2021, https://jasperbernes.substack.com/p/the-test-of-communism.

75. Bernadette Mayer, "Incidents Report Sonnet," in *Sonnets*, 55.

76. Lyn Hejinian, "The Rejection of Closure" and "Happily," in *The Language of Inquiry* (Berkeley: University of California Press, 2000), 42, 385. Hejinian uses the term "the encyclopedic impulse" to characterize her concept of the "open text."

77. Spahr, "Love Scattered," 102.

78. Both Nelson and Vickery make this suggestion throughout their chapters on Mayer's work.

79. Bernadette Mayer, "Incidents Report Sonnet #2," lines 1–3, in *Sonnets*, 56.

80. Bernadette Mayer, "Incidents Report Sonnet #2," lines 1–6, in *Sonnets*, 56.

81. Bernadette Mayer, "Incidents Report Sonnet #2," lines 7–12, in *Sonnets*, 56.

82. As Kreiner notes, the "patriarchy of the wage" offers a way to critique women's historical exclusion *and* differential inclusion in forms of wage-work. Timothy Kreiner, "The Dream Life of Value: Bernadette Mayer's Collective *Midwinter Day*," unpublished paper, 2015, 3; and Silvia Federici, *Caliban and the Witch: Women, the Body and Primitive Accumulation* (New York: Autonomedia, 2004), 68.

83. Kreiner, "The Dream Life of Value," 3.

84. Kreiner, "The Dream Life of Value," 2.

85. Kreiner, "The Dream Life of Value," 5.

86. Kreiner, "The Dream Life of Value," 5.

87. Vickery, *Leaving Lines of Gender*, 151.

88. Bernadette Mayer, *Midwinter Day* (New York: New Directions, 1999), 35.

89. As evinced, for example, in social reproduction theory's tendency to examine reproduction in terms that nearly always translate to the expressly concrete: the embodied, the biological, the physical and arduous tasks of cooking, cleaning, and caring, whether in the frame of a single household or in the context of global migration and labor patterns. The call to "return the control of our sensuous, tactile, creative capacity to labor, to where it truly belongs—to ourselves" not only suggests a view of labor as ontological—a natural activity common to all societies as opposed to a social

relation and an abstraction specific to capitalism—but opposes the "sensuous" to the abstract in implicitly ethical terms. See *Social Reproduction Theory: Remapping Class, Recentering Oppression*, ed. Tithi Bhattacharya (London: Pluto Press, 2017), 93.

90. Vishmidt, "Bodies in Space," 34.

91. Endnotes, "The Logic of Gender," 86.

92. The Marxian economist Alfred Sohn-Rethel first developed the concept of real abstraction, underlining Marx's point in *Capital* that the exchange abstraction arises not via thought but through people's actions. See Alfred Sohn-Rethel, *Intellectual and Manual Labour: A Critique of Epistemology*, ed. and trans. M. Sohn-Rethel (London: Macmillan, 1978), 33–34.

93. Bernadette Mayer, *Memory* (Plainfield: North Atlantic Books, 1976), 30–31.

94. Endnotes, "The Logic of Gender," 86.

95. The formal inventiveness of her most insistently personal work has also been ignored by those who find its lyric qualities to be a political limit, however. As a sexist observation by Barrett Watten in 1984 had it, "while the advantage of Mayer's techniques [in the late 1970s] is their adherence to the quotidian . . . the 'permanent avant-garde' vaporizes, leading to more conventional roles. As actually happened—in the course of Mayer's later editing of United Artists, the stylistic opening-up returns all these techniques to 'the self.'" Barrett Watten, *Total Syntax* (Carbondale: Southern Illinois University Press), 56–57. I follow both Vickery and Gillian White in highlighting these remarks, which render in stark terms the more troubling and at times sexist implications of the widespread anti-lyric sentiment of 1980s Language writing.

96. White, *Lyric Shame*, 187–189.

97. Julia Kristeva famously makes this claim in her essay "Women's Time." See *The Kristeva Reader*, ed. Toril Moi (New York: Columbia University Press, 1986), 187–213. For a critique of this essay, especially its evasion of the pressures on working mothers, see Carol Watts, "Time and the Working Mother: Kristeva's 'Women's Time' Revisited," *Radical Philosophy* 91 (1998): 6–17.

98. Christopher Nealon, *The Matter of Capital: Poetry and Crisis in the American Century* (Cambridge, MA: Harvard University Press, 2011), 4.

99. Nealon, *The Matter of Capital*, 7.

100. I borrow this last phrase from Seb Franklin's theorization of relations of form and formlessness as both discursive and concrete racializing operations. See Seb Franklin, *The Digitally Disposed: Racial Capitalism and the Informatics of Value* (Minneapolis: University of Minnesota Press, 2021).

101. Kay Gabriel, *A Queen in Bucks County* (New York: Nightboat Books, 2022).

102. Jordy Rosenberg, "Pleasure and Profit: Kay Gabriel Interview," *Salvage*, 18 April 2018, https://salvage.zone/online-exclusive/never-not-a-matter-of-taking-sides-kay-gabriel-interview-with-jordy-rosenberg/.

103. Louis Cabri, "Concealment and Disclosure: Nancy Shaw's *Scoptocratic*," *The Capilano Review* 3, no. 2 (2014): 120–124.

104. See Nothing, *Street Transvestite Action Revolutionaries*; and for a more recent

commentary on the connection between queer femme aesthetics and anticapitalist politics, see Meg Wesling, "Queer Value," *GLQ: A Journal of Lesbian and Gay Studies* 18, no. 1 (2012): 107–126.

105. Holly Lewis, *The Politics of Everybody: Feminism, Queer Theory, and Marxism at the Intersection* (London: Zed Books, 2016), 126.

106. Kay Gabriel, "The Vampire Mortgage," in A Queen in Bucks County, 21–22.

107. Kay Gabriel, "Travel Advisory for Constance Augusta," in *A Queen in Bucks County*, 28.

108. Kay Gabriel, "Bath 1," in *A Queen in Bucks County*, 37–38.

109. Kay Gabriel, "I Could Go On," in *A Queen in Bucks County*, 60.

110. Kay Gabriel, "I Do My Best to Cheat," in *A Queen in Bucks County*, 7.

111. Kay Gabriel, "Shklovsky 2," in *A Queen in Bucks County*, 31.

112. Emma Heaney, "The Trans Allegory and International Studies."

113. Kay Gabriel, "You Say Wife," in *A Queen in Bucks County*, 55.

114. Gabriel, "You Say Wife," 55.

115. Gabriel, "You Say Wife," 55.

116. Gabriel, "You Say Wife," 57.

117. Gabriel, "You Say Wife," 56.

118. Gertrude Stein, *Tender Buttons* (Mineola: Dover Publications, 1997), 32.

119. Natalia Cecire, "Ways of Not Reading Gertrude Stein," *ELH* 82, no. 1 (2015): 301.

120. Sianne Ngai, "Visceral Abstractions," *Theory of the Gimmick* (Cambridge, MA: Harvard University Press, 2020), 191.

121. Marx, *Capital*, vol. 1, 280.

122. Salamon, *Assuming a Body*, 3.

123. Salamon, *Assuming a Body*, 2–3.

124. Gabriel, "You Say Wife," 58.

125. Diane Elson, "The Value Theory of Labour," in *Value: The Representation of Labour in Capitalism*, ed. Diane Elson (London: Verso, 2015 [1979]), 171.

Chapter 2

1. Diane Elson, "The Value Theory of Labour," in *Value: The Representation of Labour in Capitalism*, ed. Diane Elson (London: Verso, 2015 [1979]), 174.

2. Karl Marx, *Grundrisse: Foundations of the Critique of Political Economy*, ed. and trans. Martin Nicolaus (London: Penguin, 1973), 101.

3. Karl Marx, *Capital: A Critique of Political Economy*, vol. 3, trans. David Fernbach (London: Penguin, 1991), 969.

4. The umbrella term "value-form theory" thus might include the German-language school of *Wertkritik* (value critique), the more broadly defined *neue marx-lektüre* ("new reading of Marx"), as well as Anglophone strands of value-form theory.

5. Ingo Elbe, "Between Marx, Marxism, and Marxisms—Ways of Reading Marx's Theory," *Viewpoint Magazine*, 21 October 2013, https://viewpointmag.com/2013/10/21/between-marx-marxism-and-marxisms-ways-of-reading-marxs-theory/#fn73-2941.

6. Norbert Trenkle, "Value and Crisis: Basic Questions" (1998), in *Marxism and the Critique of Value*, ed. Neil Larson, Mathias Nilges, Josh Robinson, and Nicholas Brown (Chicago: MCM', 2014), 3.

7. Elbe, "Between Marx, Marxism, and Marxisms." At the same time, Elson's essay makes it easy to see how the Marxian critique of value is often characterized as a "return to Marx," since her analysis seeks to correct and clarify many aspects of Marx's theory of value as it appears in *Capital*. As Elson notes, *Capital* is "the culmination of work on the social determination of labor that began many years before, and went through various phases." Elson, "Value Theory of Labour," 130.

8. This discussion is most often attributed to Eugen von Böhm-Bawerk. As Joshua Clover summarizes:

> In its simplest form, [the transformation problem] involves the argument that the value derived in Volume I of *Capital*—that is, determined according to given amounts of socially necessary abstract labor time—could not be made to match up with prices of production developed in Volume III. Their total magnitudes are different, and commodities cannot be found to exchange according to their values. The treble effect of this claim seems devastating. Immediately, it renders value inadequate for explaining price, calling into question its usefulness as an economic category. Following from that, it undermines the claim that profit's source is in exploitation of labor, as it then becomes possible to make the argument that profit is the play of prices rather than some secret and unverifiable extraction, thus dispensing with labor theories of value. Further, the abstract argument holding that it is embodied labor which is the common element found in all commodities that renders them exchangeable also fails. All of this contra-Marxology effects to bolster the account found in marginal utility theory, with its need only of price to explain price, and the need or desire of different people for differing uses to explain profit.

See Joshua Clover, "Value in the Expanded Field," *Mediations* 29, no. 2 (2016): 161–168.

9. Elson, "Value Theory of Labour," 123.

10. Elson, "Value Theory of Labour," 126.

11. Elson, "Value Theory of Labour," 124–129.

12. Elson, "Value Theory of Labour," 128.

13. See Clover's review of Elson's essay in "Value in the Expanded Field."

14. Karl Marx and Friedrich Engels, *The German Ideology* (London: Lawrence and Wishart, 1974), 47, quoted in Elson, "Value Theory of Labour," 129.

15. Elson, "Value Theory of Labour," 129. This will also lead—not incidentally—to a contrasting (and not wholly compatible) presentation of Marx's argument in the early chapters of *Capital*, vol. 1, which provide the basis for Alfred Sohn-Rethel's argument that the very form of thought is determined by the practice of commodity exchange, whereby the abstraction of exchange-value acquires a real force. See Karl Marx, *Capi-*

tal: *A Critique of Political Economy*, vol. 1, trans. Ben Fowkes (London: Penguin, 1991 [1976]).

16. A summary of the nuts and bolts of Elson's reading of Marx—following his basic "concern to locate the substance of value"—might thus run as follows: beginning with the commodity, Marx distinguishes between the *equivalent form* as the commodity that serves as the bearer of value, and the *relative form* as the commodity whose value is represented in the equivalent form. From this point, Marx deduces that the equivalent form must be directly exchangeable. As Elson puts it, "its exchangeability (the possibility of exchanging it) must not depend on its own use-value . . . in this it must differ from all other commodities, where, as we have already seen, their use-value and the private characteristics of their owners play a role in their exchangeability." But direct exchangeability will be limited to an "embryonic form" unless this equivalent form is a *universal* equivalent, "in which all other commodities have their abstract labor objectified, their value reflected." Further, the full establishment of direct exchangeability demands a *unique* universal equivalent, a commodity whose "specific social function, and consequently its social monopoly (is) to play the part of universal equivalent in the world of commodities."

Just as it does in *Capital*, vol. 1, Elson's next observation may seem a little quaint: "On inspection we do find such a commodity: gold-money" (which can be replaced by symbols of itself in paper money). But Elson's point is partly to demonstrate how, for Marx, capitalism is not established by convention at all: "rather, he takes the view that 'money necessarily crystallises out of the process of exchange' and that it certainly cannot be treated 'as if' established 'by a convention.'" Elson casts a useful aside on the limits of empiricism here, when she notes that the fact that we do find money—a commodity with "the social monopoly of direct exchangeability"—does not prove Marx's argument, but that it does not disprove it either; it allows it to proceed, and "this is all an empirical check on the argument can ever do."

Pausing to note the misleading confusion that arises from Marx's failure to distinguish between money as a medium of exchange and the money form of value—since "money is not specific to the capitalist mode of production, and the fact that money is functioning as a medium of exchange does not mean that it is functioning as an expression of value"—Elson stresses that while gold-money always has the characteristics required for being a universal equivalent, it is only in capitalist societies, where the objectification of abstract labor requires a universal equivalent, that it actually fulfils that function. With these points established, Elson proceeds to the next step of her reading, and it is here that we really start to get an inkling of how value "dominates" over the social world—how labor becomes socially fixed in capitalist societies. Elson, "Value Theory of Labour," 161–164, quoting Marx, *Capital, vol. 1*, 181.

17. Elson, "Value Theory of Labour," 165; my italics.

18. Elson, "Value Theory of Labour," 165.

19. Marx, *Capital*, vol. 1, 150, quoted in Elson, "Value Theory of Labour," 165.

20. Elson, "Value Theory of Labour," 165; my italics.

21. Elson, "Value Theory of Labour," 150.

22. These accounts vary in their claims and positions vis-à-vis the status of labor and value, but for one engaging example see Antonio Negri's claim that "the abstract is more true than the concrete. On the other hand, only the creativity of labor (living labor in the power of its expression) is commensurate with the dimension of value." Antonio Negri, "Twenty Theses on Marx, Interpretation of the Class Situation Today," in *Marxism Beyond Marxism*, ed. S. Makdisi, C. Casarino, and R. Karl (London: Routledge, 1996), 152.

23. As Endnotes argue: "though massively significant changes to society as a whole—and to the relation between capitalism and the worker—may result from the real subsumption of the labour process under capital, it does not follow that these changes can themselves be theorised in terms of the concepts of subsumption." Endnotes, "History of Subsumption," *Endnotes* 2 (2010): 149.

24. It bears mention that Endnotes in fact calls itself a "discussion group" and describes its project as follows:

> *Endnotes* is primarily oriented towards conceptualising the conditions of possibility of a communist overcoming of the capitalist mode of production—and of the multiple structures of domination which pattern societies characterised by that mode of production—starting from present conditions. As such it has been concerned with debates in "communist theory," and particularly the problematic of "communisation" which emerged from the post-68 French ultra-left; the question of gender and its abolition; the analysis of contemporary struggles, movements and political economy; the dynamics of surplus population and its effects on capital and class; capitalist formations of "race"; value-form theory and systematic dialectics; the revolutionary failures and impasses of the 20th Century.

See Endnotes, "About Endnotes," https://endnotes.org.uk/pages/about.

25. Endnotes, "The Logic of Gender: On the Separation of Spheres and the Process of Abjection," *Endnotes* 3 (2010): 81.

26. Christopher Arthur's formulation is useful here: "the task of systematic dialectic is to organize such a system of categories in a definite sequence, deriving one from another logically . . . making transitions from one category to another in such a way that the whole system has an architectonic." See Christopher Arthur, "Systematic Dialectic," *Science and Society* 62, no. 3 (Fall 1998): 448.

27. Endnotes, "The Logic of Gender," 65.

28. Endnotes, "The Logic of Gender," 90.

29. Endnotes, "The Logic of Gender," 89–90.

30. Endnotes, "The Logic of Gender," 90n35.

31. Julia Kristeva, *Powers of Horror: An Essay on Abjection* (New York: Columbia University Press, 1982), 2.

32. Endnotes, "The Logic of Gender," 86.

33. Endnotes is not the first to mobilize the abject as a political-economic category: for previous interventions see Karen Shimakawa, *National Abjection: The Asian American Body Onstage* (Durham: Duke University Press, 2002); and Rosemary Hennessy, "The Value of a Second Skin," in *Fires on the Border: The Passionate Politics of Labor Organizing on the Mexican Frontera* (Minneapolis: University of Minnesota Press, 2013), 125–150.

34. Kristeva, *Powers of Horror*, 2.

35. It is also, in Lee Edelman's terms, figured by queerness, as "the place of the social order's death drive." See Lee Edelman, *No Future: Queer Theory and the Death Drive* (Durham: Duke University Press, 2005), 3.

36. Endnotes, "The Logic of Gender," 64.

37. Fredric Jameson, *The Political Unconscious: Narrative as a Socially Symbolic Act* (Ithaca: Cornell University Press, 1981), 49.

38. Bhanu Kapil, "Kali's Scream," *Jack Kerouac Is Punjabi*, 17 March 2013, http://jackkerouacispunjabi.blogspot.ca/2013/03/kalis-scream.html (the blog is no longer available); Bhanu Kapil, *Ban en Banlieue* (New York: Nightboat Books, 2015), 52.

39. Kapil, *Ban en Banlieue*, 30.

40. Kapil, *Ban en Banlieue*, 41, 39.

41. Kapil, *Ban en Banlieue*, 34, 36–37.

42. Kapil, *Ban en Banlieue*, 42, 66.

43. The speaker asks, for instance: "What, for example, is born in England, but is never, not even on a cloudy day, English?" Kapil, *Ban en Banlieue*, 30.

44. Kapil, *Ban en Banlieue*, 25.

45. Kapil, *Ban en Banlieue*, 59.

46. Kapil, *Ban en Banlieue*, 59.

47. Kapil, *Ban en Banlieue*, 44.

48. Kapil, *Ban en Banlieue*, 31.

49. Kapil, *Ban en Banlieue*, 20.

50. Fred Moten, "The Case of Blackness," *Criticism* 50, no. 2 (Spring 2008): 179. But Ban has a complex relationship to Blackness: "She's a girl. A black girl in an era when, in solidarity, Caribbean and Asian Brits self-defined as black. A black (brown) girl encountered in the earliest hour of a race riot" (Kapil, *Ban en Banlieue*, 30). The distinction of Brownness is important for a number of theorists including José Muñoz, Sara Ahmed, and Gayatri Spivak, who write about the specific marginalizations of Brownness. See, for example, José Esteban Muñoz, "Feeling Brown, Feeling Down," *Signs* 31, no. 3 (2006): 675–688; Gayatri Chakravorty Spivak, "Can the Subaltern Speak?" in *Colonial Discourse and Postcolonial Theory*, ed. Patrick Williams and Laura Chrisman (New York: Columbia University Press, 1993), 66–111; and Sara Ahmed, *On Being Included* (Durham and London: Duke University Press, 2012).

51. Kapil, *Ban en Banlieue*, 82.

52. Though there was not time to incorporate her insights before this book went to press, see Sarah Dowling's recent reading of *Ban en Banlieue* and the figure lying

prone in *Here Is a Figure: Grounding Literary Form* (Evanston: Northwestern University Press, 2024).

53. Kapil, "Kali's Scream."

54. Kapil, "Kali's Scream."

55. Kapil, *Ban en Banlieue*, 63.

56. Kapil, *Ban en Banlieue*, 62.

57. The question of "the possibility of locating gender and race as part of the abstract, logical, or 'essential mechanisms' of capitalism," or pursuing, on the other hand, an analysis that aims instead "to incorporate these pervasive relations as aspects of capitalism's historical and concrete unfolding" (Manning, "Closing the Conceptual Gap") is a contentious topic of debate in recent Marxist-feminist debates, as some feminists seek to "delineate categories [of gender] that are as specific to capitalism as 'capital' itself." On this question I am in full agreement with Beverley Best's argument (discussed in Chapter 1) that gender differentials emerge as a historical consequence of capital's abstracting movement even though they are not internal to its logic, and that "price-depressed" labor power is what posits gender itself when it identifies workers as male or female. See FTC Manning, "Closing the Conceptual Gap: A Response to Cinzia Arruzza's 'Remarks on Gender,'" *Viewpoint Magazine*, 4 May 2015, https://viewpointmag.com/2015/05/04/closing-the-conceptual-gap-a-response-to-cinzia-arruzzas-remarks-on-gender; and Beverley Best, "Wages for Housework Redux: Social Reproduction and the Utopian Dialectic of the Value-Form," *Theory & Event* 24, no. 4 (2021): 896–921.

58. Theodor Adorno, *Aesthetic Theory* (Minneapolis: University of Minnesota Press, 1998), 77–78.

59. Adorno, *Aesthetic Theory*, 79.

60. Theodor Adorno, *Notes to Literature* (New York: Columbia University Press, 1992), 97.

61. Fredric Jameson, "Postmodernism: Or, the Cultural Logic of Late Capitalism," *New Left Review* 1, no. 146 (1984): 77.

62. Kapil, *Ban en Banlieue*, 59.

63. Kapil, *Ban en Banlieue*, 72.

64. See Timothy Bewes, "Reading with the Grain: A New World in Literary Criticism," *differences* 21, no. 3 (2010): 1–33.

65. For critiques of the new materialism of Grosz and others, see Jordy Rosenberg's argument about the depoliticizing temporal horizons of these studies in "The Molecularization of Sexuality: On Some Primitivisms of the Present," *Theory and Event* 17, no. 2 (2014): 15–30; Sara Ahmed's response to the charge of "biophobia" in feminism, "Imaginary Prohibitions: Some Preliminary Remarks on the Founding Gestures of the 'New Materialism,'" *European Journal of Women's Studies* 15, no. 1 (2008): 23–39; Alberto Toscano's defense of Marxist materialism as an analysis of social abstractions, "Materialism Without Matter: Abstraction, Essence and Social Form," *Textual Practice* 28, no. 7 (2014): 1221–1240; and Sean O'Brien's critique of Grosz's *The Nick of Time*,

"What's the Matter with Matter? Reproduction in Contemporary Materialist Feminisms," *GUTS Magazine*, 11 August 2013, http://gutsmagazine.ca/issue-one/whats-the-matter-with-matter.

66. Angela McRobbie, *The Aftermath of Feminism* (Thousand Oaks: SAGE, 2008), 74.

67. Kapil, *Ban en Banlieue*, 48.

68. For some recent analyses of this movement, see Phil Neel, *Hinterland: America's New Landscape of Class and Conflict* (London: Reaktion Books, 2018); Chris Chen, "The Limit Point of Capitalist Economy: Notes Towards an Abolitionist Antiracism," *Endnotes* 3 (September 2013): 203–205; and Susan Ferguson and David McNally, "Precarious Migrants: Gender, Race, and the Social Reproduction of a Global Working Class," *Socialist Register* 51 (2015): 1–23.

69. Kapil, *Ban en Banlieue*, 32.

70. See Homi K. Bhabha, *The Location of Culture* (New York: Routledge, 1994).

71. Kapil, *Ban en Banlieue*, 28, 30.

72. Kapil, *Ban en Banlieue*, 31.

73. Kapil, *Ban en Banlieue*, 27.

74. Beverley Best, *The Automatic Fetish: The Law of Value in Marx's Capital* (New York: Verso, 2024), 4. Notably Best recovers an older Marxist framework of base-superstructure to conceptualize this movement, which also provides her with a way of underlining how capitalism involves a *direction* of force, how the movement of value is a form of domination.

75. Endnotes, "The Logic of Gender," 86.

76. Marina Vishmidt, "Counter (Re-)Productive Labour," *Auto Italia South East*, 4 April 2012, http://autoitaliasoutheast.org/news/counter-re-productive-labour.

77. Christopher J. Arthur, "Value, Labour and Negativity," *Capital & Class* 73 (2001): 30.

78. Arthur, "Value, Labour and Negativity," 30.

79. Arthur, "Value, Labour and Negativity," 32.

80. Vishmidt, "Counter (Re-)Productive Labour."

81. See Silvia Federici, *Revolution at Point Zero: Housework, Reproduction, and Feminist Struggle* (New York: Common Notions, 2012); Peter Linebaugh, *The Magna Carta Manifesto: Liberties and Commons for All* (Berkeley: University of California Press, 2009); and Roswitha Scholz, "Patriarchy and Commodity Society: Gender Without the Body," in *Marxism and the Critique of Value*, ed. Mathias Nilges, Josh Robinson, Neil Larsen, and Nicholas Brown (Chicago: MCM', 2009), 123–142.

82. On this point see also Gayatri Spivak's argument that it is hard to make the low-level striations of structural racism legible to those who do not experience it. Gayatri Chakravorty Spivak, "Scattered Speculations on the Question of Value," *Diacritics* 15, no. 4 (1985): 73–93.

83. See Kumkum Sangari, "Patriarchy/patriarchies," and Delia D. Aguilar, "Inter-

sectionality," in *Marxism and Feminism*, ed. Shahrzad Mojab (London: Zed Books, 2015).

84. Sangari, "Patriarchy/patriarchies," 278.

85. Sangari, "Patriarchy/patriarchies," 279.

86. Toscano is reproducing Althusser's argument with his own valences here, before likening it to Deleuze's notion that it is not the *force* that is sensed but the *sensation*, which is something completely different. See Toscano, "Materialism Without Matter," 1232–1233.

87. See Christopher Nealon, *The Matter of Capital: Poetry and Crisis in the American Century* (Cambridge, MA: Harvard University Press, 2011), 74–86.

88. Toscano, "Materialism Without Matter," 1232. Toscano elaborates on this point when he notes that Cremonini's work, "far from any 'reflection theory,'" in Althusser's reading, "is caught up in a complex play of delays, misrecognitions, over-identifications, a play shaped by a definite space." Toscano, "Materialism Without Matter," 1234. On Marx's use of the term "phantasmagoric forms," see Michael Heinrich, *How to Read Marx's Capital: Commentary and Explanation on the Beginning Chapters* (New York: Monthly Review Press, 2021), 148–149.

89. Toscano, "Materialism Without Matter," 1232.

90. Marx, *Capital*, vol. 1, 165.

91. Gilles Deleuze, *Francis Bacon: The Logics of Sensation*, ed. and trans. D. W. Smith (London: Continuum, 2003), 56–57, quoted in Toscano, "Materialism Without Matter," 1232.

92. Louis Althusser, "Cremonini, Painter of the Abstract," *Lenin and Philosophy and Other Essays*, ed. and trans. Ben Brewster (New York: Monthly Review Press, 2001), 236.

93. Toscano, "Materialism Without Matter," 1234. Toscano borrows this phrase from Etienne Balibar.

94. Toscano, "Materialism Without Matter," 1232–1233.

95. Toscano, "Materialism Without Matter," 1233.

96. Toscano, "Materialism Without Matter," 1236.

97. Toscano, "Materialism Without Matter," 1236.

98. Charles Altieri, "The Unsure Egoist: Robert Creeley and the Theme of Nothingness," *Contemporary Literature* 13, no. 2 (1972): 162–185.

99. Steve McCaffery, *North of Intention: Critical Writings 1973–1986* (New York: Roof Books, 1986), 150.

100. Ruth Jennison, "29 | 73 | 08: Poetry, Crisis, and a Hermeneutic of Limits," *Mediations* 28, no. 2 (2015): 37–46.

101. I am riffing here on the title of Jerome Rothenberg's classic anthology, *Revolution of the Word: A New Gathering of American Avant-Garde Poetry, 1914–1945* (New York: Seabury Press, 1974).

102. It is worth noting here that Marx himself often purposely blurred the boundary between economic and literary language. For a meticulous account of the literary

aspects of *Capital*, especially its status as a work of satire, see Keston Sutherland's "Marx in Jargon," in *Stupefaction: A Radical Anatomy of Phantoms* (London: Seagull Books, 2011), 26–90.

103. Alli Warren, "Acting Out," in *Here Come the Warm Jets* (San Francisco: City Lights, 2013), 1.

104. Contrary to the opinion that Marx "turned Hegel on his head," see Andy Blunden's arguments that for Hegel, concepts had purchase on reality in the form of social activity: "As a philosopher, Hegel's subject matter is ideas, concepts. But for Hegel an idea is not something which exists inside your head . . . Hegel sees concepts as forms of human social activity—ideas exist and live in the practical activity of human communities, as forms of that activity." Andy Blunden, *Hegel for Social Movements* (Chicago: Haymarket Books, 2020), 3.

105. Marx, *Capital*, vol. 1, 163.

106. Warren, "Acting Out," 2.

107. Lisa Robertson, "Wooden Houses," in *Magenta Soul Whip* (Toronto: Coach House, 2009), 39–44.

108. Warren, "Acting Out," 2.

109. Alli Warren, "Let Them Run in Cotton" and "Personal Poem," in *Here Come the Warm Jets*, 75, 95.

110. Alli Warren, "Sensorium," in *Here Come the Warm Jets*, 10.

111. Fredric Jameson, *Valences of the Dialectic* (New York: Verso, 2009), 541.

112. Warren, "Sensorium," 10.

113. Alli Warren, "A Practice Known as Churning," in *Here Come the Warm Jets*, 66.

114. Jameson, *Valences*, 69.

115. Ruth Jennison's essay, "29 | 73 | 08: Poetry, Crisis, and a Hermeneutic of Limits," is instructive here as it points to how poetry as a form of mediation "encodes in its forms and contents a vast array of 'limits to capital,'" including those "spatial and temporal barriers to the valorization of capital."

116. Elbe, "Between Marx, Marxism, and Marxisms." Here Elbe is quoting Karl Marx, *Critique of Hegel's Philosophy of Right*, trans. Annette Jolin and Joseph O'Malley (Cambridge: Cambridge University Press, 1977), xxxvii.

Chapter 3

1. Marie Annharte Baker, *Indigena Awry* (Vancouver: New Star Books, 2012), 12.

2. Marcia Crosby, "Construction of the Imaginary Indian," in *Beyond Wilderness: The Group of Seven, Canadian Identity, and Contemporary Art*, ed. John O'Brian and Peter White (Montreal and Kingston: McGill-Queens University Press, 2007), 219–222.

3. Kristina Fagan, "What's the Trouble with the Trickster?," in *Troubling Tricksters: Revisioning Critical Conversations*, ed. Deanna Reder and Linda M. Morra (Waterloo: Wilfred Laurier University Press, 2010), 3–20.

4. For a concise history of the concept's use, see Jerome Ashmore, "Three Aspects of Weltanschauung," *Sociological Quarterly* 7, no. 2 (1966): 215–228.

5. Leanne Betasamosake Simpson, *As We Have Always Done: Indigenous Freedom Through Radical Resistance* (Minneapolis: University of Minnesota Press, 2017), 23.

6. Simpson, *As We Have Always Done*, 23.

7. Karl Marx, "The Eighteenth Brumaire of Louis Bonaparte," https://www.marxists.org/archive/marx/works/1852/18th-brumaire/ch01.htm; Simpson, *As We Have Always Done*, 17.

8. Simpson, *As We Have Always Done*, 28.

9. Simpson, *As We Have Always Done*, 23.

10. Karl Marx, *Grundrisse: Foundations of the Critique of Political Economy*, ed. and trans. Martin Nicolaus (London: Penguin, 1973), 361. Frederick Harry Pitts has usefully elaborated on this claim to argue that Marx's comparison of the sphere of circulation to "the work of combustion" in *Capital*, vol. 2, suggests a more accurate way of understanding how the "form-giving" process is realized in exchange, even if it takes place at various points in the production process, conceived as a "continuum of value production." Thus, "although it has a gradually cohering identity at earlier stages, the category of productiveness is a standpoint achieved only at the culmination of this process." See Frederick Harry Pitts, "Form-Giving Fire: Creative Industries as Marx's Work of Combustion and the Distinction Between Productive and Unproductive Labour," in *Reconsidering Value and Labour in the Digital Age*, ed. Eran Fisher and Christian Fuchs (London: Palgrave Macmillan, 2015), 246–260.

11. Simpson, *As We Have Always Done*, 23.

12. Simpson, *As We Have Always Done*, 22. Coulthard defines grounded normativity as "the modalities of Indigenous land-connected practices and longstanding experiential knowledge that inform and structure our ethical engagements with the world and our relationships with human and nonhuman others over time." As Simpson also explains, Nishnaabewin is rooted in *Aki* or akinoomaage, the concept of drawing guidance from one's environmental surroundings. See Glen Coulthard, *Red Skin, White Masks: Rejecting the Colonial Politics of Recognition* (Minneapolis: University of Minnesota Press, 2014), 39; and Simpson, *As We Have Always Done*, 160–161.

13. Simpson, *As We Have Always Done*, 30.

14. Simpson quotes John Borrows's definition: "Aki: noomaage. 'Aki' means earth and 'noomaage' means to point towards and take direction from." The spiritual aspects of *akinoomaage* bear noting: in Simpson's words, knowledge "flows through the layered spirit world above the earth, the place where spiritual beings reside and the place where our Ancestors sit." Simpson, *As We Have Always Done*, 161.

15. Léopold Lambert interview with Ruth Wilson Gilmore, "Making Abolition Geography in California's Central Valley," *The Funambulist*, no. 21: "Space and Activism" (December 20, 2018): 14.

16. Simpson, *As We Have Always Done*, 16–17.

17. Marie Annharte Baker, "Medicine Lines: The Doctoring of Story and Self," *Canadian Woman Studies* 14, no. 2 (1994): 114.

18. Annharte, "Medicine Lines," 114.

19. Michel Hogue, *Metis and the Medicine Line: Creating a Border and Dividing a People* (Chapel Hill: University of North Carolina Press, 2015), 6–7.

20. Annharte, "Medicine Lines," 115.

21. Mercedes Eng, back cover blurb for *Miskwagoode* (Vancouver: New Star Books, 2022).

22. Marie Annharte Baker, "Gynegran," in *Indigena Awry*, 49–50.

23. Marie Annharte Baker, "Indigenous Verse Ability," in *Indigena Awry*, 119.

24. Marie Annharte Baker, "Mama Sasquatch," in *Indigena Awry*, 99.

25. The word "kokum" is Cree for grandmother, while "tupa" signifies "great-grandparent" in the Indigenous nsyilxcən language of the Syilx Okanagan peoples in British Columbia, and "nokomis" is the Ojibwe name for Nanabozho's (Nanabush's) grandmother. The word "gaga" appears in the Hmali' language of the Indigenous Atayal peoples of Taiwan, but it is more likely that Annharte is playfully using the term in keeping with its meaning across several European languages to denote senility or insanity. Marie Annharte Baker, "Gynegran," and "CY-BRO-GRAN-MOC," in *Indigena Awry*, 49–51.

26. Annharte, "Gynegran," 49.

27. Anthony Reed, *Freedom Time: The Poetics and Politics of Black Experimental Writing* (Baltimore: Johns Hopkins University Press, 2014), 12. Reed invokes "the abstractness of the Black subject" in a contemporary culture where the mediatized overrepresentation of Blackness and the particular versions of self-expression it makes available constitute a process of racialization, one that mediates and commoditizes Black expression while obscuring its own alignments with the needs of global capital. See Reed, *Freedom Time*, esp. 97–105.

28. Reed, *Freedom Time*, 12. Indeed, Reed distances his position from Afro-pessimist claims for a Black ontology when he notes that Black experimental writing "announces a challenge—and opportunity—to disarticulate race as a pseudo-ontological category from the ethico-political obligations thought to derive from race as 'lived experience.'" Later, in his reading of M. NourbeSe Philip's *Zong!*, he deploys Derrida's figure of hauntology, in direct contrast to the "conjuration" of ontology, as a concept for understanding genealogical accounts of history and the Middle Passage. See Reed, *Freedom Time*, 6, 55.

29. Reed, *Freedom Time*, 107.

30. Chris Chen, "The Limit Point of Capitalist Economy: Notes Towards an Abolitionist Antiracism," *Endnotes* 3 (September 2013): 203–205.

31. Chen, "The Limit Point," 206.

32. Chen, "The Limit Point," 206.

33. See also Audra Simpson, *Mohawk Interruptus: Political Life Across the Borders of Settler States* (Durham: Duke University Press, 2014); Asad Haider, *Mistaken Identity: Race and Class in the Age of Trump* (New York: Verso, 2018); and Touré Reed, *Toward Freedom: The Case Against Race Reductionism* (New York: Verso, 2020).

34. See, for example, the University of British Columbia's warning, in their guide to

land acknowledgments, that "it's important that this recognition of territory and our relationship with Indigenous people doesn't appear as just a formality," and that users "take a moment to appreciate the meaning behind the words we use." The question of whether it *is* just a formality is the question that cannot be broached here, of course. See University of British Columbia, "What Is a Land Acknowledgment and How Do You Do It?," 11 February 2021, https://vpfo.ubc.ca/news/what-is-a-land-acknowledgement/.

35. Coulthard, *Red Skin, White Masks*, 15.

36. Coulthard, *Red Skin, White Masks*, 30.

37. Frantz Fanon, *Black Skin, White Masks*, trans. Charles Lam Markmann (Boston: Grove Press, 1991 [1967]), 220, quoted in Coulthard, *Red Skin, White Masks*, 40.

38. Iyko Day, "Eco-Criticism and Primitive Accumulation in Indigenous Studies," in *After Marx: Literature, Theory and Value in the Twenty-First Century*, ed. Colleen Lye and Christopher Nealon (Cambridge: Cambridge University Press, 2022), 50.

39. See, for example, the criminalization of Indigenous land defenders in Wet'suwet'en territory by the British Columbia (BC) provincial government and the Canadian federal government in recent years: https://www.theguardian.com/world/2019/dec/20/canada-indigenous-land-defenders-police-documents and https://www.aljazeera.com/opinions/2020/3/1/it-is-not-the-wetsuweten-who-are-hurting-canada.

40. Werner Bonefeld, *Critical Theory and the Critique of Political Economy: On Subversion and Negative Reason* (London: Bloomsbury, 2014), 23.

41. Chen, "The Limit Point," 204–205.

42. Chen, "The Limit Point," 204–205.

43. Simpson, *Mohawk Interruptus*, 187. For one of the well-known organizations of the Land Back movement, see https://ndncollective.org/landback/.

44. Marie Annharte Baker, "help me I'm a poor Indian who doesn't have enough books," in *Indigena Awry*, 16.

45. Juliana Gleeson, "Abolitionism in the 21st Century: From Communization as the End of Sex, to Revolutionary Transfeminism," *Blind Field*, August 7, 2017, https://blindfieldjournal.com/2017/08/07/abolitionism-in-the-21st-century-from-communisation-as-the-end-of-sex-to-revolutionary-transfeminism.

46. See Paolo Virno, *A Grammar of the Multitude: For an Analysis of Contemporary Forms of Life*, trans. Isobella Bertoletti, James Cascaito, and Andrea Casson (Cambridge, MA: MIT Press, 2004); Giovanni Arrighi, *The Long Twentieth Century: Money, Power, and the Origins of Our Times* (New York: Verso, 1994); and David Harvey, *A Brief History of Neoliberalism* (Oxford: Oxford University Press, 2005).

47. For a sense of the sheer range of interests in abolition across scholarly, activist, and popular culture discourses, see, for example, the "Abolish Everything" curriculum by the Baltimore SURJ Political Education Group, https://actionnetwork.org/campaigns/abolish-everything-series; Yulia Gilich and Tony Boardman, "Wildcat Imaginaries: From Abolition University to University Abolition," *Critical Times: Interventions in Global Critical Theory* 5.1 (2022): 109–120; Maya Gonzalez, "Communization and the

Abolition of Gender," in *Communization and Its Discontents: Contestation, Critique, and Contemporary Struggles*, ed. Benjamin Noys (New York: Minor Compositions, 2011), 219–236; Jennifer Maas, "'Jet Lag: The Game' Team Sets Comedy Debate Series 'Abolish Everything' at Nebula," *Variety*, November 21, 2024, https://variety.com/2024/tv/news/jet-lag-nebula-comedy-series-abolish-everything-1236216689/; Karen E. Fields and Barbara J. Fields, *Racecraft: The Soul of Inequality in American Life* (New York: Verso, 2014); Robert Kurz, "Marx's Theory, the Crisis and the Abolition of Capitalism" (2010), *Libcom*, 23 October 2014, submitted by Alias Recluse, https://libcom.org/article/marxs-theory-crisis-and-abolition-capitalism-robert-kurz.

48. Denise Riley, *Am I That Name: Feminism and the Category of Women in History* (Minneapolis: University of Minnesota Press, 1988), 1.

49. Marina Vishmidt, "Maintenance of What: On Reproduction in an Extra-Systemic Sense." Paper presented at the annual meeting for the Marxist Literary Group: Institute on Culture and Society, Banff, Alberta, June 13–18, 2014.

50. Denise Riley, "A Note on Sex and 'The Reclaiming of Language," in *Marxism for Infants* (Hastings: Street Editions, 1977), 11.

51. Samuel Solomon, "Denise Riley's Socialized Biology," *Journal of British and Irish Innovative Poetry* 5, no. 2 (2014): 180.

52. Solomon, "Denise Riley's Socialized Biology," 180.

53. Gwendolyn Brooks, *Riot* (Detroit: Broadside Press, 1969); and Amiri Baraka, *Black Magic: Sabotage, Target Study, Black Art* (New York: Bobbs-Merrill, 1969).

54. See Robert Brenner, *The Economics of Global Turbulence: The Advanced Capitalist Economies from Long Boom to Long Downturn, 1945–2005* (London: Verso, 2006); and Joshua Clover, *Riot. Strike. Riot: The New Era of Uprisings* (London: Verso, 2016).

55. That is to say, as workerism did: workerism was the appropriate form of antagonism in an era in which capital was able to absorb vast amounts of labor. In much the same way as Theorie Communiste would argue that abolitionist politics assume a specific form tied to a current cycle of struggle, it is not so much that a desire for abolition—or communization—becomes suddenly visible, as opposed to submerged (as another French communization theory collective, Troploin, might have it), but that it transmogrifies into new articulations, new forms, only under conditions of economic downturn. A debate between Theorie Communiste and Troploin on these questions is collected in a series of essays published in *Endnotes* 1, 2008, https://endnotes.org.uk/issues/1.

56. Karl Marx, *Capital: A Critique of Political Economy*, vol. 3, trans. David Fernbach (London: Penguin, 1991), 317–375.

57. Endnotes, "Afterword," *Endnotes* 1, 2011, https://endnotes.org.uk/articles/afterword. This is also a framework loosely shared across a range of other recent studies of economic downturn, from Jason E. Smith's analysis of automation to Clover's theory of riot as a struggle over reproduction. See Jason E. Smith, *Smart Machines and Service Work: Automation in an Age of Stagnation* (London: Reaktion Books, 2020); and Clover, *Riot. Strike. Riot.*

58. Harry Harootunian, *Marx After Marx: History and Time in the Expansion of Capitalism* (New York: Columbia University Press, 2015), 2.

59. Harootunian, *Marx After Marx*, 3.

60. Harootunian, *Marx After Marx*, 5.

61. Harootunian, *Marx After Marx*, 6; and Jairus Banaji, "Introduction: Themes in Historical Materialism," in *Theory as History: Essays on Modes of Production and Exploitation* (Chicago: Haymarket, 2011), 9.

62. Harootunian, *Marx After Marx*, 2.

63. Real subsumption, on the other hand, refers us to capital's techniques of increasing the productivity of those processes. See Karl Marx, "Results of the Direct Production Process," in *Marx and Engels Collected Works*, vol. 34 (London: Lawrence and Wishart, 2010).

64. Harootunian, *Marx After Marx*, 13; my italics.

65. David Lloyd and Patrick Wolfe, "Settler Colonial Logics and the Neoliberal Regime," *Settler Colonial Studies* 6, no. 2 (2015): 109–118.

66. Harootunian, *Marx After Marx*, 8–9; my italics. Harootunian also notes here:

> The importance of the copresence of both formal subsumption and primitive accumulation in future presents alongside capitalist accumulation relays the vague profile of prior histories that advanced capitalism is pledged to erasing. Rosa Luxemburg hinted at this copresence early, and it constitutes one of the principal arguments of this book.

67. Harootunian, *Marx After Marx*, 9.

68. Harootunian, *Marx After Marx*, 9.

69. Coulthard, *Red Skin, White Masks*, 25.

70. Simpson, *As We Have Always Done*, 180.

71. Marie Annharte Baker, "Borrowing Enemy Language: A First Nations Woman's Use of English," in *AKA Inendagosekwe* (North Vancouver: CUE Books, 2013), 111.

72. Marie Annharte Baker, "'A Weasel Pops In and Out of Old Tunes': Exchanging Words," Interview with Larry Grauer (2006), in *AKA Inendagosekwe*, 95–107.

73. Marie Annharte Baker, "help me," in *Indigena Awry*, 19.

74. Marie Annharte Baker, "Journal: One Pariah Two Pariah," and "Guerilla Backchat with Marie Annharte Baker (with Reg Johanson)," in *AKA Inendagosekwe*, 183, 170.

75. Marie Annharte Baker, "Toulouse Art Trick," in *Indigena Awry*, 7.

76. Reg Johanson, "Introduction," in *AKA Inendagosekwe*, viii.

77. Annharte, "Toulouse Art Trick," 7.

78. Sianne Ngai, *Ugly Feelings* (Cambridge, MA: Harvard University Press), 93.

79. Ngai, *Ugly Feelings*, 97.

80. Annharte, "Toulouse Art Trick," 7.

81. Ngai, *Ugly Feelings*, 95.

82. The Kootenay School of Writing (KSW) was formed in 1984 in Vancouver and,

as a non-profit organization, offered courses in writing, editing, and publishing; sponsored colloquia and critical talks on writing and visual art; hosted a reading series; and published the influential *Writing* magazine. The school is associated with writers such as Tom Wayman, Jeff Derksen, Catriona Strang, Colin Browne, Nancy Shaw, and Lisa Robertson. For some hesitant observations regarding Annharte's association with the KSW, see Lorraine Weir, "Tracking CanLit," *Canadian Literature Review* 220 (2014): 134–135; and Rob McClellan, "Annharte's 'AKA Inendagosekwe,'" *Jacket2*, 22 January 2015, https://jacket2.org/commentary/annhartes-aka-inendagosekwe.

83. Pauline Butling and Susan Rudy, "I Make Sense of My World Through Writing: An Interview with Marie Annharte Baker," in *Poets Talk: Conversations with Robert Kroetsch, Daphne Marlatt, Erin Mouré, Dionne Brand, Marie Annharte Baker, Jeff Derksen, and Fred Wah* (Edmonton: University of Alberta, 2005), 90.

84. Butling and Rudy, "I Make Sense of My World Through Writing," 90. In this interview Annharte nevertheless recollects how the Native Alliance for Red Power was "led by a white Trotskyist and I didn't like the idea of white guys running things, nor the idea that women would just do the drudge work." Marie Annharte Baker, "I Make Sense of My World Through Writing," 96.

85. Marie Annharte Baker, "Granny Ear Rot Tick," in *Indigena Awry*, 53.

86. Annharte, "Granny Ear Rot Tick," 54.

87. See also Coulthard's critique of Dale Turner's arguments that Indigenous word warriors must engage the legal and political discourses of the settler state in *Red Skin, White Masks*, 45–47.

88. Marie Annharte Baker, "Borrowing Enemy Language: A First Nations Woman's Use of English," in *AKA Inendagosekwe*, 111.

89. Marie Annharte Baker, "bin diver art," in *Indigena Awry*, 91. At the same time, Annharte's critical writing makes clear that she is acutely aware of the constraints placed upon her as an Indigenous writer—for example when she notes how humor functions as a strategy of avoiding disapproval:

> [Sherman Alexie] validates the acceptable and possible coxcombical use of irony and satire with his quip, "people listen to anything if you're funny." Otherwise, people would not listen to him but would "run away screaming," "get angry" or "turn off." The ultra-sensitive nature of a present-day audience might be eschewed by humour.

Marie Annharte Baker, "Alternative Approaches to Indigenous Literary Criticism and Resistance Writing Practice," in *AKA Inendagosekwe*, 159.

90. Annharte, "'A Weasel Pops In and Out of Old Tunes,'" 95.

91. Marie Annharte Baker, "Squaw Guide," in *Indigena Awry*, 12.

92. Marie Annharte Baker, "Mind the War," in *Indigena Awry*, 97.

93. Annharte, "Squaw Guide," 13.

94. Marie Annharte Baker, "Borrowing Enemy Language: A First Nations Woman's Use of English," in *AKA Inendagosekwe*, 115.

95. Marie Annharte Baker, "multicultural timbit," in *Indigena Awry*, 74.

96. Annharte, "multicultural timbit," 74.

97. Annharte, "multicultural timbit," 74.

98. Jodi Melamed, *Represent and Destroy: Rationalizing Violence in the New Racial Capitalism* (Minneapolis: University of Minnesota Press, 2011), 183–184.

99. Annharte, *Indigena Awry*, 16.

100. Annharte, *Indigena Awry*, 5, 41.

101. As Bonita Lawrence also notes, "to be federally recognized as an Indian ... an individual must be able to comply with very distinct standards of government regulation." See Bonita Lawrence, "Gender, Race, and the Regulation of Native Identity in Canada and the United States: An Overview," *Hypatia* 18, no. 2 (2003): 3–31. The informative Indigenous Foundations information resource site, run from the University of British Columbia, led me to this essay by Lawrence. This particular line is quoted at https://indigenousfoundations.arts.ubc.ca/the_indian_act/.

102. Darryl Leroux, *Distorted Descent: White Claims to Indigenous Identity* (Treaty 1 Territory/Manitoba: University of Manitoba Press, 2019), 29.

103. Simpson, *Mohawk Interruptus*, 108.

104. Simpson, *Mohawk Interruptus*, 56.

105. Coulthard, *Red Skin, White Masks*, 83–91, and Joyce Green, "Canaries in the Mines of Citizenship: Indian Women in Canada," *Canadian Journal of Political Science* 34, no. 4 (2001): 728, quoted in Coulthard, *Red Skin, White Masks*, 88.

106. Isabel Altamirano-Jiménez, *Indigenous Encounters with Neo-Liberalism: Place, Women and the Environment in Canada and Mexico* (Vancouver: University of British Columbia Press, 2013), 24.

107. Altamirano-Jiménez, *Indigenous Encounters*, 4.

108. Brenna Bhandar, *The Colonial Lives of Property: Law, Land, and Racial Regimes of Ownership* (Durham: Duke University Press, 2018), 178. See also Stephen M. Best, *The Fugitive's Properties: Law and the Poetics of Possession* (Chicago: University of Chicago Press, 2004).

109. Scott Lauria Morgensen, *Spaces Between Us: Queer Settler Colonialism and Indigenous Decolonization* (Minneapolis: University of Minnesota Press, 2011), 24–25.

110. For a discussion of the controversial term "Indigenous sovereignty," see Taiaiake Alfred, "Sovereignty," in *Sovereignty Matters: Locations of Contestation and Possibility in Indigenous Struggles for Self-Determination*, ed. Joanne Barker (Lincoln: University of Nebraska Press, 2006), 33–50.

111. Coulthard, *Red Skin, White Masks*, 19–20.

112. Warrior Publications, "How the Indian Act Made Indians Act Like Indian Act Indians," *Warrior Publications*, 11 February 2012, https://warriorpublications.word press.com/2011/02/11/how-the-indian-act-madeindians-act-like-indian-act-indians/.

113. Coulthard, *Red Skin, White Masks*, 11.

114. Coulthard, *Red Skin, White Masks*, 12.

115. Coulthard, *Red Skin, White Masks*, 14.

116. Coulthard, *Red Skin, White Masks*, 14.

117. Fredric Jameson, *The Political Unconscious: Narrative as a Socially Symbolic Act* (Ithaca: Cornell University Press, 1981), 36.

118. Coulthard, *Red Skin, White Masks*, 14.

119. Marx, *Capital*, vol. 3, 967.

120. "Accumulation by dispossession" is David Harvey's well-known formulation. See David Harvey, "The 'New' Imperialism: Accumulation by Dispossession," *Socialist Register* 40 (2004): 63–87.

121. Colleen Lye and Christopher Nealon, "Introduction: Marxist Literary Study and the General Law of Capitalist Accumulation," in *After Marx: Literature, Theory, and Value in the Twenty-First Century*, ed. Colleen Lye and Christopher Nealon (Cambridge: Cambridge University Press, 2022), 14.

122. Coulthard demonstrates the limits of an argument made by Dale Turner here—briefly, a claim that the discursive practices of Indigenous "word warriors" can, through an "ethics of participation," engage with and effectively transform the legal and political discourses of the state. See Coulthard, *Red Skin, White Masks*, 45–46.

123. Coulthard, *Red Skin, White Masks*, 114.

124. Bhandar, *The Colonial Lives of Property*, 30. See also Simpson, *Mohawk Interruptus*, 56.

125. Simpson, *As We Have Always Done*, 23.

126. Simpson, *As We Have Always Done*, 23.

127. Marie Annharte Baker, "Indigenous Verse Ability," in *Indigena Awry*, 119.

128. Jeff Derksen, "Globalism and the Role of the Cultural: Nation, 'Multiculturalism,' and Articulated Locals" (PhD dissertation, University of Calgary, 2000), National Library of Canada 0-612-54774-4, 172.

129. Simpson, *Mohawk Interruptus*, 105.

130. Simpson, *As We Have Always Done*, 19–20.

131. Annharte, "Medicine Lines," 115. The preceding passage from Annharte's essay is worth including at length for the ways it speaks laterally to the arguments of this chapter:

> [T]he emergence of a shared culture is fascinating. The fusion of Swampy Cree-Ojibway traditions which have come to be known as "Saulteaux" is an interesting example of how peoples come together to share a language and stories and a territory. To look only at racial mixing and posit some ideology that might make sense of it is suspect. I am not only a mixed blood, that is, part white. I am actually a product of celtic confusion. I think of what wonderful stories I might conjure by researching the use of smoking pipes by older Scottish settler ladies. My great grandmother had a pipe with a beautiful white tassel. With only one symbol in hand, I find that picture of her to be so inspiring. She was a settler, colonizer, invader, and whatever non-feminist label might fit. I see also that she was privileged

to have a pipe and a ritual of her own. I do not see her as hooked to a plough and cultivating the land. I see her not as a matriarch. I may begin to see her as a woman of celtic creation . . . linking back to her own prior generations of warrior queens. I then think of my Saulteaux auntie making cabbage rolls. I remember a friend's Dakota mother who had a craving for matzoh ball soup one day.

Chapter 4

1. Carolyn Lesjak, "Reading Dialectically," *Criticism* 55, no. 2 (Spring 2013): 247

2. Lesjak, "Reading Dialectically," 245, 237.

3. Lesjak, "Reading Dialectically," 248.

4. Hannah Black, "Open Letter," reprinted in "The Painting Must Go: Hannah Black Pens Open Letter to the Whitney About Controversial Biennial Work," *Art News*, 21 March 2017, https://www.artnews.com/artnews/news/the-painting-must-go-hannah-black-pens-open-letter-to-the-whitney-about-controversial-biennial-work-7992/.

5. Hannah Black, "Hannah Black in Conversation with Estelle Hoy," *Flash Art* 56, no. 345 (Winter 2023–2024): 87.

6. Lesjak, "Reading Dialectically," 239

7. Lesjak, "Reading Dialectically," 238; Fredric Jameson, *Valences of the Dialectic* (New York: Verso, 2009), 531.

8. Fredric Jameson, *The Modernist Papers* (New York: Verso, 2007), 3–4.

9. Jameson, *Modernist Papers*, 8.

10. See George Hartley, *Textual Politics and the Language Poets* (Bloomington: Indiana University Press, 1989); and Rob Halpern, "Restoring China," *Jacket* 39 (2010), http://jacketmagazine.com/39/perelman-halpern.shtml.

11. Jameson, *Valences*, 498.

12. Jameson, *Modernist Papers*, 209.

13. For a discussion of Stevens's nevertheless ambiguous relationships to these editors and journals, see Paul Bauer, "The Politics of Reality, 1948: Wallace Stevens, Delmore Schwartz, and the New Criticism," *Wallace Stevens Journal* 13, no. 2 (1989): 206–225.

14. Virginia Jackson and Yopie Prins, *The Lyric Theory Reader: A Critical Anthology* (Baltimore: Johns Hopkins University Press, 2014), 5.

15. Jameson, *Modernist Papers*, 18.

16. Jameson, *Modernist Papers*, 47.

17. Jameson, *Modernist Papers*, 208.

18. Jameson, *Modernist Papers*, 5.

19. Jameson, *Modernist Papers*, 4. Modernist authors are, for Jameson, at least less sanguine than the Romantics about their capacities to recover a sense of history, unity, or the Absolute from within their "technologically mediated sensorium," however. As G. S. Sahota observes, though it shared a promethean sensibility with an earlier Romantic moment of metaphysical consolations and a Kantian sense of moral superior-

ity over Nature, "modernism does not seek so much to revitalize the religiosity of old as to absorb and thereby overcome it. This amounts to evoking the usual awe and angst, but the evocations of wondrous, yet rapidly depleting, nature are now no longer required." See G. S. Sahota, "Review of Fredric Jameson, *The Modernist Papers*," *Bryn Mawr Review of Comparative Literature* 8, no. 1 (2009): 4.

20. Jameson, *Modernist Papers*, 4.

21. Joshua Clover, "The Irreconcilable: Marx After Literature," in *After Marx: Literature, Theory and Value in the Twenty-First Century*, ed. Colleen Lye and Christopher Nealon (Cambridge: Cambridge University Press, 2022), 112.

22. In Sahota's words, "all that lies beyond its internal limits, beyond the views validated by literary study and its established canons, beyond Western languages, beyond the West itself." Sahota, "Review of *The Modernist Papers*," 2.

23. Jameson, *Valences*, 531.

24. Jameson, *Modernist Papers*, 208.

25. Jameson, *Valences*, 496.

26. Jameson, *Valences*, 497; my italics.

27. See Paul Ricoeur, "The Human Experience of Time and Narrative," *Research in Phenomenology* 9 (1979): 17–34. See also Joshua Clover's argument, spanning several articles, that narrative has been the privileged cultural form within capitalism, but no longer holds the representational and explanatory power it once did, since in the age of capitalism's terminal decline "capitalism no longer exists in the way it did to grant privilege to narrative." Joshua Clover, "A Conversation with Sianne Ngai and Joshua Clover," in "Narrative and Crisis" (special issue), ed. Benjamin Crais, Veronica Davis, and Carson Welch, *Polygraph: An International Journal of Culture and Politics* 29 (13 May 2024): 18. See also Joshua Clover, "Autumn of the System: Poetry and Financial Capital," *Journal of Narrative Theory* 41, no. 1 (Spring 2011): 34–52; and his "Retcon: Value and Temporality in Poetics," *Representations* 126, no. 1 (Spring 2014): 9–30.

28. Gillian White, *Lyric Shame: The "Lyric" Subject of Contemporary American Poetry* (Cambridge, MA: Harvard University Press, 2014), 3.

29. On the relationship between modernist abstraction and racial fetishism, see especially Anne Anlin Cheng's extensive work, especially her book, *Second Skin: Josephine Baker and the Modern Surface* (Oxford: Oxford University Press, 2011). For recent pertinent studies, see Virginia Jackson's intervention, *Before Modernism: Inventing American Lyric* (Princeton: Princeton University Press, 2023); and Christopher Chen's critique of Kenneth Goldsmith's controversial conceptual poem, "The Body of Michael Brown," in *Literature and Race in the Democracy of Goods: Reading Black and Asian North American Poetry* (London: Bloomsbury Academic, 2022), 18–19.

30. See Theodor Adorno's arguments concerning the subjective and changeable nature of truth in *Negative Dialectics* (New York: Continuum, 1981). For a knowledgeable overview of his arguments on this question, see Deborah Cook, *Theodor Adorno: Key Concepts* (Durham: Acumen, 2008).

31. Michael Inwood, *A Hegel Dictionary* (Oxford: Blackwell, 1992), 200.

32. Marina Vishmidt and Zoe Sutherland, "(Un)making Value: Reading Social Reproduction Through the Question of Totality," in *Totality Inside Out: Rethinking Crisis and Conflict Under Capital*, ed. Kevin Floyd, Jen Hedler Phillis, and Sarika Chandra (New York: Fordham University Press, 2022), 80.

33. Fred Moten, "Not In Between," in *Black and Blur* (Durham: Duke University Press, 2017), 2.

34. C. L. R. James, *The Black Jacobins: Toussaint L'Ouverture and the San Domingo Revolution* (New York: Vintage, 1989), 314–315, quoted in Moten, "Not In Between," 5–6.

35. Moten, "Not In Between," 2, 6.

36. Moten, "Not In Between," 2.

37. Moten, "Not In Between," 3.

38. Fred Moten, "The Case of Blackness," *Criticism* 50, no. 2 (Spring 2008): 185. Moten makes a similar point of linking the resistance of the (Black) object and the commodity's scream in *In the Break: An Aesthetics of the Black Radical Tradition* (Minneapolis: University of Minnesota Press, 2003), 12.

39. Moten, "Not In Between," 6.

40. Vishmidt and Sutherland, "(Un)making Value," 79.

41. Moten, "Not In Between," 6.

42. As Reed puts it:

Moten's textual metaphors are therefore symptomatic of the degree to which Blackness for him is abstracted from the quotidian and historical contingencies of social life. Akin to Derridean *différance*, Blackness differs/defers meaning, prevents conceptual closure, inhabits those fields of thought from which it seems excluded. The misfit—indeed, the indistinction—between the general and the specific makes Blackness nominal. Moten elevates the idea that Black performance, rooted in colonial slavery, carries secret meanings opaque to the white disciplinary gaze to the place of the West's self-reproduction as self-identical and modern. Doing so makes Blackness a proxy for philosophical problems, which in turn confers on it a curious form of autonomy: every potential example is true; plus, the heuristic value of any example is already subsumed by the concept's generality. From within this theoretical frame, it is difficult to see how Blackness can be anything other than a position in discourse.

Anthony Reed, "The Black Situation: Notes on Black Critical Theory Now," *American Literary History* 34, no. 1 (2022): 289.

43. Moten, "Not In Between," 6.

44. Moten, "Not In Between," 8–9.

45. Moten, "Not In Between," 9.

46. Jameson, *Valences*, 497.

47. Moten, "Not In Between," 10. "Freedom's Basis in the Indeterminate" is the title

of an influential article by Homi K. Bhabha, but Moten instead footnotes this citation by reference to Arif Dirlik's 1994 critique of postcolonial theory's emergent currency in the academy, in which Dirlik emphasizes:

> the complicity of postcolonial in hegemony lies in postcolonialism's diversion of attention from contemporary problems of social, political, and cultural domination, and in its obfuscation of its own relationship to what is but a condition of its emergence, that is, to a global capitalism that, however fragmented in appearance, serves as the structuring principle of global relations.

It bears noting, too, in the context of Dirlik's article, that "not-in-between" is likely a riff on Bhabha's opening question, in his 1994 book *The Location of Culture*, in which he asks, "How are subjects formed 'in-between,' or in excess of, the sum of the 'parts' of difference (usually intoned as race/class/gender, etc.)?" See Arif Dirlik, "The Postcolonial Aura: Third World Criticism in the Age of Global Capitalism," *Critical Inquiry* 20 (1994): 331; Homi K. Bhabha, "Freedom's Basis in the Indeterminate," *October* 61 (1992): 46–57; and Homi K. Bhabha, *The Location of Culture* (London: Routledge, 1994), 2.

48. Moten, "Not In Between," 10.
49. Moten, "Not In Between," 12.
50. Lesjak, "Reading Dialectically," 263–264, 259.
51. Moten, "Not In Between," 11.
52. C. L. R. James, *The Black Jacobins*, xi, quoted in Moten, "Not In Between," 11.
53. Moten, "Not In Between," 11.
54. Moten, "Not In Between," 11.
55. Jameson, *Valences*, 68.
56. Andrea Brady, *Poetry and Bondage: A History and Theory of Lyric Constraint* (Cambridge: Cambridge University Press, 2021), 254.
57. Brady, *Poetry and Bondage*, 265.
58. Brady, *Poetry and Bondage*, 279–280.
59. Moten, "Not In Between," 12.
60. This is Beverley Best's phrase. See Beverley Best, *The Automatic Fetish: The Law of Value in Marx's Capital* (New York: Verso, 2024), 4.
61. Jackson and Prins, *Lyric Theory Reader*, 7.
62. Sianne Ngai, "Ambiguous Lever," *PMLA* 137, no. 3 (2022): 529.
63. "Intuition" is Christopher Nealon's preferred term for this process, which in his reading of Stephanie Young's 2019 collection, *Pet Sounds*, he also describes as "the compassion [the poem] both invites and gives out." See Christopher Nealon, "Abstraction, Intuition, Poetry," *ELH* 88, no. 2 (2021): 389.
64. Brady, *Poetry and Bondage*, 280.
65. Notably, this is the same dialectical impulse Jameson reads in *Paterson*.
66. Lesjak, "Reading Dialectically," 250.
67. This framing helps to clarify a practice of ideological critique that challenges

what Lesjak calls "the assumption that ideological critique is primarily a practice of unveiling in which surface appearances are shown to be illusory, and the hidden or latent meaning beneath the surface the truth." Lesjak, "Reading Dialectically," 245.

68. Lesjak, "Reading Dialectically," 251.

69. Werner Bonefeld, *Critical Theory and the Critique of Political Economy: On Subversion and Negative Reason* (London: Bloomsbury, 2014), 56.

70. Anna Kornbluh, *Immediacy: Or, The Style of Too Late Capitalism* (New York: Verso, 2024), 151.

71. "Uprisings: Hannah Black Interviewed," interview by Hannah Zeavin, *Bomb Magazine*, 7 February 2022, https://bombmagazine.org/articles/2022/02/07/uprisings-hannah-black-interviewed/.

72. Jackson and Prins, *Lyric Theory Reader*, 6.

73. Jackson and Prins, *Lyric Theory Reader*, 2.

74. As Juliana Spahr writes, "this desire to articulate those moments where meaning is slipping away is lyric's great tradition." See Juliana Spahr, "Introduction," in *American Women Poets in the 21st Century: Where Lyric Meets Language* ed. Juliana Spahr and Claudia Rankine (Middletown: Wesleyan University Press, 2002), 2.

75. Lesjak, "Reading Dialectically," 253. It would be fair to surmise that Lesjak is taking issue here with the range of data-driven, often empiricist (though oft-named "materialist") interpretive methods that have sprung up in the field of digital humanities—the target in her later critique of Franco Moretti's work on distant reading and bourgeois culture. See Lesjak, "All or Nothing: Reading Franco Moretti Reading," *Historical Materialism* 24, no. 3 (2016): 185–205.

76. Lesjak, "Reading Dialectically," 264.

77. Lesjak, "Reading Dialectically," 260.

78. Hannah Black, *Tuesday or September or The End* (New York: Capricious, 2022), 9.

79. Black, *Tuesday or September or The End*, 10.

80. Black, *Tuesday or September or The End*, 11.

81. Black, *Tuesday or September or The End*, 14.

82. Black, *Tuesday or September or The End*, 14.

83. See Jane Hu, "True Grift," *Bookforum*, Summer 2023, https://www.bookforum.com/print/3001/emma-cline-s-novel-of-a-sex-worker-who-s-never-off-the-clock-25221.

84. Black, *Tuesday or September or The End*, 15.

85. Jonathan Swift, *Gulliver's Travels* (London: Jones and Company, 1826), 10.

86. See Dianne Swann-Wright, *A Way Out of No Way: Claiming Family and Freedom in the New South* (Charlottesville: University of Virginia Press, 2002). As Moten notes, this African American folk saying also features saliently in Deborah McDowell's Black feminist memoir, *Leaving Pipe Shop*. See Deborah McDowell, *Leaving Pipe Shop: Memories of Kin* (New York: W. W. Norton, 1998); and Moten, *Black and Blur*, 153.

87. Black, *Tuesday or September or The End*, 13.
88. Black, *Tuesday or September or The End*, 12–13.
89. Black, *Tuesday or September or The End*, 12.
90. Black, *Tuesday or September or The End*, 15.
91. Barbara Johnson, "Muteness Envy," in *The Feminist Difference: Literature, Psychoanalysis, Race, and Gender* (Cambridge, MA: Harvard University Press, 1998), 130.
92. Black, *Tuesday or September or The End*, 31.
93. Black, *Tuesday or September or The End*, 32.
94. Black, *Tuesday or September or The End*, 10–12.
95. Black, *Tuesday or September or The End*, 30–31.
96. Black, *Tuesday or September or The End*, 35–36.
97. Black, *Tuesday or September or The End*, 34.
98. Black, *Tuesday or September or The End*, 35.
99. Black, *Tuesday or September or The End*, 33.
100. Black, *Tuesday or September or The End*, 34.
101. Black, *Tuesday or September or The End*, 35.
102. Karl Marx, *Capital: A Critique of Political Economy*, vol. 1, trans. Ben Fowkes (London: Penguin, 1991 [1976]), 247n1.
103. Jeff Diamanti, *Climate and Capital in the Age of Petroleum: Locating Terminal Landscapes* (London: Bloomsbury, 2021), 33.
104. Black, *Tuesday or September or The End*, 35.
105. Black, *Tuesday or September or The End*, 31.
106. Rosenberg quotes Marx here: "in this way the Enlightenment endeavoured . . . to remove the appearance of strangeness from the mysterious shapes assumed by human relations whose origins they were unable to decipher." Marx, *Capital*, vol. 1, 186, quoted in Jordy Rosenberg, *Critical Enthusiasm: Capital Accumulation and the Transformation of Religious Passion* (Oxford: Oxford University Press, 2011), 5.
107. Rosenberg, *Critical Enthusiasm*, 3.
108. Rosenberg, *Critical Enthusiasm*, 4.
109. Rosenberg, *Critical Enthusiasm*, 4.
110. Ngai, "Ambiguous Lever," 529.
111. Black, *Tuesday or September or The End*, 16–17.
112. Black, *Tuesday or September or The End*, 63.
113. Black, *Tuesday or September or The End*, 125.
114. Black, *Tuesday or September or The End*, 132.
115. Rosenberg, *Critical Enthusiasm*, 6–7.
116. Black, *Tuesday or September or The End*, 65, 61.
117. Black, *Tuesday or September or The End*, 65–66.
118. Moten, "Not In Between," 9.
119. Black, *Tuesday or September or The End*, 66.
120. Black, *Tuesday or September or The End*, 66–67.
121. Moten, "Not In Between," 11.

122. Black, *Tuesday or September or The End*, 62–65.
123. Black, *Tuesday or September or The End*, 70.
124. Black, *Tuesday or September or The End*, 74.
125. Black, *Tuesday or September or The End*, 75.
126. Black, *Tuesday or September or The End*, 77.
127. Black, *Tuesday or September or The End*, 77.
128. Black, *Tuesday or September or The End*, 77–78.

129. Lesjak, "Reading Dialectically," 260, quoting Jameson, *Valences*, 69. Lesjak notes how Fernand Braudel's history of the Mediterranean informs Jameson's concept of spatial dialectic, where "one way of seeing these intersecting gaps or incommensurabilities is by extending the very frame of time, as Braudel does when he attends to three temporalities in his study of the Mediterranean: the long durée of geological time, the middle time of institutional practices, and the short durée of historical events." Lesjak, "Reading Dialectically," 259.

130. Beverley Best, "Distilling a Value Theory of Ideology from Volume Three of *Capital*," *Historical Materialism* 23, no. 3 (2015): 104.

131. See Marx, "The Commodity," 168, as well as Michael Heinrich's helpful emphasis on these aspects of capitalist totality in his reading of chapter 2 of *Capital*, vol. 1. Michael Heinrich, "Chapter 2: The Process of Exchange," in *How to Read Marx's Capital: Commentary and Explanations on the Beginning Chapters*, trans. Alexander Locascio (New York: Monthly Review Press, 2021), 187–202.

Index

abjection, 36, 37, 88–90, 99, 100
abolition, 38, 78, 124, 211–212n47, 212n55; of abstract identity categories, 38, 124, 132, 53; Annharte, 38, 114, 135; Chen, 123; Coulthard, 143; of gender, 54-55, 125, 211n47; Hannah Black, 39; Indigenous feminist, 32, 114, 129; "The Limit Point of Capitalist Equality: Notes Toward an Abolitionist Antiracism" (Chen), 120–121; paradox of, 124–132; poetics grounded in Nishnaabewin, 132; of race, 123, 125; rejection of reformist demands, 48; Sojourner Truth, 12; *Tuesday or September or The End* (Black), 169, 170, 173–174
abolitionist poetics, 38, 117, 123, 124, 127, 132
absence, 7, 8, 104, 133, 193n5; determinate, 103
abstraction, function of, 3, 35, 50, 53, 112, 142, 183n13
abstraction, modernist, 154, 218n29
abstraction and difference, 21, 50–57
abstractions, capitalist, 8, 21, 87, 122; feminized poets inventively theorized, 36; Gabriel, 78; Jameson, 61; linked to feminization, 46; Marx, 1, 79; Ngai, 77; Toscano, 102; Warren, 111

abstractions, poetic, 79
abstractions, real, 50, 71, 85; Althusser, 104; capital's function of, 43, 46, 109; Cremonini, 103; Marx, 79; Sohn-Rethel, 19, 183n13, 199n92; Vishmidt, 8, 67
aching gaps (Sedgwick), 34, 165, 175. *See also* elsewheres; hidden abodes; polytemporal pacts
"Acting Out" (Warren), 37, 102, 105–108, 110
activity of sex, 69–74
Adorno, Theodor, 5, 20, 25, 60, 96, 184n24, 218n30; abstraction, 19; *Aesthetic Theory*, 24, 95; *Notes to Literature*, 24, 95; trans-aesthetic subject, 45
aesthetic experience, 2, 9, 22, 24, 32, 44, 45, 95, 104
affect, 45, 70, 110, 144, 145, 166; abjection, 89, 101; in "Acting Out" (Warren), 37, 105; in *Ban en Banlieue* (Kapil), 93, 94; negative, 6, 21
Africa, 130
African Americans. *See* Blackness
Aki/akinoomaage, 117, 209n12, 209n14. *See also* Nishnaabeg peoples
Alderson, Lynn, 47

Altamirano-Jiménez, Isabel, 139
Althusser, Louis, 82, 85, 103, 207n86, 207n88; Althusserian approach, 16; "Ideology and Ideological State Apparatuses," 15; "Materialism Without Matter: Abstraction, Absence and Social Form," 102, 104; model of structural causality, 142; structuralism, 15; technicist reading of Marx, 81; theories of interpellation, 17, 56
anarchism, 32, 125, 170, 178; "coyotrix granarchist" (Eng), 119
Anishinaabemowin, 114. See also Ojibwe peoples/language
Anishinaabe peoples, 9, 37, 39, 113, 114, 118, 123, 124, 131, 137. See also Nishnaabewin
Annharte, 9, 34, 39, 131–134, 140; on abolitionism, 38, 114, 135; abolitionist poetics of, 122–124; granny boot camp poems, 13, 119, 120, 136, 210n25; *Indigena Awry*, 38, 137, 138, 143, 144; "Indigenous Verse Ability," 144; on kwe-as-theorist, 117–119, 145; "Medicine Lines," 146, 216n131; on Native Alliance for Red Power, 214n84; poetry resonates with Marxian understandings, 37; "Squaw Guide," 113; use of humor, 214n89
Another Mother Tongue: Gay Words, Gay Worlds (Grahn), 140
antagonism, 26, 35, 52, 123; in Annharte's work, 113, 144; in *Ban en Banlieue* (Kapil), 93, 97; class, 48; in Dene communities, 141; Indigenous, 131; in Mayer's work, 65, 68; in *Politics and Broken Windows* (Black), 148; proletarian-capitalist, 21; temporal, 64; workerism as form of, 212n55
apostrophe, 70, 72, 132–138, 154, 168
appearance, 4, 34–35, 38, 79, 87, 106, 122, 143; capital's, 44, 108; of the commodity, 5, 12, 14, 48, 55–56, 84, 103, 106, 156, 202n16; of conjunctural/aleatory moments, 130–131; effects/sensations reduced to, 107; forms of, 8, 11–12, 14, 18, 19, 31, 77, 86, 163, 178; fragmented, 219–220n47; as illusory, 220–221n67; of individuals, 128; inverted world of, 56, 163, 183n12; poems as poets', 60; racializing, 123; reading, 164; social forms of, 3, 30, 32–33, 55–56; of sociality, 151; of society, 44; of strangeness, 222n106; of value, 82, 84, 120, 183n12, 186n36; wife as sequence of, 76; world in nonidentity of, 179
Arthur, Christopher, 19, 80, 99, 100, 203n26
Ashbery, John, 102
Asia, 92, 93, 96, 98, 124, 130, 193n5, 204n50
Asia, Southeast, 139
As We Have Always Done: Indigenous Freedom Through Radical Resistance (Simpson), 114
Atlantic slave trade, 124, 170. See also Blackness; slavery
Aufhebung, 159, 175
autonomist Marxism/*Operaismo*, 17, 128
avant-garde, 23, 60, 68, 135, 136, 181n3, 199n95
Awkward-Rich, Cameron, 12

Backhaus, Hans-Georg, 5, 19
Bacon, Francis, 103
Baker, Marie Annharte. See Annharte
Ban en Banlieue (Kapil), 36, 80, 90, 91, 94, 96, 97, 100, 111
banlieue, global, 80, 101, 111
Baraka, Amiri, *Black Magic: Sabotage, Target Study, Black Art*, 126–127
Baroque style, 106
Barrett, Michèle: *The Politics of Truth: From Marx to Foucault*, 16; *Women's Oppression Today: The Marxist/Feminist Encounter*, 15

Becoming Undone (Grosz), 96
Bergen County, New Jersey, 71
Bergson, Henri, 96
Bernes, Jasper, 60, 61, 197–198n72; *The Work of Art in the Age of Deindustrialization*, 6
Best, Beverley, 4, 10–11, 17, 22, 55, 57, 67, 99, 206n74; function of abstraction, 3, 183n13; on gender differentials, 54, 205n57; "Wages for Housework Redux: Social Reproduction and the Dialectic of the Value-Form," 53, 186n36
Bewes, Timothy, 96–97
Bhandar, Brenna, 140, 144
Biiskabiyang, 114. *See also* Nishnaabewin
binary, gender-sex, 11, 47–48, 50, 57, 58
Binizaá peoples, 139
Bird and Dog. *See Tuesday or September or The End* (Black)
Black, Hannah, 161; *Tuesday or September or The End*, 39, 40, 148, 154, 162–163, 165–178
The Black Jacobins (James), 40, 148, 155, 157
Black Lives Matter movement, 124
Black Magic: Sabotage, Target Study, Black Art (Baraka), 127
Black Mountain school, 104
Blackness, 7, 8, 204n50, 210n27, 221n86; chattel slavery, 120, 121, 124, 156, 170, 219n42; diaspora, 160; police killings, 93; politics of naming, 175; radicalism, 32, 40, 148, 154, 155, 157; sorrow songs, 32, 154, 160, 161
Black US poetry, 126
Bonefeld, Werner, 19, 20, 44–45, 52
bpNichol, 136
Brady, Andrea, 160, 162; *Poetry and Bondage*, 6
Braidotti, Rosi, 15
Brecht, Bertolt, 95
Brenner, Robert, 33, 127

Brooks, Cleanth, 150, 160
Brooks, Gwendolyn, 108; *Riot*, 126
Brownmiller, Susan, 47
Brownness, 8, 93, 98, 204n50
"But He Says I Misunderstood" (Notley), 27
Butler, Judith, 14, 76, 77, 186n38
Butling, Pauline, 136

Cabri, Louis, 70
Caliban and the Witch (Federici), 21
California, 79, 102
Canada, 38; Canadian Indian Youth Council, 136; the commons, 141; First Nations/Indigenous peoples in, 38, 118, 121, 123, 132, 138, 139; *Globe and Mail* (newspaper), 137; government, 138, 141, 145; Indian Act, 117, 138, 139, 144; Indigenous writers in, 136; Ontario, 114; parliamentary law, 124; prairie provinces, 114; Quebec, 137; Quebecois people, 38; settler-colonialism in, 131, 142; Toronto, 71, 137; Vancouver, 117, 135, 136, 213–214n82
The Cantos (Pound), 150
capaciousness, 2, 10, 16, 36, 131, 148, 168
Capital (Marx), 29, 35, 130; abstraction in, 183n13; abstract vs. concrete labor, 84, 199n92; accumulation and reproductive labor, 53–54; commodity fetishism, 103; exchange as social synthesis, 20; hidden abodes and inner bonds, 13–14, 187n45; M-C-M' as prime mover, 4–5; mirrored in "Acting Out," 105, 107; money as universal equivalent, 202n16; New Reading of Marx, 5, 19, 200n4; Sohn-Rethel on, 201–202n15; theory of value, 201n7, 209n10; transformation problem, 201n8; Trinity Formula, 30; value as hidden determinant of society, 3, 8, 83; *Wertkritik* readings, 81, 200n4

capital, logic of, 2, 3, 52, 80, 173
capital accumulation, 6, 13, 14, 19, 20, 37, 50, 90, 128; social struggle and, 127
capital as social modality, 34, 51, 79, 183n13
capitalism, global racial, 23
capitalism, social forms of, 2, 8, 12, 14, 52, 79, 101, 127, 128
capitalist mode of production, 3, 14, 50, 112, 202n16, 203n24
capitalist societies, 1, 2, 127, 128, 154, 202n16
capitalist totality, 19, 29, 36, 44, 57, 58, 68, 78, 125, 170
capital-labor relation, 34, 101, 128, 129
capital's abstracting movement, 1, 54, 80, 109, 205n57
capital's internal logics, 2, 86, 91
care work, 13, 51, 88, 89
Caribbean, 32, 40, 165, 204n50; Haitian revolution, 155
Cecire, Natalia, 76
Céline, Louis-Ferdinand, *Voyage au bout de la nuit*, 151
Chen, Christopher, 38, 121, 122, 123, 191n99; "The Limit Point of Capitalist Equality: Notes Toward an Abolitionist Antiracism," 120; *Literature and Race in the Democracy of Goods*, 6
Chicago, Illinois, 46–47
"China" (Perelman), 149
cisness, 30, 101, 186–187n43; *Feminism Against Cisness* (Heaney), 31
class relations, 7, 9, 20, 25
Clover, Joshua, 6, 127, 152, 189n69, 201n8, 218n27
Clueless (film), 60
Coast Salish, 141
colonialism, 93, 116, 128, 141–142, 143, 154; postcolonialism, 219–220n47. *See also* settler-colonialism

Combahee River Collective, "Statement of the Combahee River Collective," 49
commodity fetishism, 48, 56
communism, 37, 86, 124, 203n24
communization theory, 86, 124, 125, 127, 211n45, 211n47, 212n55
"Consciousness" (Gornick), 42
consciousness-raising, 19, 32, 35, 42, 43, 49, 55, 56. *See also* Marxist interpretation/reading method
contemporary poetics, 1, 6, 152, 191n99
A Contribution to the Critique of Political Economy (Marx), 19
cosmology, 40, 117, 165, 168, 171, 172; identity and, 174–179. *See also* Utopia
Coulthard, Glen, 116, 141–144, 209n12, 216n122; *Red Skin, White Masks: Rejecting the Colonial Politics of Recognition*, 121, 140
COVID-19 pandemic, 33, 165, 171
Coward, Rosalind, 16, 188n52
Cremonini, Leonardo, 102–104, 207n88
critical social theory, 5
Crosby, Marcia, 113
Culler, Jonathan, 22, 135, 189n73

Dalla Costa, Mariarosa, 18, 50; "Women and the Subversion of the Community," 17
Dancing on Our Turtle's Back (Simpson), 115
Das Kapital (Marx). *See Capital* (Marx)
Day, Iyko, 122
decolonization, 28, 113, 114, 134, 142
deindustrialization, 9, 98, 124, 125, 129
Deleuze, Gilles, 15, 58, 103, 207n86
Dene peoples, 116, 141
dereification, 149
Derksen, Jeff, 145
Derrida, Jacques, 22, 58, 181–182n3, 210n28, 219n42; *Of Grammatology*, 155

The Desires of Mothers to Please Others in Letters (Mayer), 57, 59, 60, 62
determinations, 80, 82, 192n110; concept of, 83; experiential concrete, 96; form-determination, 36, 37, 81, 107, 112; self-determination, 115, 138; social, 21, 36, 201n7; structural, 15; value-form, 35
devaluation, 10, 52, 122, 156
The Dialectic of Sex: The Case for Feminist Revolution (Firestone), 47, 194n20
dialectics, 155, 169, 172, 203n24; of abstract/concrete, 103; of aesthetic experience, 2, 9, 96, 104; of affirmation/negation, 148; dialectical activity, 24; dialectical reading, 9, 103, 147, 148, 150–151, 162; dialectical totality, 61, 155; dialecticians, 9, 103, 178; dialecticization, 99; *The Dialectic of Sex: The Case for Feminist Revolution* (Firestone), 47, 194n20; of (dis)identification with gendered social forms, 36; of feminization, 70; of form and content, 95; of form and formlessness, 70; of (formless) hidden abodes, 85; of forms of value, 81; of historical materialism, 157; of identification with the feminine, 46; Marxist, 39, 40; in Moten's reading of C. L. R. James, 155-160; of negativity, 100; "Reading Dialectically" (Lesjak), 147, 154; recasting, 154–160; of social form, 85; *Valences of the Dialectic* (Jameson), 7, 32, 39, 148, 149, 160; "Wages for Housework Redux: Social Reproduction and the Dialectic of the Value-Form" (Best), 53
Diamanti, Jeff, 172
différance, 22, 40, 157, 219n42
differentials, 21, 22, 52, 53, 56, 87, 109, 189n69; gender, 53, 54, 205n57; and shifting patriarchal distributions, 101; of valuation, 191n99; wage, 123, 198n82
Dinners and Nightmares (Di Prima), 25–26
Di Prima, Diane, *Dinners and Nightmares*, 25–26
directly market-mediated (DMM) sphere, 88, 89f, 90, 101. *See also* indirectly market-mediated (IMM) sphere
dispossession, 21, 38, 41, 48, 52, 118, 122, 142-143; "Indigenous Verse Ability" (Annharte), 146
Du Bois, W. E. B., 160

Eastern Bloc, 19
Economic and Philosophic Manuscripts of 1844 (Marx), 107
economic downturn, 6, 127, 212n55, 212n57
economic stagnation, 6, 25, 90, 125
Elbe, Ingo, 81, 112
elsewheres, 8, 34, 35, 44, 144. *See also* aching gaps (Sedgwick); hidden abodes; polytemporal pacts
Elson, Diane, 19, 37, 58–60, 66, 77, 79, 86, 112, 201n7; on capitalist exploitation, 2; reading of Marx, 202n16; "The Value Theory of Labour," 36, 80–85
embodiment, 8, 11
Endnotes collective, 33, 37, 50, 97, 99, 203n23, 203n24; "The Logic of Gender," 36, 85–89
Eng, Mercedes, 119
enthusiasm, 172–173
Europe: bourgeois culture, 133 134, 157, 161; colonization, 38; Enlightenment, 40; Eurocentrism, 133–134; model of patrilineal descent, 139; proletariat, 158
Europeanized lyric, 161–162
expression, social forms of, 55

230 Index

Fagan, Kristina, 113
Fanon, Frantz, 93, 121, 140, 143
Federal Reserve Bank, 124
Federici, Silvia, 21, 28, 50, 51, 65, 100; "Wages Against Housework," 13, 17, 18, 27, 186–187n43
feminism, Marxist. *See* Marxist feminism
feminism, revolutionary, 35, 46, 47, 48, 194n20, 194n24
feminism, socialist, 15, 35, 46–47, 48
feminism, trans, 12, 30, 31
feminism, value-critical, 35, 90, 112
Feminism Against Cisness (Heaney), 31
feminist literary criticism, 9, 17
feminized poetry, 8, 36, 58, 86, 168; amid crises of capitalism and daily life, 69; Annharte's critique of maternal stereotypes, 12–13; *Ban en Banlieue* (Kapil), 37; breath-lines, 110; critique of irrational rationality, 45; dialectical modes of perception and, 24; identity formation under capital in, 57; of Kapil and Warren, 90; on mediation of gender, race, and Indigeneity, 6; poetic abstractions and value critique, 79; *A Queen in Bucks County* (Gabriel), 70; on racialized representation and absence, 7; recompositions of gender and, 28–29; on reproductions of gender, race, and class, 9–10; scansion, 106; social forms, 32, 52, 56; subversion of sonnet forms, 64–65; trans body, 35, 71, 78; value-determined forms, 2; value's dissimulating movement, 4, 80. *See also* figuration; lyric poetry
femme, 60, 70, 78, 148. *See also* lesbians
Ferguson, Michaele, 49
figuration, 37, 77, 80, 102, 108, 153, 158, 160–161, 163.
Firestone, Shulamith, *The Dialectic of Sex: The Case for Feminist Revolution*, 47, 194n20

First Nations, 38, 122, 132, 134, 139, 145; Anishinaabe, 9, 37, 39, 113, 114, 118, 123, 124, 131, 137; Métis, 137, 138; Michi Saagiig, 114, 115; Ojibwe, 37, 114, 116, 119, 137, 210n25; Plains Métis, 118. *See also* Canada; Indigenous peoples
Flatley, Jonathan, 45
Floyd, Kevin, 16
Fordism, 17, 34, 65, 125
form-determination, 36–37, 81, 107, 112; form-determined by value, 2, 3, 100
Fortunati, Leopoldina, 50
Foucault, Michel, 14, 15, 59; *The Politics of Truth: From Marx to Foucault* (Barrett), 16
fragmentation, 117, 149, 219–220n47; in Black's work, 166; of experience, 2, 8, 77, 162; first-personalism, 163; in Gabriel's work, 76; Jameson on, 4; in Kapil's work, 92; psychic, 175
Francophone culture, 137–138
Frankfurt School, 5, 19, 128
Franklin, Seb, 184n23, 199n100; on form and formlessness, 70
Fraser, Nancy, 49, 54
French feminism, 15
Freud, Sigmund, 90–91
function of abstraction, 3, 35, 50, 53, 112, 142, 183n13

Gabriel, Kay, 9, 34, 44, 57, 72, 79; consciousness-raising, 43; "I Do My Best To Cheat," 73; *A Queen in Bucks County*, 35, 46, 70, 71, 73, 74; on sexual difference, 2–3, 46, 70; "You Say Wife," 74–78
gay men, 75, 185n34; *Another Mother Tongue: Gay Words, Gay Worlds* (Grahn), 140; Gay Liberation Front, 49; *A Queen in Bucks County* (Gabriel), 70

gender, 12, 19, 52; abolition of, 54, 55, 125; differentials, 53, 54, 205n57; logic of, 85–91; "The Logic of Gender" (Endnotes collective), 36, 85–89; mediation of, 6, 24, 35; processual reproductions of, 10; production of, 50, 53, 57, 62, 67, 68, 70, 86, 101; recompositions of, 6, 28–29, 100; as social form, 6, 78
gendering, 3, 25, 35, 51, 53, 65, 97
genderqueer, 114
The German Ideology (Marx), 83
German Romanticist thought, 114
Gilmore, Ruth Wilson, 117
Gleeson, Juliana, 124–125
global economy, 25, 33, 34, 79, 98, 165
global financial crisis of 2008, 2, 33, 121
Global North, 24, 33, 39, 125, 129, 131, 140, 197–198n72
Goethe, Johann Wolfgang von, 164
The Golden Book of Words (Mayer), 60
Gonzales, Maya, 14
Gornick, Vivian, 47, 193n5; "Consciousness," 42
Grahn, Judy, *Another Mother Tongue: Gay Words, Gay Worlds*, 140
"granny boot camp" (Annharte), 119, 120, 136, 210n25
Grosz, Elizabeth, 97; *Becoming Undone*, 96
Grundrisse (Marx), 1, 19, 34, 81, 83, 107, 130

Haitian revolution, 155
Hall, Stuart, 12; "Race, Articulation, and Societies Structured in Dominance," 16
Halpern, Rob, 149
Hamer, Fannie Lou, 27
Hansen, Alvin, 166
Haraway, Donna, 11
Harootunian, Harry, 129, 130, 131, 143, 144, 213n66; deprovincializing Marx, 38, 124, 128
Hartley, George, 149
Heaney, Emma, 30–31, 73; *Feminism Against Cisness*, 31
Hegel, G. W. F., 157; idea of lyric as pure representation of subjectivity, 164; influence on James, 158; influence on Marx, 1, 9, 29, 154–155; language of leaps, 159; logic of moments, 61, 106; master-slave dialectic, 121; model of a dialectical unity, 114; reality of the appearance, 4, 35; recognition paradigm, 140; Schellingian critiques of, 30; sees concepts as forms of human social activity, 208n104; on sublation of living labor, 100
Heidegger, Martin, 156
Heinrich, Michael, 19, 183n12, 207n88, 223n131
Hejinian, Lyn, 9
Hennessy, Rosemary, 10, 11, 185n34
Here Come the Warm Jets (Warren), 36, 105, 109, 111
heres, 35, 144. *See also* elsewheres
hidden abodes, 34, 78, 85, 100; of capitalist whole, 36; of feminization, 68; of production, 14; of reproduction, 14, 19; of social reproduction, 6, 52. *See also* aching gaps (Sedgwick); elsewheres; polytemporal pacts
hierarchy and difference, social forms of, 54, 86
Hogue, Michel, 118
homophobia, 11, 70, 74, 75
Hurston, Zora Neale, 23

ideology: in Althusserian structural causality, 142; Althusser's concept of, 15–16; attacks on humanities, 147; capitalist, 149; of cisgender, 30; and dialectical reading, 147, 162–163; *The

ideology (*cont.*)
  German Ideology, 83; and hidden abode of reproduction, 19; as historical modality of capital (Best), 44, 178; ideological critique, 220–221n67; of linguistic freedom as fallacy, 63; linked to economic transformations, 34; in Marxist-feminist theory, 15–17; in Marxist literary criticism, 104; Ngai as critic of, 184n24; vs. "perceptual economy" and "objective thought-forms" (Best), 57; of racial mixing, 216n131; as reification (Lukács), 16; of secular rationalism vs. religious fanaticism, 172–173; sexual, 66
"Ideology and Ideological State Apparatuses" (Althusser), 15
"I Do My Best To Cheat" (Gabriel), 73
imperialism, 40, 43, 154, 197n62
impersonal compulsions/domination, 8, 19, 21, 31, 35, 36, 52-53, 85-86, 142, 153, 171, 174, 194n14
incels, 75
"Incidents Report" (Mayer), 61, 62, 63, 64, 68
India, 9, 91, 93, 96, 98; New Delhi, 92. *See also* Punjab/Punjabi-British subjects
Indigena Awry (Annharte), 38, 137, 138, 143, 144
Indigeneity, 6, 38, 39, 113; identification and, 138–146; racializing, 120–124
Indigenized concepts, 38, 120
Indigenous cultural identities, 38, 121
Indigenous peoples, 121, 122, 132, 140, 142, 143, 210–211n34, 215n101; Anishinaabemowin, 114; Anishinaabe peoples, 9, 37, 39, 113, 114, 118, 123, 124, 131, 137; Binizaá, 139; Coast Salish peoples, 141; Dene, 116, 141; identity, 118; Imaginary Indian, 113; Indian Act, 117, 138, 139, 144; Invisible/Hollywood, 137; Little Saskatchewan First Nation of Manitoba, 114, 131; Michi Saagiig, 114, 115; Mohawk Nation of Kahnawà:ke, 139; National Indian Youth Council, 136; Native Alliance for Red Power, 136, 214n84; Nishnaabeg, 38, 114–117, 146. *See also* First Nations
"Indigenous Verse Ability" (Annharte), 144
indirectly market-mediated (IMM) sphere, 88, 89f, 90, 101. *See also* directly market-mediated (DMM) sphere
inner bond/*inneres Band*, 6, 13, 14, 18, 52, 78, 100, 187n45
Intellectual and Manual Labour: A Critique of Epistemology (Sohn-Rethel), 19
International Wages for Housework Campaign, 13, 28, 29f
The Intimacies of Four Continents (Lowe), 22
intuition, 9, 29, 36, 68, 70, 112, 162, 176
Inwood, Michael, 155
Italian feminists, 50

Jackson, Virginia, 22, 23, 150, 163–164
James, C. L. R., 158, 159, 160, 161, 176; *The Black Jacobins*, 40, 148, 155, 157
James, Selma, 18; "Women and the Subversion of the Community," 17
Jameson, Fredric, 21, 44, 153, 161–164; on capitalist abstractions, 61; on dialectics and spatio-temporal movement, 155, 158; on historical consciousness, 111; on historical time/narrative history, 110; on Modernist authors, 149–152, 217n19; *The Modernist Papers*, 149, 150, 152; on poetry and abstraction, 173; *The Political Unconscious: Narrative as a Socially Symbolic Act*,

32, 154; "Postmodernism: Or, the Cultural Logic of Late Capitalism," 96, 149; and reading method, 154; on representation/fragmentation/lived experience under late capitalism, 4; spatial dialectic, 40, 155, 223n129; *Valences of the Dialectic*, 7, 32, 39, 148, 149, 160; on violent intersections of temporalities, 159; Western Marxism of, 184n24
Jeffreys, Sheila, 47
Jennison, Ruth, 105, 208n115
Johanson, Reg, 134
Johnson, Barbara, 167, 168
Johnson, Marsha P., 31, 49
Jones, Grace, 60
Jordan, June, "1977: Poem for Mrs. Fannie Lou Hamer," 27

Kapil, Bhanu, 2, 9, 34, 37, 79, 93, 112; *Ban en Banlieue*, 36, 80, 90, 91, 94, 96, 97, 100, 111; fragmentation, 92; metaphor use, 98, 99
Kearney, Douglas, 120
Keats, John, 168
Kelley, Robin, 120
Keynesianism, 125
Klein, Melanie, 96
Kootenay School of Writing, 135, 213–214n82
Kornbluh, Anna, 163
Kreiner, Timothy, 65–66, 198n82
Kristeva, Julia, 89–90; *Powers of Horror: An Essay on Abjection*, 89
Kurz, Robert, 80
kwe/woman, 37–38, 116, 145; kwe-as-theorist (Simpson), 117–119

labor, abstract, 14, 34, 80, 83, 85, 100, 107, 112, 201n8, 202n16; expressions of, 84; as only source of value, 191n107
labor, counterproductive, 99, 100, 156

labor, counter-reproductive, 98–101
labor, feminized, 10, 11, 31, 61
labor, gendered division of, 19, 27, 66
labor, productive, 52, 87, 99
labor, reproductive, 46, 50, 51, 87, 88, 97, 156
labor, unwaged, 18, 19, 50, 54, 57, 86, 88, 89
labor process, 82, 85, 86, 128
Land Back movement, 123
Language poetry, 9, 34, 104, 149, 151, 181–182n3
Latin America, 139
Lectures in America (Stein), 149
Leroux, Darryl, 138
lesbians, 47, 140, 181n1, 185n34
Lesjak, Carolyn, 159, 162, 167, 172, 177, 179, 220–221n67, 221n75, 223n129; on dialectical reading/critique of surface reading, 10, 147–148, 163; on knowing vs. realizing, 164–165; on narrative/temporality/coexistence of subjectivities, 148–149; "Reading Dialectically," 147, 154
Lewis, Holly, 71
Life in a Box Is a Pretty Life (Martin), 7
"The Limit Point of Capitalist Equality: Notes Toward an Abolitionist Antiracism" (Chen), 120
literary criticism, 5–6, 56, 69, 132, 145, 147, 164; feminist, 9, 17; Marxist, 2, 31, 90, 104, 147, 152, 161
Little Saskatchewan First Nation of Manitoba, 114, 131. See also Anishinaabe peoples
Lloyd, David, 129
logic of gender, 85–91
"The Logic of Gender" (Endnotes collective), 36, 85–89
London, UK, 17, 47, 165, 174; *les banlieues*, 91; Southall suburb, 92
long downturn, 6, 127, 212n55, 212n57

L'Ouverture, Toussaint, 155, 158
Lowe, Lisa, *The Intimacies of Four Continents*, 22
Lukács, Georg, 16, 56, 183–184n22
lyricism, 40, 154, 155, 163
Lyric Pedagogy and Marxist-Feminism (Solomon), 6
lyric perversion, 160–165
lyric poetry, 8, 23, 63, 68, 108, 135, 150, 161
lyric reading, 23, 40, 163-164, 168,
lyric studies, 22, 23

Martin, Dawn Lundy, 8, 9; *Life in a Box Is a Pretty Life*, 7
Marx, Karl, 1–223 passim; abstract labor, 80, 85; analytical categories, 46, 79, 83; category of labor, 99; *A Contribution to the Critique of Political Economy*, 19; critique of political economy, 20, 55, 81; critique of "things and their men," 48, 103; *Economic and Philosophic Manuscripts of 1844*, 107; Elson's reading of, 202n16; fetishistic objectification of social relations, 50; formal subsumption, 128, 130; form-giving, 209n10; *The German Ideology* (Marx/Engels), 83; *Grundrisse*, 1, 19, 34, 81, 83, 107, 130; "On the Jewish Question," 173; labor as value, 43; labor in capitalism, 115; "Machinery and Large-Scale Industry," 190n87; magical qualities of commodities, 106; personal vs. impersonal domination, 171; physiognomy of our *dramatis personae*, 77; real abstraction, 199n92; real subsumption, 86, 130; theory of value, 65, 82, 84, 100, 201n7; thought-forms, 201–202n15; value forms, 184n24. *See also Capital* (Marx)
Marxism, 14, 33, 40; critiques of, 6, 30; Cultural, 34; dissident, 19; Indigenous, 9; in literary studies, 7; Open, 5; poetry, 9; queer, 10; Soviet, 142; value-critical, 31, 32; Western, 15, 128, 130, 184n24
Marxism for Infants (Riley), 126
Marxist critique, 31, 52, 96, 164, 186–187n43
Marxist dialectics, 39, 40
Marxist feminism, 14–16, 39; on capital's abstractions becoming concrete, 28; on consciousness-raising and its limits, 43; critique of abstract identity, 132; critiques of value, 50; dialectics, 85; dissociation thesis, 55; economic concept of the abject, 96; and feminized poetry, 13; on feminizing work, gender, and poetic refusals, 52; formless/obscured histories as starting point, 21; on gender, race, and capitalism's logic, 205n57; on gender as social form, 19; in "The Logic of Gender" (*Endnotes* collective), 87; postwar feminist poets and, 25; reconfiguration of racist, cissexist, and heteronormative categories, 101; trans people inclusion in, 186–187n43; unitary theories of, 142–143; value-critical, 9, 86, 97; and value's dissimulating movement, 17
Marxist interpretation/reading method, 2, 7–8, 31, 40, 42, 56, 90, 104; conjunctural relations (Harootunian), 124, 130-131, 138, 144; consciousness and, 15, 18-19, 31-31, 35, 43-44, 48-49, 55-56, 70, 109, 111, 144, 157, 173, 178-179; cycles of accumulation and struggle, 127; "Materialism Without Matter" (Toscano), 102–104; mediation, 11, 16, 24, 35, 37, 86, 95, 102, 104, 151, 163, 172, 208n115; omitted in literary criticism, 69; reading dialectically, 147–154, 161–165, 177–179; real abstraction, 19-20, 43, 46, 50, 67, 103-104, 183n13, 199n92;

the reality of the appearance, 4, 8, 35, 44, 56, 79, 143, 163, 183n12; vs. real subsumption, 86, 128-130, 184n24, 203n23; recasting dialectics, 127, 132, 155, 158. *See also* impersonal compulsions/domination and not-in-between (Moten)

Marxist literary criticism, 2, 31, 90, 104, 147, 152, 161

Marxists, 31, 48, 155; autonomist, 128; British, 80; millenarian, 125

materialism, 103, 148, 155, 221n75; historical, 96, 157; new, 16, 32, 59, 96, 97

"Materialism Without Matter: Abstraction, Absence and Social Form" (Toscano), 102, 104

Mayer, Bernadette, 9, 34, 35, 43, 44, 58, 199n95; *The Desires of Mothers to Please Others in Letters*, 57, 59, 60, 62; formal experimentation in work of, 192n113; Gabriel's work inherits inventions of, 70; *The Golden Book of Words*, 60; "Incidents Report," 61, 62, 63, 64, 68; *Memory*, 57, 60–62, 64, 67, 68; *Midwinter Day*, 46, 60, 62, 64, 65, 66, 68; on nonidentical experiences and capitalist social forms, 79; *Sonnets*, 57, 62, 67; spiritual and mystical rituals, 69; *Unnatural Acts*, 60

McClanahan, Annie, 34

M-C-M, 5

McNeil, Sandra, 47

McRobbie, Angela, 97

Memory (Mayer), 57, 60, 61, 62, 64, 67, 68

metamorphoses, 98; sensuous, 102–110

metaphors, 2, 35, 77, 168; feminized backs as, 181n1; in Kapil's work, 98, 99; in Mayer's work, 70; meaning as, 171; in *Midwinter Day* (Mayer), 66; in Moten's work, 219n42; strength of the British Pound, 2, 94

Métis, 137, 138

Métis, Plains, 118

Mexico, maquiladora workers in, 10–12, 185n34

Michi Saagiig peoples, 114, 115. *See also* Nishnaabewin

Midwinter Day (Mayer), 46, 60, 62, 64, 65, 66, 68

Mill, John Stuart, 23, 161

misogyny, 47, 74, 75, 94, 98, 136

The Modernist Papers (Jameson), 149, 150, 152

Mohawk Nation of Kahnawà:ke, 139

Morgensen, Scott Lauria, 140

Moten, Fred, 93, 172, 175, 178, 219n42; lyric perversion, 160–165; not-in-between, 40, 155–159, 161, 164, 219–220n47

narrative, 110, 172, 175; vs. lyric, 39-40, 148-159, 161, 163-164, 168, 178. *See also The Political Unconscious: Narrative as a Socially Symbolic Act* (Jameson)

Native Alliance for Red Power, 136, 214n84

Native peoples. *See* Indigenous peoples

Nealon, Christopher, 9, 29, 69, 102, 198n73

Neel, Phil, 33

negative dialectics, 19, 37, 46, 56, 100, 159, 160, 163, 178–179

negative totality, 156

Negri, Antonio, 6, 17, 203n22

Nelson, Maggie, 58, 59, 60, 66

neoliberalism, 88, 108, 125, 138, 139

New Criticism, 150, 160, 161, 162; Southern Agrarian New Critics, 23

New Delhi, India, 92

New Narrative movement, 154

new reading of Marx/*neue Marx-lektüre*, 5, 19, 200n4

New York City, 9, 17, 42, 46, 49, 70, 165, 174, 185n34

Ngai, Sianne, 24, 25, 26, 45, 135, 162, 173, 194n14; socially binding or plasticizing action of capitalist abstractions, 77; *Ugly Feelings*, 6, 184n24
Nicholsen, Shierry Weber, 25
"1977: Poem for Mrs. Fannie Lou Hamer" (Jordan), 27
Nishnaabeg peoples, 38, 114–117, 146. *See also* Simpson, Leanne Betasamosake
Nishnaabewin, 114, 115, 116, 132, 135, 209n12. *See also* Anishinaabe peoples
Nixon, Richard, 166
nonidentity, 11, 32, 34, 44, 131, 168, 179
North America, 6, 71, 119. *See also* Canada; Mexico; United States (US)
"A Note on Sex and 'The Reclaiming of Language'" (Riley), 126
Notes to Literature (Adorno), 24, 95
not-in-between (Moten), 40, 155-161, 164, 200n47
Notley, Alice, 27, 28, 69
Nuevo Laredo, Mexico, 10

O'Brien, Sean, 33
Occupy movement, 124
Of Grammatology (Derrida), 155
Ojibwe peoples/language, 37, 114, 116, 119, 137, 210n25
Olson, Charles, 59; "Projective Verse," 104
Ontario, Canada, 114; Toronto, 71, 137
Oppen, George, 59

Pakistan, 98
Panzieri, Raniero, 17
Paris, France, 91
parody, 13, 113, 135, 138
Paterson (Williams), 149, 150–151
patriarchies, 48, 49, 100–101, 141, 142; capitalism, 54; violence, 94, 95; of the wage, 65, 198n82
perceptual physics/perceptual economy, 3, 4, 24, 51, 57, 75, 183n13

Perelman, Bob, "China," 149
performativity, 13, 14, 145
Pinker, Stephen, 147
Plato, Ann, 23
poetics, 13, 34, 35, 70, 102, 112; of abolition, 38, 117, 123, 124, 127, 132; abstract, 181–182n3; anti-capitalist, 58; Black, 23; Black Mountain, 104; contemporary, 1, 6, 152, 191n99; of the global *banlieue*, 80, 111; Kootenay School of Writing, 135; Language poetry, 9, 34, 104, 149, 151, 181n3; racialized, 36. *See also* speech
poetry, feminized. *See* feminized poetry
Poetry and Bondage (Brady), 6, 160
political economy, 20, 55, 81, 90, 99, 203n24; of appositional collision, 155; bourgeois, 13; *A Contribution to the Critique of Political Economy* (Marx), 19; elision of critiques of, 6; slow death, 166
The Political Unconscious: Narrative as a Socially Symbolic Act (Jameson), 32, 154
politics of recognition, 38, 120, 140, 143, 145; *Red Skin, White Masks: Rejecting the Colonial Politics of Recognition* (Coulthard), 121
"The Politics of Recognition" (Taylor), 121
The Politics of Truth: From Marx to Foucault (Barrett), 16
polytemporal pacts, 34, 176. *See also* aching gaps (Sedgwick); elsewheres; hidden abodes
Pope, Alexander, 167
Posmentier, Sonya, 23
postcolonial aura (Dirlik), 158
"Postmodernism: Or, the Cultural Logic of Late Capitalism" (Jameson), 96, 149
Postone, Moishe, 19, 51

postwar era, 6, 24, 25, 33, 59, 61, 65, 197–198n72
Pound, Ezra, *The Cantos*, 150
Powers of Horror: An Essay on Abjection (Kristeva), 89
"A Practice Known as Churning" (Warren), 111
Prins, Yopie, 150, 163–164
production of gender. *See* gender
productivity rates, 3, 33, 90, 127, 189n69, 213n63,
"Projective Verse" (Olson), 104
proletariat, 20, 21, 30, 31, 48, 49, 127, 129, 141, 158
Prometheanism, 154, 217–218n19
Prosser, Jay, 11
psychoanalysis, 14, 15, 77, 90, 108, 191n98
Punjab/Punjabi-British subjects, 32, 36, 79, 91; the two Punjabs (Kapil), 98. *See also Ban en Banlieue* (Kapil); India

Quaker (religion), 107
Quebec, Canada, 137
Quebecois people, 38
A Queen in Bucks County (Gabriel), 35, 46, 70–71, 73, 74
queens, 35; Radical Queens, 49
queerness, 3, 13, 32, 49, 72, 124, 136; femininity, 60; liberation, 140; Marxism, 10; politics, 70; *The Reification of Desire: Toward a Queer Marxism* (Floyd), 16; sexual desire, 74; theory, 30. *See also* trans*

"Race, Articulation, and Societies Structured in Dominance" (Hall), 16
racial capitalism, 23
racial categories, 9, 23, 38, 122
racialization, 7–8, 54, 184n23, 185n33, 199n100; abjection and, 37, 91; animatedness and, 135; in Annharte's work, 13, 38, 113, 119, 133, 135; as ascriptive process (Chen), 38, 120–123, 191n99; Cheng, 218n29; enables land access, 138; feminized labor and, 10; in feminized poetry, 7; identity categories, 119; of Indigeneity, 120–124, 138–139; in Kapil's work, 92; low-waged women, 100; in lyric, 23, 36, 161, 164; mediatized representation of Blackness, 210n27; modernism and, 152, 154; regulation/discipline/murder of subjects, 97; relation with feminization and class relation, 9; in *Tuesday or September or The End* (Black), 154; violence and, 95; by white settler culture, 38, 113
Rankine, Claudia, 120
Ransom, John Crowe, 150, 160
"Reading Dialectically" (Lesjak), 147, 154
Red Deer College, 136
Red Power movement, 136, 214n84
Red Skin, White Masks: Rejecting the Colonial Politics of Recognition (Coulthard), 121, 140
Reed, Anthony, 120, 156, 210n27, 210n28, 219n42
Rees, Jeska, 47, 48
reification, 19, 78, 85; of capitalist logics, 163; concepts that are, 173; of consciousness, 15; in Jameson's work, 150; Lukács's concept of, 16, 183–184n22; protocols of reading, 162; reification of language, 149
The Reification of Desire: Toward a Queer Marxism (Floyd), 16
Ricoeur, Paul, 39, 153
Rifkin, Libbie, 60
Riley, Denise, 46, 125; *Marxism for Infants*, 126; "A Note on Sex and 'The Reclaiming of Language,'" 126
Riot (Brooks), 126
Riot Grrrl, 60

Rivera, Sylvia, 49
Roberts, Luke, *Living in History*, 6
Robertson, Lisa, "Wooden Houses," 107–8
Robinson, Cedric, 157, 158
Romantics, 66, 72, 96, 217–218n19; German, 114
Rosenberg, Jordy, 172, 174, 222n106
Rubin, I. I., 81, 82
Rubles, Mamie, 12, 186n40
Rudy, Susan, 136
RuPaul's Drag Race (TV series), 60

Sahota, G. S., 152, 217–218n19, 218n22
Salamon, Gayle, 45, 77
Sangari, Kumkum, 100, 101
second skin, 10, 11
Sedgwick, Eve Kosofsky, 30, 41, 164, 165, 169, 179; *Tendencies*, 22
"Sensorium" (Warren), 109, 110
sensory perception, 7, 9, 22, 29, 65, 80, 164
settler-colonialism: audience, 134; colonialism, 128, 142, 146; colonial settler states, 113; culture, 113, 122, 144; figure of the settler, 113; Idle No More, 125; imposed stereotypes, 135; Land Back movement, 123, 211n43; perceptions of theory, 116–117; settler-colonial cultural economies, 132; settler-Indigenous relations, 118, 123, 141; settlers, 144, 216–217n131; societies, 129, 131, 140; version of Indigeneity, 38, 39, 139, 140, 145. *See also* politics of recognition
sex class, 35, 46–49, 50, 194n20
sexual difference, 3, 12, 31, 46, 70, 71, 74
sexuality, 22, 47, 48, 58, 64, 140, 194n20; childhood, 63
Shaw, Nancy, 70
Sheldon, Caroline, 48
SIC collective, 33
Simpson, Audra, 138, 139, 144

Simpson, Leanne Betasamosake, 37, 114–116, 121, 131, 145, 209n12, 209n14; *Dancing on Our Turtle's Back*, 115; kwe-as-theorist, 117–119; *As We Have Always Done: Indigenous Freedom Through Radical Resistance*, 114
slavery, 121, 156, 219n42; Atlantic slave trade, 124, 170. *See also* Blackness
Smith, Adam, 30
Smith, Jason E., 33
Smithson, Robert, 58
social difference, 2, 7, 24, 54
social factory, 17
socialism, 39, 56, 158, 166, 169, 170, 171, 174, 194n24; Eastern Bloc, 19; socialist feminism, 15, 35, 46–47, 48
social reproduction, 6, 12, 45; as abject and immaterial "non-labor," 97; Althusser's model of, 16; emphasis on embodied/biological labor, 198n89; ethically coded versions of, 67; Hegel's categories and, 182n5; hidden abodes of, 6, 52; in literature, aesthetics, and abjection, 90–91; *Lyric Pedagogy and Marxist-Feminism: Social Reproduction and the Institutions of Poetry* (Solomon), 6; Mayer as signal poet of, 57; in *A Queen in Bucks County* (Gabriel), 70; as shaped by value, 85; social reproduction theory, 51, 198n89; value's relation to, 36, 188n62; Vishmidt on, 51, 125, 195n36; "Wages for Housework Redux: Social Reproduction and the Dialectic of the Value-Form" (Best), 53, 186n36
social totality, 4, 9, 13, 16, 46, 51, 71, 79
Socratic dialogue, 154, 169
Sohn-Rethel, Alfred, 20, 183n13, 199n92, 201–202n115; *Intellectual and Manual Labour: A Critique of Epistemology*, 19
Solomon, Samuel, 48–49, 126; *Lyric Pedagogy and Marxist-Feminism*, 6

Sonnets (Mayer), 57, 62, 67
sorrow songs, 32, 154, 160, 161
Southeast Asia, 139
Southern Agrarian New Critics, 23. *See also* New Criticism
Spahr, Juliana, 58, 62, 189n69
speech, 40; everyday/vernacular, 44, 63, 131, 136; "organ speech" (Freud), 91; poetic, 23, 150–151; speech acts, 189n73; vs. writing, 60, 155–157
Spivak, Gayatri, 15, 204n50
"Squaw Guide" (Annharte), 113
Stalin, Joseph, 19
"Statement of the Combahee River Collective," 49
Stein, Gertrude, 181n3; *Lectures in America*, 149; *Tender Buttons*, 76
stereotypes, 13, 135, 146
Stevens, Wallace, 150–152, 160, 162
Street Transvestite Action Revolutionaries (STAR), 49
subjectivity, 15, 41, 45; Annharte poetry grounded in, 37; in *Ban en Banlieue* (Kapil), 92; Best on, 17; capitalism's subjectivizing powers, 56; formed through collective labor/social practices, 115; gender/race mediate formation of, 12; as historically/socially mediated formations of capital, 44; intersubjectivity, 24; kwe generates, 117; lyric as pure representation of, 164; in Mayer's and Gabriel's poems, 79; as simultaneous and coexisting across discrete temporalities, 149, 152; in *Tuesday or September or The End* (Black), 177; of the worker, 99
surplus populations, 33, 52, 54, 90, 92, 99, 111, 203n24
surplus value, 3, 5, 10, 11, 13, 14, 20, 86, 130, 142
Sutherland, Zoe, 51, 155, 156
Swann-Wright, Dianne, 167

Sweezy, Paul, 81, 82
SWERF, 70
Swift, Jonathan, 167
systematic totality/whole, 2, 16, 80, 165, 203n26

Taylor, Charles, "The Politics of Recognition," 121
temporalities, incommensurable, 39, 41, 160
Tendencies (Sedgwick), 22
Tender Buttons (Stein), 76
TERF, 70, 75
Theorie Communiste, 127, 212n55
Till, Emmett, 148
Tiqqun, 61
Toronto, Ontario, 71, 137
Toscano, Alberto, 37, 102, 103, 104, 207n86, 207n88
totality feminism, 13–25
totality-thinking, 8, 57, 59, 61, 78; rich totality, 34, 192n110
"To the First of August" (Plato), 23
Toulouse-Lautrec, Henri de, 133–135
trans*, 74, 124; activists, 125; body, 11, 30, 35, 78, 186–187n43; exclusionary radical feminisms, 194n20; "felt sense" (Salamon), 45, 77; Marsha P. Johnson, 31; second skin (Prosser and Hennessy), 10-11; spaces of social reproduction, 70; Street Transvestite Action Revolutionaries (STAR), 49; writers, 32. *See also* transfeminism
transfeminism, 12, 30-31, 49, 124-125, 185n33, 185n34, 186n40, 186n43, 194n20
transindividuality, 32, 41, 164, 179
transphobia, 34, 47, 70, 186n43
Trenkle, Norbert, 80, 81
trickster figure, 113, 114, 119
Trinity Formula, 30, 56
Tronti, Mario, 17

Troploin, 127, 212n55
Truth, Sojourner, 12
Tuesday or September or The End (Black), 39, 40, 148, 154, 162–163, 165–178
Turner, J. M. W., 72
Turner, Lana (actor), 72
Turtle Island (North America), 131
Two-Spirit, 140

Ugly Feelings (Ngai), 6, 184n24
United Kingdom (UK), 5, 19, 49; *Ban en Banlieue* (Kapil), 2, 36, 91, 94; Bhanu Kapil, 9, 79; British Marxists, 80; England, 91, 128; Hannah Black, 39; London, 14, 17, 91, 92, 165, 174; Lynn Alderson, 47
United States (US), 5, 10, 19, 23, 33, 39, 47, 74, 114; American life, 109; American lyric, 160; American modernist poetry, 197n62; Bay Area, California, 79, 102; Black chattel slavery in, 120; Black poetry of, 126; border between Canada and, 118; Chicago, Illinois, 46–47; consciousness-raising, 49; electoral politics, 165; police killing of Black people in, 93; queer white writers in, 140; soldiers, 118; universities, 181–182n3. *See also* New York City
Unnatural Acts (Mayer), 60
Utopia, 40, 58, 156, 162, 163; abolition of gender and, 54; in *The Dialectic of Sex* (Firestone), 194n20; failed, 150; in *Tuesday or September or The End* (Black), 173, 174; type of language, 149; value-form and, 53. *See also* cosmology

Valences of the Dialectic (Jameson), 7, 32, 39, 148, 149, 160
value, capitalist, 7, 10, 17, 86, 89f; counter-capitalist values, 51. *See also* value-form
value critique, 30–32, 36, 43, 56, 79, 80, 81, 200–201n4, 201n7; value-critical approach, 97. *See also* Wertkritik
value-form, 2, 8, 35, 43, 53, 85, 99; appearance of, 82; capitalist, 111, 125; theory, 106, 112, 200–201n4, 203n24
value theory, 17, 77, 80, 81, 82, 86, 100, 130, 184n24, 201n7
"The Value Theory of Labour" (Elson), 36, 80–85
Vancouver, British Columbia, 117, 135, 136, 213–214n82
Vickery, Ann, 59, 66, 199n95
Vishmidt, Marina, 25, 60, 79, 99, 100, 155, 156; on real abstractions, 8, 67; on social reproduction, 51, 125
Voyage au bout de la nuit (Céline), 151

"Wages Against Housework" (Federici), 13, 17, 18, 27, 186–187n43
"Wages for Housework Redux: Social Reproduction and the Dialectic of the Value-Form" (Best), 53, 186n36
Walker, Gavin, 61
Warren, Alli, 36, 79, 80, 90, 104, 112; "Acting Out," 37, 102, 105–108, 110; *Here Come the Warm Jets*, 36, 105, 109, 111; "A Practice Known as Churning," 111; "Sensorium," 109, 110
Warrior, Betsy, 28, 29f
Warrior Publications, 141
Weltanschauung, 114
Wertkritik, 80, 200n4
Whitby, Stephen, 92
White, Gillian, 59–60, 68, 199n95
whiteness, 9, 120
Williams, William Carlos, 59; *Paterson*, 149, 150–151
Wolfe, Patrick, 129

"Women and the Subversion of the Community" (Dalla Costa/James), 17
women's liberation movement, 46, 47, 48, 49
Women's Oppression Today: The Marxist/Feminist Encounter (Barrett), 15
"Wooden Houses" (Robertson), 107–8

Wordsworth, William, 159, 161, 175
Wright, Melissa, 10

"You Say Wife" (Gabriel), 74–78

Zeavin, Hannah, 163
Žižek, Slavoj, 159

Post

Jeremy Rosen, *Genre Bending: The Plasticity of Form in Contemporary Literary Fiction*

Sara Kippur, *New York Nouveau: How Postwar French Literature Became American*

Francisco E. Robles, *Coalition Literature: Aesthetics on the Move in Midcentury US Multiethnic Writing*

Myka Tucker-Abramson, *Cartographies of Empire: The Road Novel and American Hegemony*

Michael Shane Boyle, *The Arts of Logistics: Artistic Production in Supply Chain Capitalism*

Adam Kelly, *New Sincerity: American Fiction in the Neoliberal Age*

Adrienne Brown, *The Residential Is Racial: A Perceptual History of Mass Homeownership*

Patrick Whitmarsh, *Writing Our Extinction: Anthropocene Fiction and Vertical Science*

Rebecca B. Clark, *American Graphic: Disgust and Data in Contemporary Literature*

Palmer Rampell, *Genres of Privacy in Postwar America*

Joseph Darda, *The Strange Career of Racial Liberalism*

Jordan S. Carroll, *Reading the Obscene: Transgressive Editors and the Class Politics of US Literature*

Michael Dango, *Crisis Style: The Aesthetics of Repair*

Mary Esteve, *Incremental Realism: Postwar American Fiction, Happiness, and Welfare-State Liberalism*

Dorothy J. Hale, *The Novel and the New Ethics*

Christine Hong, *A Violent Peace: Race, U.S. Militarism, and Cultures of Democratization in Cold War Asia and the Pacific*

Sarah Brouillette, *UNESCO and the Fate of the Literary*

Sophie Seita, *Provisional Avant-Gardes: Little Magazine Communities from Dada to Digital*

Guy Davidson, *Categorically Famous: Literary Celebrity and Sexual Liberation in 1960s America*

Joseph Jonghyun Jeon, *Vicious Circuits: Korea's IMF Cinema and the End of the American Century*

Lytle Shaw, *Narrowcast: Poetry and Audio Research*

Stephen Schryer, *Maximum Feasible Participation: American Literature and the War on Poverty*

Margaret Ronda, *Remainders: American Poetry at Nature's End*

Jasper Bernes, *The Work of Art in the Age of Deindustrialization*

Annie McClanahan, *Dead Pledges: Debt, Crisis, and Twenty-First-Century Culture*

Amy Hungerford, *Making Literature Now*

J. D. Connor, *The Studios After the Studios: Neoclassical Hollywood (1970–2010)*

Michael Trask, *Camp Sites: Sex, Politics, and Academic Style in Postwar America*

For a complete listing of titles in this series, visit the Stanford University Press website, www.sup.org.

The authorized representative in the EU for product safety and compliance is:
Mare Nostrum Group
B.V Doelen 72
4831 GR Breda
The Netherlands

www.ingramcontent.com/pod-product-compliance
Lightning Source LLC
Chambersburg PA
CBHW022005220426
43663CB00007B/961